Designs for Excellence in Education:

The Legacy of B.F. Skinner

Limited Edition

Editors: Richard P. West and L.A. Hamerlynck

ISBN #0-944584-52-7

Published and Distributed by

SOPRIS WEST, INC.

1140 Boston Avenue
Longmont, CO 80501
(303) 651-2829

Contents

za

Burrhus Frederic Skinner
(1904 - 1990)

Introduction

Dr. B.F. Skinner wrote in 1989, "We know how to build better schools" (p. 96). This volume is dedicated to that proposition. It is designed to provide a comprehensive picture of the range of verified educational practices which derive from Dr. Skinner's lifelong pursuit of a science of learning and behavior. Chapters are written by leading researchers who describe the historical development of the practice and its current status in schools or other educational settings. An attitude of educational reform characterizes this volume, but it is a hopeful attitude. Each practice that is described is the outgrowth of extensive research that clearly documents the benefits of the approach. This hopeful attitude is tempered, however, by our own experience. As Skinner himself wrote in 1968,

> . . . the advances which have recently been made in our control of the learning process suggest a thorough revision of classroom practices and, fortunately, they tell us how the revision can be brought about. This is not, of course, the first time that the results of an experimental science have been brought to bear upon the practical problems of education. The modern classroom does not, however, offer much evidence that research in the field of learning has been respected or used (p. 19).

Skinner's concern seems to echo that of another educational critic, John Amos Comenius, who wrote:

> For more than a hundred years much complaint has been made of the unmethodological way in which schools are conducted, but it is only within the last thirty that any serious attempt has been made to find a remedy for this state of things. And with what results? Schools remain exactly as they were.

Comenius included these words in his book, *The Great Didactic*, written in 1632, more than four hundred years ago (quoted in Silberman, 1971). It appears that the more things change, the more they stay the same.

1

The idea that a science of learning might emerge from a partnership of psychology and education is simply describing history. According to Baer and Bushell (1981),

> *Psychology has been a partner in education almost as long as it has existed as an applicable social science. During that time, psychology has changed often and profoundly, and virtually all its changes have been applied somehow to educational practice. But psychology changes more often by the addition of something new than by the disappearance of something old. Indeed, the rate at which concepts leave the discipline is clearly much slower than the rate at which new concepts enter it. Consequently, education is by now accustomed to some number of psychologies, even to the fact that the number increases, slowly but reliably (p. 259).*

They go on to explain that Skinner's approach to the analysis of behavior and learning has experienced an uneasy relationship with education.

> *Thus, the appearance in psychology of something new referred to variously as reinforcement, operant conditioning, behavior modification, or, best of all, behavior analysis and applied behavior analysis, soon led to its application to educational theory and to educational practice. However, in a number of ways this new discipline proved to be uncomfortable to education (and, indeed, to psychology as well). Too quickly it moved from helping with to challenging the traditional mission. The challenge suggested not only a new mission but also a new set of techniques with which to achieve that (or any) mission. Because no ongoing institution with a long history of acceptance and habit responds easily to a change in mission or method, a demand to change both at once and for similar reasons must seem particularly arrogant (p. 259).*

In 1968, Dr. Sidney Bijou addressed the Division of School Psychologists at the annual convention of the American Psychological Association. His address, later published as an article in the *Journal of Applied Behavior*

Analysis, was entitled, "What Psychology has to Offer Education—Now." He opened his remarks by saying:

> *Some day, the question, 'What does psychology have to offer education—now?' will be answered by psychologists with some measure of agreement. But at the present the answer to this question depends almost entirely on the particular orientation of the individual to whom the question is put, for psychologists differ enormously in the conception of the subject matter and objectives of their discipline.*

He then promised several outcomes if education were to employ a behavior analytic approach to school and instructional issues. Teachers would derive new satisfaction from teaching because they would see student progress in concrete terms. They would know what to do when students were found not to make satisfactory progress in learning. They

> *... could not help but gain new confidence in [themselves] because [they] would know what [they were] doing and why [they were] doing it.*

> *There would be a common basis for discussion of problems among those working with the teacher—the principal, the psychologist, the counselor, and the school social worker. A common approach to all aspects of education would certainly advance teaching as a profession.*

> *Children would reach the fourth grade able to read at a functional level.*

This prediction was made when only 20 to 40% of the school population could be expected to demonstrate such competence. Bijou added that

> *... it would reverse the spiraling increases in budgets for remedial services. [The] ultimate result, of course, would be a better educated community.*

In the more than twenty years since Bijou made these predictions, it has become very apparent that the situation in our nation's schools has not improved substantially; in fact, things may even be worse. The 1983 report of the National Commission on Excellence in Education known as "The Nation at Risk" has certainly catalogued deficiencies in the areas in which

Bijou promised excellence. These problems have been documented in dozens of additional reports from numerous national commissions, federal agencies, and private foundations.

The disappointing, even tragic, fact is that Bijou was not promising outcomes that couldn't be achieved. The approaches described in this volume enjoy an impressive record of producing behavioral improvement, documented in hundreds of research studies conducted in every area of the country and in nearly every reasonable combination of school, student, and community variables. The means for realizing Bijou's goals of teachers' satisfaction in their work, a common language for all educational professionals, and student competence in reading (and in other basic skills), have all been demonstrated time after time. Unfortunately, many of these demonstrations have been in small, isolated programs, with populations of atypical students. Educational professionals continue to find reasons to reject these results and to deny the potential positive impact of behavior analysis on educational practice. Their unjustified affirmations that behavior analysis has not been sufficiently proven is more than a challenge for behavior analysts to overcome. It is a statement that clearly places these professionals with their feet planted firmly in midair.

The Challenge

This volume begins with a critique of our American system of education, and a challenge to improve it. Dr. Skinner, writing in *The Shame of American Education*, reminds us that "the average achievement of our high school students on standardized tests is now lower than it was a quarter of a century ago, and students in American schools compare poorly with those in other nations in many fields." As the National Commission on Excellence in Education (1983) put it, America is threatened by "a rising tide of mediocrity." Many solutions to this problem have been offered, but, writes Skinner, "as many of us have learned to expect, there is a curious omission in that list: It contains no suggestion that teaching be improved. There is a conspiracy of silence about teaching as a skill."

Skinner goes on to explain how a science of behavior and learning can be used to improve education. His positive approach is based upon a "good program of instruction [that] guarantees a great deal of successful action. . . . Students do not have to be made to study. Reinforcement is enough, and good programming provides it. . . . If given a chance, teachers can also be interesting and sympathetic companions. It is a difficult assignment in a classroom in which order is maintained by punitive sanctions. The word *discipline* has come a long way from its association with *disciple* as one who understands."

Selection I

In *Programmed Instruction and Teaching Machines*, Ernest A. Vargas and Julie S. Vargas trace the history of teaching machines from an early steam-powered, mechanical computer to today's computers. The history of programmed instruction is also detailed, beginning with Skinner's simple practice machine which provided the student with immediate feedback on the accuracy of each response. Skinner's subsequent efforts to program instruction utilized thematic prompts and presented items in a sequence that built upon prior knowledge. These have become the hallmarks of programmed instruction. While the popularity of programmed instruction appears to have waned, numerous instructional procedures that are widely used today share a common heritage. Among these are Precision Teaching, Direct Instruction, and the Keller Personalized System of Instruction. A number of reasons are given for the failure of the programmed instruction movement to emerge as a powerful force in shaping American education. The authors also suggest ways of evaluating curricula designed for microcomputers, the teaching machines of today, in order to assess their ability to program instruction effectively.

Selection II

Wesley C. Becker, a pioneer in the direct instruction movement, reviews the development of this approach in *Direct Instruction*. His early collaboration with Siegfried Engelmann resulted in the DISTAR reading program. This revolutionary approach, Direct Instruction (DI), is based upon procedures which increase the efficiency of teaching time through fast-paced lessons.

The historical foundations of the development of Direct Instruction as an educational approach lie in the studies of Carl Bereiter and Siegfried Engelmann at the University of Illinois in the early 1960s. Their empirical approach to problems of instruction was later merged with behavior analysis through contact with Wesley Becker and Douglas Carnine. Direct Instruction stands today as a systematic approach to the design and delivery of a range of procedures for building and maintaining basic cognitive skills. The central visible feature of DI is small-group instruction, with frequent responding by the students as teachers and aides follow scripts in an active, participation-oriented classroom.

Selection III

Richard P. West and K. Richard Young describe the approach known as *Precision Teaching*. In his 1938 book, *The Behavior of Organisms*, Skinner claimed that the "rate of responding is the principal measure of the strength of an operant," and therefore, the "main datum to be measured in the study of . . . an operant is . . . the rate of responding" (p. 58). He studied the effects of environmental events on response rates by plotting responses per units of time, and studying the slopes of the lines formed by the data. Skinner used mostly infrahuman subjects in his research, usually rats or pigeons. One of his graduate students, Ogden Lindsley, was an early advocate of using Skinner's research methodology in investigations of human behavior. In the approach he developed, called Precision Teaching, Lindsley utilized a graphic display similar to the one used by Skinner, in which responses per minute per day were plotted. Lindsley, like Skinner, advocated the study of the slopes of the lines formed by the daily data points. In this way, the effects of environmental events on response rates could be seen. If the approach were used in school classrooms, the effects of teaching strategies could be seen almost immediately on the daily academic performance of the students. Precision Teaching, while not really "teaching" at all, has since been used in many varied applications to improve the effectiveness of instruction.

In this paper, Drs. West and Young describe the heritage Precision Teaching owes to Skinner's behaviorism, and the ways in which a knowledge of behavioral principles can contribute to a study of human learning. The strategies employed by precision teachers are presented and discussed, with recommendations for using the data from daily performance probes to maximize the positive effects of the instructional tactics used in the classroom.

Selection IV

Kenneth E. Lloyd and Margaret E. Lloyd, in *Behavior Analysis and Technology in Higher Education*, present a review of research and evaluations investigating the various aspects of Personalized Systems of Instruction (PSI). The PSI approach, developed by Dr. Fred S. Keller, is a type of individualized instruction that includes the distinguishing features of operant behavior analysis. The behaviors that are to be strengthened are clearly specified, and the learner receives timely feedback on the appropriateness of each response. When the learner's performance is judged to be unsatisfactory, the deficient skills are remediated through retraining. This highly individualized mastery approach has been used effectively for college coursework, and in high school and junior high applications.

In this paper, the Lloyds explain what constitutes a Personalized System of Instruction and how the system is related to Skinner's behaviorism; they review the history of the various applications of the system; and they analyze the research on the elements of the PSI model. They then recommend applications that are best suited for PSI, and describe how the PSI approach can be used most effectively.

Selection V

Sidney W. Bijou offers his perspective in *Early Childhood and Parent Education*. Educators, developmental psychologists, and the general public agree that early childhood education and parent education are important. However, they do not necessarily agree on their importance relative to other educational activities, hence there is no well-coordinated drive to establish an explicit national policy concerning these activities. Dr. Bijou contends that "early childhood education and parent education are essential to the proper social, emotional, and intellectual development of *all* children in a highly industrialized society; therefore, we need more explicit and vigorous policies to promote them within and outside of the educational establishment." According to Dr. Bijou, the psychological development that occurs between two and six years of age has powerful and enduring effects: " . . . this is the period in which a child's basic psychological equipment is formed, namely, motor abilities, language style, and social behavior patterns, as well as attitudes, values, and beliefs. Upon these foundations are established the great mass of psychological behaviors that constitute his or her unique individuality, referred to as personality, character, and intelligence." Only through proper education and training can this most important period of life adequately prepare the child to meet the challenges he or she will encounter later in life.

This selection begins with a brief account of the historical roots of preschool and parent education, focusing on the influences of behaviorally-oriented philosophers, psychologists, and educators, but Dr. Bijou also addresses the contributions of researchers and theorists whose views are not behavioral but, nevertheless, may have influenced national trends and priorities. Dr. Bijou assesses the current situation, looking especially closely at the impact of the behavioral approach, and he describes his concerns for the future of early childhood and parent education and his predictions.

Selection VI

In *Influences and Effects of the Behavioral Paradigm in Special Education*, Eugene Edgar and Stephen Sulzbacher identify and explain the influences of behaviorism on special education, and highlight the contributions of some of the leaders in special education who claim a behavioral heritage. As a discipline, special education is more "behavioral" than other disciplines, even those traditionally linked to education, such as psychology, deaf education, and elementary and secondary education. In other words, special education treatment programs and curricula are likely to contain more of the defining characteristics of behavioral analysis than are programs emanating from other disciplines. Other disciplines are more likely to rely upon complex hypothetical constructs to explain learning and teaching phenomena, and their treatment programs are more likely to be based upon a cognitive framework.

The authors claim the following seven characteristics are generally present in treatment programs and curricula based upon a behavior analytic model: (1) reliance upon standard, absolute units of behavior; (2) use of reinforcement to strengthen behavior; (3) emphasis on the functional relationship consisting of a response and its consequence; (4) a schedule of reinforcements that programs the delivery of reinforcements; (5) the use of successive, small approximations in the development of complex behaviors; (6) the provision of ample opportunities to respond to stimuli and receive consequences; and (7) the use of frequent and direct measures of performance to evaluate the impact of the treatment program and to decide whether the impact is satisfactory. Some of these components are obvious in virtually every special education classroom in the country (behavioral specification, use of reinforcers, shaping); some are not as noticeable as others (reinforcement schedules, contingencies); and some of the components are found only occasionally (response opportunities, data-based decision making) but seem to be gaining in popularity.

A number of the most popular special education models are then reviewed to determine if they contain the components described above. The authors have contacted the leaders in the field of special education who have developed or refined these models. They have asked the "experts" to explain why the model is effective and how it makes use of the technology of behavior analysis. The authors include reviews of Direct Instruction, Precision Teaching, behavioral approaches in educating children with emotional disorders and/or severe and multiple disabilities, programmed instruction, and computer-based instruction.

Selection VII

In *Applied Behavior Analysis in Sport and Physical Education: Past, Present, and Future,* Garry L. Martin reviews the application of the principles of behavior analysis to sport and physical education, and he recommends future applications of this technology. His review is brief, because the history is brief. It is limited almost entirely to the work of two persons, Brent Rushall and Daryl Siedentop. Their collaboration resulted in a book, published in 1972, that contained numerous practical strategies for shaping new sport skills, managing contingencies to maintain existing skills at high levels, and generalizing practiced skills to competitive settings. Much of the literature in this area is concerned with describing and promoting techniques, with little attention devoted to research investigating the impact of the techniques on performance. Several of the nonresearch papers have offered the reader a detailed task analysis of the behaviors taught in physical education settings. Others have focused on the teaching behaviors that are presumed to be effective in developing athletic skills.

Recently, more attention has been given to research. Dr. Martin identifies three areas in which progress in research can be documented. First is the development of reliable observation systems for monitoring the behavior of physical education teachers and students. This permits the researcher to learn more about what is going on in the gym. Second, behavioral teaching skills (e.g., praising, prompting, and systematic corrections) are more widely accepted now in sport and physical education applications than they have been in the past. Many procedures that have long been used in other instructional settings are now being tested for use in sport and physical education. Third, behavior change strategies are now used more widely to reduce or eliminate various problem behaviors in the physical education environments. Researchers are beginning to focus more on the elimination of disturbing behaviors that compete for reinforcements with desirable behaviors. While considerable progress has been made in the areas listed above, Dr. Martin notes that there is still room for some improvement. In spite of pleas for physical educators to take specific, detailed, and frequent measures of student performance, and for them to use those measures as the primary means for evaluating the effectiveness of specific teaching tactics, there appears to be little accountability for student performance gains placed on teachers.

Dr. Martin recommends that future applications of behavior analysis in sport and physical education should emphasize skill development, increasing the frequency of practice and exercising, decreasing the rate of problem behaviors in competitive and training environments, and assessing and developing the behavior modification skills of coaches.

Selection VIII

R. Douglas Greer discusses how experimental and applied behavior analysis can contribute to teaching and learning in *The Teacher as Strategic Scientist: A Solution to Our Educational Crisis?* According to Dr. Greer, *Skinner's Behavior of Organisms* (1938) is all about teaching. Dr. Greer believes that teaching is the deliberate attempt to develop specific behavioral repertoires under certain stimulus conditions and not under other stimulus conditions. The author then explains the strategies and tactics a teacher must use to become a "strategic scientist," one who uses effective techniques to produce capable learners. These strategies include: (1) strategies of measurement and evaluation; (2) strategies for observing and analyzing contingencies; (3) strategies of data analysis; (4) tactics for implementing strategies; (5) epistemological bases of strategies; (6) strategies for developing and analyzing curricular goals; and (7) strategies for the design and selection of instructional materials.

Dr. Greer explains how he has trained teachers to use each of the strategies effectively. He also suggests guidelines for designing and conducting preservice and inservice training in behavior analysis, and effecting system-wide change through personnel development.

This volume describes the advances in educational technology and practice which Skinner, Bijou, and Baer have anticipated and participated in developing. However, we are far from achieving the condition of common practice. Proof of a better mousetrap does not sell in a society that is convinced that mice are housepets or that an increase in the wages and workday of mice watchers will take care of the "problem." Those who recognize the potential impact of this approach are often confused by the lack of interest by others: the situation appears hopeless, but no one thinks it is serious. Nevertheless, Skinner (1968) offers us hope once again that we are now prepared to affect meaningful change in our educational system. Our current situation

> . . . is no doubt partly due to the limitations of earlier research. But it has been encouraged by a too hasty conclusion that the laboratory study of learning is inherently limited because it cannot take into account the realities of the classroom. In the light of our increasing knowledge of the learning process we should, instead, insist upon dealing with those realities and forcing a substantial change in them. Education is perhaps the most important branch of scientific technology. It deeply affects the lives of all of us. We can no longer allow the exigencies of a practical situation to suppress the tremendous improvements which are within reach. The practical situation must be changed (p. 19).

It is to this proposition, and to him who issued it, that this volume is dedicated: "We know how to build better schools." Let's be about the business of doing it!

References

Baer, D.M. & Bushell, D., Jr. (1981). The future of behavior analysis in the schools? Consider its recent past, and then ask a different question. *School Psychology Review, 10*(2), 259-270.

Bijou, S.W. (1970). What psychology has to offer education—Now. *Journal of Applied Behavior Analysis, 3*(1), 65-71.

Comenius, J.A. (1632). The great didactic. In C.E. Silberman (1971), *Crisis in the classroom: The remaking of American education* (chap. 5). New York: Vintage Books.

National Commission on Excellence in Education (1983). *A nation at risk: The imperative for educational reform.* Washington, DC: U.S. Department of Education.

Rushall, B.S. & Siedentop, D. (1972). *The development and control of behavior in sport and physical education.* Philadelphia, PA: Lea & Febinger.

Skinner, B.F. (1938). *The behavior of organisms.* Englewood Cliffs, NJ: Prentice-Hall.

Skinner, B.F. (1968). *The technology of teaching.* Englewood Cliffs, NJ: Prentice-Hall.

Skinner, B.F. (1989). The school of the future. In B.F. Skinner (Ed.), *Recent issues in the Analysis of Behavior* (pp. 85-96). Englewood Cliffs, NJ: Prentice-Hall.

The Shame of American Education

B.F. Skinner (1904-1990), Harvard University

O n a morning in October, 1957, Americans were awakened by the beeping of a satellite. It was a Russian satellite, Sputnik. Why was it not American? Was something wrong with American education? Evidently so, and money was quickly voted to improve American schools. Now we are being awakened by the beepings of Japanese cars, Japanese radios, phonographs, and television sets, and Japanese wristwatch alarms, and again questions are being asked about American education, especially in science and mathematics.

Something does seem to be wrong. According to a recent report of a National Commission on Excellence in Education (1983), for example, the average achievement of our high school students on standardized tests is now lower than it was a quarter of a century ago and students in American schools compare poorly with those in other nations in many fields. As the Commission put it, America is threatened by "a rising tide of mediocrity."

The Challenge

The first wave of reform is usually rhetorical. To improve education we are said to need "imaginative innovations," a "broad national effort" leading to a "deep and lasting change," and a "commitment to excellence." More specific suggestions have been made, however. We are said to need better teachers, and to get them we should pay them more, possibly according to merit. They should be certified to teach the subjects they teach. Scholarship standards should be raised to get better students. The school day should be extended from six to seven hours, more time should be spent on homework, and the school year should be lengthened from 180 to 200 or even 220 days. We should change what we are teaching. Social studies are all very well, but they should not take time away from basics, especially mathematics.

As many of us have learned to expect, there is a curious omission in that list: It contains no suggestion that teaching be improved. There is a conspiracy of silence about teaching as a skill. The *New York Times* publishes a quarterly survey of education. The last three issues[1] contained 18 articles about the kinds of things being taught in schools, 11 articles about the financial problems of students and schools, ten about the needs of special students, from the gifted to the disadvantaged, and smaller numbers about the selection of students, professional problems of teachers, and sports and other extracurricular activities. Of about 70 articles, only two had anything to do with how students are taught or how they could be taught better. Pedagogy is a dirty word.

In January, 1981 Frederick Mosteller, president of the American Association for the Advancement of Science, gave an address called "Innovation and Evaluation." He began with an example of the time which can pass between a scientific discovery and its practical use. The fact that lemon juice cures scurvy was discovered in 1601, but more than 190 years passed before the British navy began to use citrus juice on a regular basis and another 70 before scurvy was wiped out in the mercantile marine—a lag of 264 years. Lags have grown shorter but, as Mosteller pointed out, are often still too long. Perhaps unwittingly he gave another example. He called for initiatives in science and engineering education, and said that a major theme of the 1982 meeting of the Association would be a "national commitment to educational excellence in science and engineering for all Americans."

1 November 14, 1982, January 9, 1983, and April 24, 1983.

When Mosteller's address was published in *Science*, I wrote a letter to the editor calling attention to an experiment in teaching algebra in a school in Roanoke, Virginia, in which an eighth-grade class using simple teaching machines and hastily-composed instructional programs went through *all* of ninth-grade algebra in *half* a year. Their grades met ninth-grade norms, and when tested a year later they remembered rather more than usual. Had American educators decided that that was the way to teach algebra? They had not. The experiment was done in 1960, but education had not yet made any use of it. The lag was already 21 years long.

A month or so later I ran into Mosteller. "Did you see my letter in *Science* about teaching machines?" I asked. "Teaching machines?" he said, puzzled. "Oh, you mean *computers*—teaching machines to *you*." And, of course, he was right. Computers are now badly misnamed. They were designed to compute, but they are not computing when they are processing words, or displaying Pac-Man, or aiding instruction (unless the instruction is in computing). "Computer" has all the respectability of the white-collar executive, while "machine" is definitely blue-collar, but let us call things by their right names. Instruction may be "computer-aided" and all good instruction must be "interactive," but machines that teach are teaching machines.

I liked the Roanoke experiment because it confirmed something I had said a few years earlier to the effect that with teaching machines and programmed instruction one could teach what is now taught in American schools in half the time with half the effort. I shall not review other evidence that this is true. Instead I shall demonstrate my faith in a technology of teaching by going out on a limb. I claim that the school system of any large American city could be so redesigned, at little or no additional cost, that students would come to school and apply themselves to their work with a minimum of punitive coercion and, with very rare exceptions, learn to read with reasonable ease, express themselves well in speech and writing, and solve a fair range of mathematical problems. I want to talk about why that has not been done.

The teaching machines of 25 years ago were crude, of course, but that is scarcely an explanation. The calculating machines were crude, too, yet they were used until they could be replaced by something better. The hardware problem has now been solved, but resistance to a technology of teaching survives. The rank commercialism which quickly engulfed the field of teaching machines is another possible explanation. Too many people rushed in to write bad programs and make promises that could not be kept. But that should not have concealed the value of programmed instruction for so many years. There is more than that to be said for the marketplace in the selection of a better mousetrap.

I shall argue that educators have not seized this chance to solve their problems because the solution conflicts with deeply-entrenched views of human behavior, and that these views are too strongly supported by current psychology. Humanistic psychologists, for example, tend to feel threatened by any kind of scientific analysis of human behavior, particularly if it leads to a "technology" that can be used to intervene in people's lives. A technology of teaching is especially threatening. Carl Rogers has said that teaching is vastly overrated, and Ivan Illich has called for the deschooling of society. I dealt with the problem in *Beyond Freedom and Dignity*. To give a trivial example: We do not like to be told something we already know, for we can no longer claim credit for having known it.

To solve that problem Plato tried to show that students already possess knowledge and have only to be shown that they possess it. But the famous scene in Plato's *Meno*, in which Socrates shows that the slaveboy already knows Pythagorus's theorem for doubling the square, is one of the great intellectual hoaxes of all time. The slaveboy agrees with everything Socrates says, but there is no evidence whatsoever that he could then go through the proof by himself. Indeed, Socrates says that he would need to be taken through it many times before he could do so.

Cognitive psychology is causing much more trouble, but in a different way. It is hard to be precise because the field is usually presented in what we may call a cognitive style. For example, a pamphlet of the National Institute of Education (1980) quotes with approval the contention that "at the present time, modern cognitive psychology is the dominant theoretical force in psychological science as opposed to the first half of the century when behavioristic, antimentalistic stimulus-response theories of learning were in the ascendance." (The writer means "ascendant.") The pamphlet tells us that cognitive science studies learning, but not in quite those words. Instead, it is said to be "characterized by a concern with understanding the mechanisms by which human beings carry out complex intellectual activities including learning." The pamphlet also says that cognitive science can help construct tests that will tell us more about what a student has learned and hence how to teach it better, but here is the way it says it: "Attention will be placed on two specific topics: Applications of cognitive models of the knowledge structure of various subject matters and of learning and problem-solving to construction of tests that identify processes underlying test answers, analyze errors, and provide information about what students know and don't know, and strategies for integrating testing information with instructional decisions." Notice especially the cognitive style in the last phrase—the question is not "whether test results can suggest better ways of teaching" but "whether there are strategies for integrating testing information with instructional decisions."

A more recent example can be found in the announcement of a Biennial Program Plan covering the period 1 May 1983 to 30 April 1985 of a Commission on Behavior, Social Sciences, and Education of the National Research Council (1984). The Commission will take advantage of "significant advances . . . in the cognitive sciences." Will it study learning? Well, not exactly. The members will "direct their attention to studies of fundamental processes underlying the nature and development of learning." Why do cognitive psychologists not tell us frankly what they are up to? Is it possible that they themselves do not really know?

Cognitive psychology is certainly in the ascendant. The word cognitive is sprinkled through the psychological literature like salt—and, like salt, not so much for any flavor of its own as to bring out the flavor of other things, things which a quarter of a century ago would have been called by other names. The heading of an article in a recent issue of the *Monitor* (1983) tells us that "cognitive deficits" are important in understanding alcoholism. In the text we learn simply that alcoholics show losses in perception and motor skills. Perception and motor skills used to be fields of psychology; now they are fields of cognitive science. Nothing has been changed except the name, and the change has been made for suspicious reasons. There is a sense of profundity about "cognitive deficits," but it does not take us any deeper into the subject.

Much of the vogue of cognitive science is due to advances in computer technology. The computer offers an appealing simplification of some old psychological problems. Sensation and perception are reduced to input, learning and memory to the processing, storage, and retrieval of information, and action to output. It is very much like the old stimulus-response formula patched up with intervening variables. To say that students process information is to use a doubtful metaphor, and how they process it is still the old question of how they learn.

Cognitive psychology also gains prestige from its alignment with brain research. Interesting things are certainly being discovered about the biochemistry and circuitry of the brain, but we are still a long way from knowing what is happening in the brain as behavior is shaped and maintained by contingencies of reinforcement, and that means that we are a long way from help in designing useful instructional practices.

Cognitive science is also said to be supported by modern linguistics, a topic to which I am particularly sensitive. Programmed instruction emerged from my analysis of verbal behavior (Skinner, 1957), which linguists, particularly generative grammarians, have, of course, attacked. So far as I know they have offered no equally effective practices. One might expect them to have improved the teaching of languages, but almost all language laboratories still work in particularly outmoded ways, and language instruction is one of the principal failures of precollege education.

Psycholinguistics moves in essentially the same direction in its hopeless commitment to development. Behavior is said to change in ways determined by its structure. The change may be a function of age, but age is not a variable that one can manipulate. The extent to which developmentalism has encouraged a neglect of more useful ways of changing behavior is shown by a recent report in which the number of studies concerned with the development of behavior in children was found to have skyrocketed, while the number concerned with how children *learn* has dropped to a point at which the researcher could scarcely find any examples at all (Siegler, 1983).

There are many fine cognitive psychologists who are doing fine research, but they are not the cognitive psychologists who for 25 years have been promising great advances in education. A short paper published in *Science* last April (Resnick, 1983) asserts that "recent advances in cognitive science suggest new approaches to teaching in science and mathematics," but the examples given, when expressed in noncognitive style, are simply these:

1. Students who solve textbook problems in physics are not always effective in dealing with the physical world.

2. Students tend to fall back upon theories they have already learned.

3. Many problems cannot be solved exclusively with mathematics.

4. Students must learn more than isolated facts; they must learn how facts are related to each other.

5. Students must relate what they are learning to what they already know.

And that is all. If these are *recent* findings, where has cognitive science been?

Cognitive psychology is frequently presented as a revolt against behaviorism, but it is not a revolt; it is a retreat. Everyday English is full of terms derived from ancient explanations of human behavior. We spoke that language when we were young. When we went out into the world and became psychologists, we learned to speak in other ways but made mistakes for which we were punished. But now we may relax. Cognitive psychology is old home week. It brings us back among friends speaking the language we spoke when we were growing up. We can talk about love and will and ideas and memories and feelings and states of mind, and no one will ask us what we mean; no one will raise an eyebrow.

Psychological theories come into the hands of teachers through schools of education and teachers' colleges, and it is there, I think, that we must lay the major blame for what is happening in American education. In a recent article in the *New York Times* (June 5, 1983), President Leo Botstein of Bard College proposed that schools of education, teachers' colleges, and departments of education simply be disbanded. But he gave a different reason. He said that schools of that sort put too much emphasis on "pedagogical techniques and psychological studies," where they should be teaching the subjects the teachers would eventually teach. But disbanding them is certainly a move in the wrong direction. It has long been said that college teaching is the only profession for which there is no professional training. Would-be doctors go to medical schools, would-be lawyers go to law schools, would-be engineers go to institutes of technology, and would-be college teachers—just start teaching. Fortunately it is recognized that grade- and high school teachers need to learn to teach. The trouble is, they are not being taught in effective ways. The commitment to humanistic and cognitive psychology is only part of it.

Equally damaging is the assumption that teaching can be adequately discussed in everyday English. The appeal to laymanship is attractive. One member of the "Convocation on Science, Mathematics, and the Schools" called by the National Academies of Sciences and Engineering (Raizen, 1983) said that "what we need are bright, energetic, dedicated young people, trained in mathematics . . . science . . . or technology, mixing it up with six- to thirteen-year-old kids in the classroom." The problem is too grave to be solved in any such way. The first page of the report notes with approval that "if there is one American enterprise that is local in its design and control it is education." That is held to be a virtue. But certainly the Commission would not approve similar statements about other professional fields, such as medicine, law, or science and technology. Why should the community decide how children are to be taught? The Commission is actually pointing to one explanation of why education is failing.

We must beware of the fallacy of the good teacher and the good student. There are many good teachers, who have not needed to learn to teach. They would be good at almost anything they tried. There are many good students, who scarcely need to be taught. Put a good teacher and a good student together and you have what seems to be an ideal instructional situation. But it is disastrous to take it as a model to be followed in our schools, where hundreds of thousands of teachers must teach missions of students. Teachers must learn how to teach, and they must be taught by schools of education. They only need to be taught more effective ways of teaching.

We could solve our major problems in education if students learned more during each day in school. That does not mean a longer day or year or more homework. It simply means using time more efficiently. Such a solution is not considered in any of the reports I have mentioned—whether from the National Institute of Education, the American Association for the Advancement of Science, the National Research Council, or the National Academies of Sciences and Engineering. Nevertheless, it is within easy reach. Here is all that needs to be done.

1. **Be clear about what is to be taught**. When I once explained to a group of grade-school teachers how I would teach children to spell words, one of them said, "Yes, but can you teach spelling?" For him, students spelled words correctly not because they had learned to do so but because they had acquired a special ability. When I told a physicist colleague about the Roanoke experiment in teaching algebra, he said "Yes, but did they learn algebra?" For him, algebra was more than the solving of certain kinds of problems; it was a

mental faculty. No doubt the more words you learn to spell the easier it is to spell new words, and the more problems you solve in algebra the easier it is to solve new problems. What eventually emerges is often called "intuition." We do not know what it is but we can certainly say that no teacher has ever taught it directly, nor has any student ever displayed it without first learning to do the kinds of things it replaces.

2. **Teach first things first.** It is tempting to move too quickly to final products. I once asked a leader of the "new math" what he wanted students to be able to do. He was rather puzzled, and then said, "I suppose I just want them to be able to follow a logical line of reasoning." That does not tell a teacher where to start or, indeed, how to proceed at any point. I once asked a colleague what he wanted his students to do as a result of having taken his introductory course in physics. "Well," he said, "I guess I've never thought about it that way." I'm afraid he spoke for most of the profession.

Among the ultimate but useless goals of education is "excellence." A candidate for President recently said that he would let local communities decide what that meant. "I am not going to try to define excellence for them," he said, and wisely so. Another useless ultimate goal is *creativity*. It is said that students should do more than what they have been taught to do. They should be creative. But does it help to say that they must acquire creativity? More than 300 years ago, Moliere wrote a famous line: "I am asked by the learned doctors for the cause and reason why opium puts one to sleep, to which I reply that there is in it a soporific virtue, the nature of which is to lull the senses." Two or three years ago an article in *Science* pointed out that 90 percent of scientific innovations were accomplished by fewer than 10 percent of scientists. The explanation, it was said, was that only a few scientists possess creativity. Moliere's audiences laughed. Eventually some students behave in creative ways, but they must have something to be creative with and that must be taught first. They can be taught to be creative by multiplying the variations which give rise to new and interesting forms of behavior. (Creativity, incidentally, is often said to be beyond a science of behavior, and it would be if that science were a matter of stimulus and response, but by emphasizing the selective action of consequences, the experimental analysis of behavior deals with the creation of behavior precisely as Darwin dealt with the creation of species.)

3. **Stop making all students advance at essentially the same rate**. The phalanx was a great military invention, but this has long been out of date, and it should be out of date in American schools, but students are still expected to move from kindergarten through high school in twelve years. We all know what is wrong: Those who could move faster are held back, and those who need more time fall farther and farther behind. We could double the efficiency of education with one change along—by letting each student move at his or her own pace. (I wish I could blame that costly mistake on developmental psychology, because it is such a beautiful example of its major principle, but the timing is out of joint.)

No teacher can teach a class of thirty or forty students and allow each to progress at an optimal speed. Tracking is too feeble a remedy. We must turn to individual instruments for part of the school curriculum. The report of the convocation on precollege education held by the National Academies of Sciences and Engineering refers to "new technologies . . . which can be used to extend the educational process, to supplement the teacher's role in new and imaginative ways," but no great enthusiasm is shown. Thirty years ago educational television was promising, but the promise has not been kept. The report alludes to "computer-aided instruction" but calls it the latest "rage of education," and insists that "the primary use of the computer is for drill." (Properly programmed instruction is **never** drill if that means going over material again and again until it is learned.) The report also contains a timid allusion to "low-cost teaching stations that can be controlled by the learner," but evidently they are merely to give the student access to video material rather than to programs.

4. **Program the subject matter**. The heart of the teaching machine, call it what you will, is the programming of instruction—an advance not mentioned in any of the reports I have cited. Standard texts are designed to be read by the student, who will then discuss what they say with a teacher or take a test to see how much has been learned. Material prepared for individual study is different. It first induces students to say or do the things they are to learn to say or

do. Their behavior is thus "primed" in the sense of being brought out for the first time. Until the behavior has acquired more strength, it may need to be prompted. Primes and prompts must then be carefully "vanished" until the behavior occurs without help. At that point the reinforcing consequences of being right are most effective in building an enduring repertoire.

Working through a program is really a process of discovery, but not in the sense in which that word is currently used in education. We discover many things in the world around us, and that is usually better than being told about them, but as individuals we can discover only a very small part of the world. Mathematics has been discovered very slowly and painfully over thousands of years. Students discover it as they go through a program, but not in the sense of doing something for the first time in history. Trying to teach mathematics or science as if the students themselves were discovering it for the first time is not an efficient way of teaching the very skills with which, in the long run, a student may, with luck, actually make a genuine discovery.

When students move through well-constructed programs at their own pace, the so-called problem of motivation is automatically solved. For thousands of years students have studied to avoid the consequences of not studying. Punitive sanctions still survive, disguised in various ways, but the world is changing and they are no longer easily imposed. The great mistake of progressive education was to try to replace them with natural curiosity. Teachers were to bring the real world into the classroom to arouse the students' interest. The inevitable result was a neglect of subjects in which children were seldom naturally interested—in particular, the so-called basics. One solution is to make some of the natural reinforcers—goods or privileges—artificially contingent upon basic behavior, as in a token economy. Such contingencies can be justified if they correct a lethargic or disordered classroom, but there should be no lethargy or disorder. It is characteristic of the human species that successful action is automatically reinforced. The fascination of video games is adequate proof. What would industrialists not give to see their workers as absorbed in their work as young people in a video arcade? What would teachers not give to see their students applying themselves with the same eagerness? (For that matter, what would any of us not give to see ourselves as much in love with our work?) But there is no mystery; it is all a matter of the scheduling of reinforcements.

A good program of instruction guarantees a great deal of successful action. Students do not need to have a natural interest in what they are doing, and subject matters do not need to be dressed up to attract attention. No one really cares whether Pac-Man gobbles up all those little spots on the screen. Indeed, as soon as the screen is cleared, the player covers it again with little spots to be gobbled up. What is reinforcing is successful play, and in a well-designed instructional program students gobble up their assignments. I saw them doing that when I visited the project in Roanoke with its director, Allen Calvin. We entered a room in which thirty or forty eighth-grade students were at their desks working on rather crude teaching machines. When I said I was surprised that they paid no attention to us, Calvin proposed a better demonstration. He asked me to keep my eye on the students, and then went up on the teacher's platform, jumped in the air, and came down with a loud bang. Not a single student looked up. Students do not have to be made to study. Abundant reinforcement is enough, and good programming provides it.

Individually programmed instruction has much to offer teachers. It makes very few demands upon them. Paraprofessionals may take over some of their chores. That is no reflection on teachers or a threat to their profession. There is much that only teachers can do, and they can do it as soon as they have been freed of unnecessary tasks.

One thing they can do is talk and listen and read what students write. A recent study is said to have found that teachers are responding to things that students say during only five percent of the school day (Goodlad, 1983). If that is so, it is not surprising that one of the strongest complaints against our schools is that students do not learn to express themselves.

If given a chance, teachers can also be interesting and sympathetic companions. It is a difficult assignment in a classroom in which order is maintained by punitive sanctions. The word "discipline" has come a long way from its association with "disciple" as one who understands.

Success and progress are the very stuff on which programmed instruction feeds. They should also be the stuff that makes teaching worthwhile as a profession. Must as students must not only learn but know that they are learning, so teachers must not only teach but know that they are teaching. Burnout is usually regarded as the result of abusive treatment by students, but it can be as much the result of looking back upon a day in the classroom and wondering what one has accomplished. Along with a sense of satisfaction goes a place in the community. One proposed remedy for American education is to give teachers greater respect, but that is putting it the wrong way around.

Let them teach twice as much in the same time and with the same effort, and they will be held in greater respect.

The effect on the educational establishment may be much more disturbing. Almost sixty years ago Sidney Pressey invented a simple teaching machine and predicted the coming "industrial revolution" in education. In 1960, he wrote to me, "Before long the question will need to be faced as to what the student is to do with the time which automation will save him. More education in the same place or earlier completion of full-time education?" Earlier completion is a problem. If what is now taught in the first and second grades can be taught in the first (and I am sure that it can), what will the second grade teacher do? What is now done by the third or fourth grade teacher? At what age will the average student reach high school, and at what age will he or she graduate? Certainly a better solution is to teach what is now taught more effectively and to teach many other things. Even so, students will probably reach college age younger in years, but they will be far more mature. That change will more than pay for the inconvenience of sweeping administrative changes.

The report of the National Commission on Excellence in Education repeatedly mistakes causes for effects. It says that "the educational foundations of our society are being eroded by a rising tide of mediocrity," but is the mediocrity causing the erosion? Should we say that the foundations of our automobile industry are being eroded by a rising tide of mediocre cars? Mediocrity is an effect, not a cause. Our educational foundations are being eroded by a commitment to laymanship and to theories of human behavior which simply do not lead to effective teaching. The report quotes President Reagan as saying that "this country was built on American respect for education . . .. Our challenge now is to create a resurgence of that thirst for education that typifies our nation's history." But is education in trouble because it is no longer held in respect or is it not held in respect because it is in trouble? Is it in trouble because people do not thirst for education or do they not thirst for what is being offered?

Everyone is unhappy about education, but what is wrong? Let us look at a series of questions and answers rather like the series of propositions in what logicians call a sorites:

1. Are students at fault when they do not learn? No, they have not been well taught.

2. Are teachers then at fault? No, they have not been properly taught to teach.

3. Are schools of education and teachers' colleges then at fault? No, they have not been given a theory of behavior that leads to an effective technology.

4. Are behavioral scientists then at fault? No, a culture too strongly committed to the view that a technology of behavior is a threat to freedom and dignity is not supporting the right behavioral science.

5. Is our culture then at fault? But what is the next step? Let us review the sorites again and ask what can be done. Shall we . . .

   - punish students who do not learn by flunking them? Or
   - punish teachers who do not teach well by discharging them? Or
   - punish schools of education which do not teach teaching well by disbanding them? Or
   - punish behavioral science by refusing to support it? Or
   - punish the culture that refuses to support behavioral science—but how?

You cannot punish a culture. A culture is punished by its failure or by other cultures which take its place in a continually evolving process. There could scarcely be a better example of the point of my book *Beyond Freedom and Dignity*. A culture that is not willing to accept scientific advances in the understanding of human behavior, together with the technology which emerges from it, will eventually be replaced by a culture that is. If that is our culture that will be replaced, it would be a tragic end because there are many good things about it that might be lost.

When the National Commission on Excellence in Education says that "the essential raw materials needed to reform our educational system are waiting to be mobilized," it speaks more truly than it knows, but to mobilize them it calls for "leadership." That is as vague a word as excellence. Who, indeed, will make the changes that must be made if education is to play its proper role in American life? It is reasonable to turn to those who suffer most from the present situation:

1. First of all, there are those who pay for education—primarily taxpayers and the parents of children in private schools. They can simply demand their money's worth.

2. There are those who use the products of grade- and high school education—colleges and universities on the one hand and business and industry on the other. As consumers of education they cannot refuse to buy, but they can be more discriminating.

3. There are the teachers. Good teaching will survive only if it is a rewarding profession. Teachers must not only be reasonably well paid; they must enjoy a sense of accomplishment. Their power over the educational establishment is the power to withdraw, and too many are already exercising it individually. The organized withdrawal of a strike is usually a demand for higher wages, but it could also be a demand for better instructional facilities and administrative changes that would improve classroom practices.

But why must we always speak of *demand*? Higher standards for students, merit pay for teachers, and all the other versions of punitive sanctions—they are the things one thinks of first, and they will no doubt make teachers and students work harder, but they will not necessarily have a better effect. They are more likely to lead to further defection. There is a better way: Give students and teachers better reasons for learning and teaching. That is where the behavioral sciences can make a contribution. They can develop instructional practices so effective and so attractive in other ways that no one—student, teacher, or administrator—will need to be coerced into using them.

Young people are by far the most important natural resource of a nation, and the development of that resource is left to education. It is not doing a good job. Each of us is born needing to learn what others have learned before us, and much of it needs to be taught. We should all be better off if education played a far more important part in transmitting our culture. That would make for a stronger America (remember Sputnik), but may we not look forward to the day when the same issues can be discussed with respect to the world as a whole—when all peoples behave well with respect to each other not because they are forced to do so but because they have been taught something of the ultimate advantages of a peaceful world?

References

Botstein, L. (1983, June 5). Nine proposals to improve our schools. *New York Times Magazine*, p. 64.

Goodlad, J.L. (1983). *A place called school.* New York: McGraw-Hill.

Mosteller, F. (1981). Innovation and evaluation. *Science, 212,* 881-886.

National Commission on Excellence in Education (1983). *A nation at risk: The imperative for educational reform.* Washington, DC: U.S. Department of Education.

National Institute of Education (1980). Science and technology and education. In *The five-year outlook: Problems, opportunities and constraints in science and technology* (Vol. 2). Washington, DC: National Science Foundation.

National Research Council, Commission on Behavioral and Social Science and Education (1984). *Biennial program plan, May 1, 1983–April 30, 1985* (p. 41). Washington DC: National Academy Press.

Pressey, S. (1960). Personal communication.

Raizen, S. (1983). *Science and mathematics in the schools: Report of a convocation.* Washington, DC: National Academy Press.

Resnick, L.B. (1983). Mathematics and science learning: A new conception. *Science, 220,* 477.

Rushton, E.W. (1965). *The Roanoke experiment.* Chicago: Encyclopedia Britannica Press.

Siegler, R.S. (1983). Five generalizations about cognitive development. *The American Psychologist, 38,* 263-277.

Skinner, B.F. (1957). *Verbal behavior.* New York: Appleton-Century.

Skinner, B.F. (1971). *Beyond freedom and dignity.* New York: Knopf.

Skinner, B.F. (1982). Innovation in science teaching. *Science, 212,* 283.

Turkington, C. (1983). Cognitive defecits hold promise for prediction of alcoholism. *APA Monitor, June,* 16.

PART ONE

Designs for Excellence:
Behavior Analysis and Teaching

Programmed Instruction and Teaching Machines

Ernest A. Vargas and Julie S. Vargas
West Virginia University

❦

A n extraordinary excitement permeated the beginning of programmed instruction (PI) and its corollary tool, the teaching machine. Conferences were held, new journals published, companies started, machines of every variety invented, and students of every level and background taught. For a while a brave new educational world was glimpsed; a world in which each individual could be taught at her or his own pace and with respect to her or his own needs, yet held to the highest standards society could demand. But after all the excitement over reaching what the vision promised, it turned out to be a mirage. Or was it? No answer is possible without examining what happened, and what effects linger in current educational practices. Was programmed instruction destined to a dead end? An answer unfolds from examining its current status, and the reasons given for the sudden crash of its high-flying success. Can the instructional technology called "programmed instruction" be revitalized? That answer lies ultimately in the future, and perhaps, in part, is predictable, and, in part, with proper prescription, is determinable.

ટ્ર

Historical Development

Some great ideas are born before their time. Take, for example, Babbage's notion of the "analytical engine," the contraption he invented early in the nineteenth century. This machine, to be powered by steam, was a mechanical computer. Unlike any computational devices before it, including Babbage's own "difference engine" on which one could calculate polynomials like $X + X^2 = 35$, the new machine was designed to be programmable. Patterns of holes on punched cards determined the operations the machine was to perform. In addition, Babbage planned his machine to handle branching so that one operation could depend upon the outcome of another calculation. Babbage spent forty years trying to fund and build his analytical engine, but died with only a few parts actually constructed. The engineering techniques of his time could not handle the fine tolerances required for the myriad of cogwheels and levers required (Bernstein, 1981).

Innovations, even when they solve critical problems, succeed only when supportive technology exists. A century passed before technology caught up with Babbage's scheme and made feasible the operations that Babbage envisioned. The history of teaching machines and programmed instruction resembles the story of Babbage's computer: The machine required to teach effectively according to Skinner's conception could not be feasibly built with the technology of the time.

Origins

A Practice Machine. The history of programmed instruction started on November 11, 1953 in a fourth grade classroom: Father's Day at Shady Hill School. Milling among those parents visiting the fourth grade math lesson was B. F. Skinner. He described the class as follows:

> *The students were at their desks solving a problem written on the blackboard. The teacher walked up and down the aisles, looking at their work, pointing to a mistake here and*

*there. A few students soon finished and were impatiently
idle. Others, with growing frustration, strained. Eventually
the papers were collected to be taken home, graded, and
returned the next day (Skinner, 1983, p. 64).*

Having spent eighteen years researching and shaping behavior in the
laboratory, it appalled Skinner to watch what was (and probably still is) a
typical math class. As he later put it,

> *. . . the teacher was violating two fundamental principles:
> the students were not being told at once whether their work
> was right or wrong (a corrected paper seen 24 hours later
> could not act as a reinforcer), and they were all moving at
> the same pace regardless of preparation or ability.*
>
> *But how could a teacher reinforce the behavior of each of
> 20 or 30 students at the right time and on the material for
> which he or she was just then ready? (Skinner, 1983, p.64).*

Clearly automation was needed.

Skinner reacted immediately. Herrnstein in a later recollection mentions that he and another graduate student were to meet Skinner that same
day for a lecture at the Massachusetts Institute of Technology. Arriving
early, they found him sitting in an empty auditorium, busy cutting up manila
folders. When asked what he was doing, Skinner replied, "I'm making a
model of a teaching machine" (Herrnstein, 1984).

From the manila folder model, Skinner built his first teaching machine.
The machine, while lacking elegant looks, nevertheless solved the problem
of providing feedback and letting students go at their own rates (see Machine
A in Figure 1.1). This first machine provided drill and practice: Students
were to have learned how to solve problems before working on the machine.
Though not designed to build new behaviors, it would replace the exercises
that dismayed Skinner during his visit to the math class.

When ready to work on the machine, a student would bring a pile of
cards to it. Inserting a card brought a problem to the window. The student
moved sliders to set the two digits of his or her answer in the space off to
the right of the problem. When the student was ready to check an answer,
he or she pressed a button, locking the sliders in place and turning on a light.

If the student answered correctly, the light showed through a hole in the card, making the answer visible to the student. If the answer was not correct, releasing the lever enabled the student to rearrange the sliders and to try again. The student went on to the next problem by replacing the card in the machine with another from the pile.

The critical characteristics of the first of Skinner's teaching machines were thus three: it required responses that were composed (later called "constructed") as opposed to multiple-choice; it provided immediate feedback to the student on the correctness of his or her response without revealing the correct answer in case of error; and it permitted each student to progress at his or her own rate.

Revisions appeared quickly. A larger version soon replaced the first model. This larger machine permitted problems with answers of up to nine digits. A second improvement used paper tape instead of punched cards. The use of tape provided the opportunity to sequence problems—and the possibility of *building* behavior rather than just providing practice (see Figure 1.1, Machine B).

Earlier Drill and Practice Machines. Long before Skinner's first paper on teaching machines, many other "teaching" devices had been invented. The U.S. Patent Office records dozens of patents for teaching devices prior to 1900, beginning with "Mode of Teaching to Read" in 1809, and these efforts continued into the 1900s. The machines were as varied as the concerns of their inventors. For example, in 1914, Maria Montessori obtained a patent in this country on a device to teach the sense of touch, and others offered apparatuses to teach walking, dancing, and boxing (Mellan, 1960). The military also made early use of devices to teach. In 1918, H.B. English used a column of liquid to give visual feedback to soldiers on how well they were squeezing rifle triggers. If the column rose smoothly, they were squeezing evenly, if it jerked, the pull was uneven (Porter, 1960). No doubt, other earlier teaching instruments of the same sort appeared, that is, devices that primarily used feedback to enhance practice effects (without any clear analysis of the functional effect of the postcedent stimulus, for example, as reinforcer or punisher).

In 1923, Sidney Pressey, working at Ohio State University, invented "A Simple Apparatus Which Gives Tests and Scores—and Teaches" (Pressey, 1926). When Pressey saw Skinner's demonstration of the disk machine at the American Psychological Association in 1957, he wrote

FIGURE 1.1

Skinner's "Slider" Machines

A Skinner's first machine (1953) had two sliders containing the numbers 0 through 9 with which the student composed the answer to simple arithmetic problems on cards inserted one at a time.

B An improved version demonstrated at the University of Pittsburgh (March, 1954). A problem, such as 3+4=__, appears in the square window on a paper tape. The boy moves sliders to fill in the missing numbers and then turns a knob. If correct, the knob turns freely and a new problem comes into view. If incorrect, the knob will not turn, and the boy must reset the sliders. Note that, unlike randomly presented problems, the tape controlled the sequence, so that a program could build behavior through successive approximation.

Skinner and included copies of articles he had written about his machine. Pressey's machine presented items with up to four multiple-choice options, and could tally not only correct answers but the number of tries for incorrect answers. In addition, Pressey reported in his article,

> ... the device ... tells the subject at once when he makes a mistake (there is no waiting several days, until a corrected paper is returned, before he knows where he is right and where wrong). It keeps each question on which he makes an error before him until he finds the right answer; he must get the correct answer to each question before he can go on to the next (Pressey, 1926).

Items mastered could be dropped from those the student encountered on repeated testings, and the machine even included a metal chute, out of which candy would drop when the subject made a preset number of correct responses.

In the 1920s, Pressey also tried using punchboards that held an answer sheet on top of thick cardboard containing holes for the answer key. When a student pressed a pin or pencil under his or her choice, it would puncture the paper only if over a correct answer hole, but leave marks for wrong answers (Pressey, 1950). A 1948 variant revealed a red spot through correct holes (Angell & Troyer, 1960). In 1931, a student of Pressey's, J. C. Peterson, devised "chemo-sheets," answer sheets that turned blue when the spot for the correct multiple-choice answer was correct, but turned red if incorrect (Peterson, 1960). Another of Pressey's students, Leslie J. Briggs, worked with the Air Force in designing a "Subject-matter Trainer." This large machine consisted of a panel with twenty windows, each window with a button next to it. A question or name appeared in the window, and the trainee, standing in front of the panel, pushed the button for the matching response.

In all of the devices deriving from Pressey's work, the questions and answers did teach, but the instruction could not be called programmed in any sense: The machines simply gave feedback following multiple-choice items presented in random order. The items did not use formal or thematic prompting nor did the items build in any kind of sequence. When the devices were used for training, students typically made many errors and retook the same sets of problems over and over before reaching mastery.

In spite of their inability to allow for shaping, these early multiple-choice testing machines, compared to quizzes without feedback, increased scores on final exams. Devices, and studies using them, proliferated after 1954 along with teaching machines designed for programmed instruction.

From Drill to Shaping. On March 12, 1954, just four months after visiting his younger daughter's class, Skinner presented his first paper on teaching machines, "The Science of Learning and the Art of Teaching," at a conference at the University of Pittsburgh. He described the teaching technology evolving from the experimental analysis of behavior and set forth the basis for that technology. Skinner demonstrated the paper tape version of the teaching machine (Figure 1.1, Machine B) and listed its important features. They included the constructed response, the go-at-your-own-rate and immediate-reinforcement features from earlier machines, but also some additional advantages:

> *The device makes it possible to present carefully designed material in which one problem can depend upon the answer to the preceding problem and where, therefore, the most efficient progress to an eventually complex repertoire can be made. Provision has been made for recording the commonest mistakes so that the tapes can be modified as experience dictates. Additional steps can be inserted where pupils tend to have trouble, and ultimately the material will reach a point at which the answers of the average child will almost always be right (Skinner, 1954, p. 95).*

Thus, Skinner described the two new features: sequencing problems in complexity and cybernetic feedback (whereby student behavior provided data to improve just those parts of a sequence that were ineffective). That year, he published the paper in the *Harvard Educational Review*.

The spring of 1955 found Skinner on sabbatical leave at Putney, Vermont, finishing his analysis of language soon to be published as *Verbal Behavior* (1957). He realized that a number of things he was saying in *Verbal Behavior* applied to the instructional setting. The teaching of the kinds of verbal behaviors that made up a large part of most subject matters involved subtleties of stimulus control like those he was discussing under the headings of prompting, probing, priming, vanishing, and fading. Skinner began to differentiate between simply presenting harder and harder problems and an "entirely new type of educational program" that would use the principles detailed in *Verbal Behavior* to shape new behavior (Skinner, 1983, p. 95). The first time a response was to be written it had to be "primed" by providing directions and/or examples using the student's imitative or direction-following repertoire to guarantee a correct response. After having written the correct response under conditions which essentially gave away the answer, the student would probably still need formal prompting (being given part of the response) or thematic prompting ("hints" related to the relevant variables controlling the desired response). These aids would be gradually withdrawn *by removing parts* of text or drawings (called "vanishing") or by making them increasingly *hard to see* by lightening print, decreasing size or contrast, or other equivalent actions ("fading"). Linear programming, as Skinner's careful sequencing of frames came to be called, was born—gradually.

The slider machine could not handle complex responses. Earlier, at Putney, in writing a little program about procrastination for his younger daughter Deborah, Skinner used cards with blanks to fill in—his first nonmachine programmed instruction. By April 1955, Skinner had built a new "disk" machine that enabled students to write or draw answers to frames (see Figure 1.2 for a later model):

> *The material is printed on twelve-inch disks exposed one sector at a time. The pupil writes an answer on an exposed strip of paper, then moves a lever which covers his answer with a transparent mask, and reveals the correct answer. If he is right, he moves the lever in a different direction. This punctures the paper to record his judgment, and moves a detent so that the material does not appear again, or will appear only once again as the disk revolves. [When the lever was moved back in place, a new frame appeared.] After finishing the disk, the student tears out the strip of paper and puts it in a file to record his progress (Skinner, 1983, p. 97).*

The development of programmed instruction and its distinctive characteristic as a shaping technique marks the advance from Skinner's first slider teaching machine to the disk machine. The first machine, though able to sequence problems, emphasized drill and practice, that is, strengthening the topography of a repertoire already in place. The disk machine emphasized the development of a new, complex verbal repertoire through gradual build-up of its parts. Behavior could be shaped, using the techniques outlined in *Verbal Behavior*.

FIGURE 1.2

Skinner's "Disk" Machine

A A student putting a disk into the model of the disk machine shown at the APA convention, 1957.

B A student working at the machine. A question appears in the window to the left. The student composes his answer and then moves the lever in his left hand to check it. The written answer moves under plexiglass (where it cannot be changed) and the correct answer is exposed. If the student judges his answer correct, he moves the lever to the right, if incorrect he moves it down again.

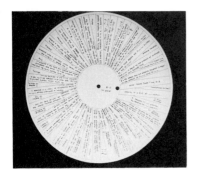

C A disk. This one is on physics. Note that in addition to the materials inserted into the machine, panel books were also referred to, so that detailed diagrams, illustrations, etc., could be used as part of the material to which a student responded.

D Students working on disk machines around 1958.

Development

Software and Hardware. In the fall of 1956, several small grants were pieced together to support a teaching machine project. Skinner moved the project into an old ramshackle place called Batchelder House. Joining the project were Lloyd Homme, on leave for a year from the University of Pittsburgh, Irving Saltzman on leave from Indiana University, and several graduate students (Sue Meyer [later Markle], Douglas Porter, and Matthew Israel). Terminology evolved. "Frame" was coined. Providing examples and asking the student to derive the rules (induction) was named "egrule"— with its opposite "ruleg" (deduction). "Size of step" referred to how rapidly a program built a repertoire (roughly the inverse of the number of frames required to teach a particular skill), and was tied to "density of errors" (the percent of frames on which mistakes were made by a particular student population). "Branching" was also explored for students who made errors.

Many programs were written:

> By the end of the year [the academic year 1956-1957] we had constructed short programs in kinematics, trigonometry, coordinate systems, basic French words and material to teach French dictation, phonetic notation, vocabulary and rudimentary grammar, as well as single demonstration disks in geography, anatomy, and poetry (Skinner, 1983, p. 120).

Skinner also hired a machinist who produced ten disk machines, one of which was demonstrated, along with a geography program, at the American Psychological Association conference of 1957 (see Figure 1.2).

Jim Holland joined the project for its second year (1957-1958), replacing Homme who returned to Pittsburgh. Holland describes those early days:

> For me it began when I arrived, in the fall of 1957, at a gray clap-board building, Batchelder House. Batchelder House, then in decay, had been a rambling residence just across the street from Harvard's Memorial Hall where the Psychology Department, including Skinner's office and laboratory, was housed. . . . Memories of those days in Batcheldor House give me a special verification of humorist Francis Parkinson's claim that active, productive and innovative activities are to be found, not in new buildings

which instead house moribund organizations, but in small,
converted, understaffed, and unkept buildings (Holland,
1976, p. 323).

Holland's task consisted of helping Skinner put his course, Natural Sciences 114, on machine. The thirty wedges they could fit on a disk encouraged brevity and a high density of responding by students. Most frames asked students to fill in a missing word or to supply a technical term, a definition, or example. New principles emerged. Blanks for responses should occur near the end of a sentence to avoid the slight averseness of going back to write. Only stimuli required for the response should be included in a frame. To find out what part of a frame was critical for correct responding, Holland came up with the blackout technique. Portions of a frame were inked out to see how well students could perform with those parts missing (Holland and Kemp, 1965).

The next semester, spring 1958, Harvard and Radcliffe students went to the machine room and worked on the disks before attending Skinner's lectures (see Figure 1.2). By the end of the semester each of the two hundred and fifty students had generated about 3,000 answers, providing Holland and Skinner with precise data on the items most frequently missed, as well as alternative correct answers. After three cycles of tryout and revision, the program was published (in 1961) in book form (see Figure 1.3 for a sample page).

Others were also busy. Following the 1957 launching of Sputnik by the Russians, interest in improving education ran high. In the fall of 1958, Eugene Galanter organized a conference on teaching machines and the papers were published a year later (Galanter, 1959). By 1960, a number of psychologists and educators, primarily in universities, pursued work in teaching machines and programmed instruction all across the United States, and there were beginnings in Europe, primarily in England. (Lumsdaine and Glaser's 723-page source book, *Teaching Machines and Programmed Learning*, 1960, contains papers reflecting development efforts in educational institutions, in the military, and in business.)

Manufacturing and Marketing. From 1954 on, Skinner tried to get a company to manufacture a device that could handle programmed instruction. He negotiated first with International Business Machines (IBM) to produce a slider machine. It assigned the machine to the typewriter division. In the fall of 1955, Skinner received a request as to whether a punched card

FIGURE 1.3

Sample Pages from Popular Programmed Instruction Books

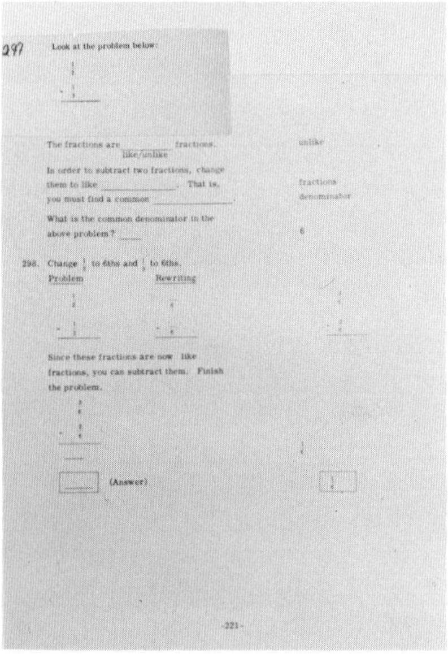

297 Look at the problem below:

The fractions are ______ fractions. (like/unlike) — unlike

In order to subtract two fractions, change them to like ______. That is, you must find a common ______. — fractions, denominator

What is the common denominator in the above problem? ____ — 6

298. Change to 6ths and to 6ths.

Problem — Rewriting

Since these fractions are now like fractions, you can subtract them. Finish the problem.

(Answer)

-221-

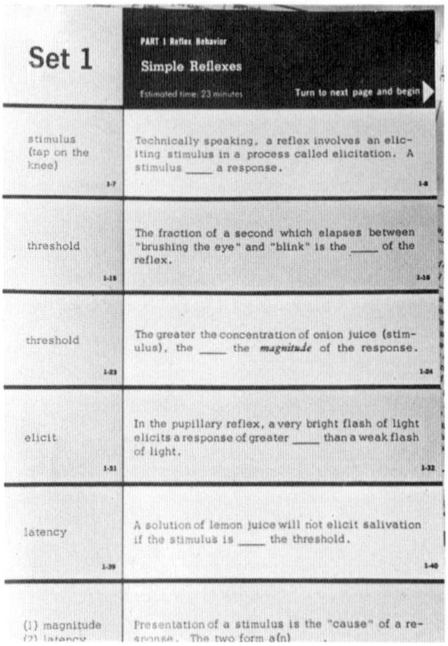

Set 1

PART I Reflex Behavior

Simple Reflexes

Estimated time: 23 minutes

Turn to next page and begin

stimulus (tap on the knee) 1-7	Technically speaking, a reflex involves an eliciting stimulus in a process called elicitation. A stimulus ____ a response. 1-8
threshold 1-15	The fraction of a second which elapses between "brushing the eye" and "blink" is the ____ of the reflex. 1-16
threshold 1-23	The greater the concentration of onion juice (stimulus), the ____ the *magnitude* of the response. 1-24
elicit 1-31	In the pupillary reflex, a very bright flash of light elicits a response of greater ____ than a weak flash of light. 1-32
latency 1-39	A solution of lemon juice will not elicit salivation if the stimulus is ____ the threshold. 1-40
(1) magnitude (2) latency	Presentation of a stimulus is the "cause" of a response. The two form a(n)

A Two frames from *Basic Mathematics* (O'Malley, 1963, p.220-221) showing the initial stages of teaching adding and subtracting fractions. The prompts which help the student through this problem are later withdrawn so he or she must compute without being reminded of the rules. This program like the Programmed Reading, used a slider to cover correct answers.

B A page from Holland and Skinner's *The Analysis of Behavior* (1961). The student answers the first item and then turns the page. The correct answer is printed on the same level next to the next item to answer.

verifier could be used for prototype testing models. It could not, Skinner replied, and also mentioned that a year had already passed since their first discussion of machines. A schedule was made but nothing happened. (Plans were to construct ten machines by fall 1956, try them out in schools in spring 1957, and produce a version for sale in fall 1958). In 1956, IBM turned the machines over to a private model builder. Still no action. Finally in 1959, one machine (instead of ten promised) was sent to Skinner, and Sue Meyer used it with children in the Somerville schools with great success. Nevertheless, in 1960, IBM terminated work on teaching machines.

Initially, Skinner experienced a bit better luck with the Rheem Company. The company first contacted him in May 1958, and by June 1959 it approved a plan to develop an improved model of the machine Skinner was using for his courses. (IBM had been shown the disk machine but expressed no interest in it.) An early version of the Rheem disk machine, called the Didak, was displayed at the 1959 American Psychological Association meetings in Cincinnati, but it presented problems about which Skinner wrote to the company. Three month later no changes had been made. By the summer of 1960, Skinner wrote to Rheem,

> ... complaining that I had given Rheem the names of more than six hundred people who had asked about teaching machines and that the company had not written to any of them. As a result, I was receiving letters which were almost abusive, and people who wanted my machines were buying other models (Skinner, 1983, p. 189).

The letter resulted in a trip to California, entertainment, and a drafting table on which Skinner designed a model for production. Several months later Rheem informed him that the machine he designed was nearly ready. When the machines finally arrived, a mechanic had to change parts to ready the machines for Skinner's course. In March 1962, Rheem transferred Skinner to another office. A year later "our association came to an end" (Skinner, 1983, p. 237).

Shorter discussions with General Motors (which sent an engineer to spend a summer with Skinner's operation at Harvard) and the Comptometer Company in 1959 bore no better results.

Others, however, produced machines, especially for linear programs. Lloyd Homme, after returning to Pittsburgh from Harvard, moved to Albuquerque and founded Teaching Machines, Inc. The company produced both machines and programs and then was bought by Grolier. Charlie Ferster designed an inexpensive cardboard teaching machine that sold widely. They were not alone. The entrepreneurial rush was on, and a variety of small companies proliferated overnight to design, build, advertise, and sell teaching machine products and instruction.

Dissemination

The spread of programmed instruction and all sorts of teaching devices in the 1960s and early 1970s can only be described as a "boom." Money was available for research and development. "Programmed instruction" became a catchy label (though often a misleading one) for any instruction broken into steps. Varieties of programmed instruction proliferated. In overviewing the kinds, instructional designers classified programming into two types: linear and branching.

A linear program taught the student with a minimum of errors, using Skinner's techniques of prompting, priming, etc. and through tryouts and revisions. The "linear" referred to the tight building of behavior, not to a formal ordering of items since a student could be skipped ahead or brought back to some point in the program if necessary. Most linear programs required the student to write or compose a response rather than select it, and most were field tested and rewritten until remedial branching was not necessary. However, some linear programs branched, some asked for multiple-choice responses, and some used panels or long passages to read before responding. Nevertheless, their defining feature was insistence upon a low error rate. All linear programmers shared Skinner's philosophy that the program should bear the burden of teaching so that mistakes would not be made.

Instructional programmers divided the instructional material into units called "frames." Frames in linear programming tended to be small (usually no longer than a fifth of a page, including the response). Program designers included only the textual material necessary for a response, leading to a high density of responding (few words to read per constructed response [see Figure 1.3 for an example]). Standard practice demanded that any frame missed by more than five percent of the students be rewritten, or its content broken into smaller steps.

Branching programs, in contrast, consisted of passages to read followed by multiple-choice test questions. In a sense they resembled the programs in Pressey's machines, except that instead of asking students to read the whole assignment before taking all test items, questions were interspersed throughout, with remedial loops for those items missed. Students were to learn from the text passages, but if they failed, presumably they could learn from their mistakes. Branching programs thus divided instruction into larger chunks and planned for errors.

Typically a branching program frame occupied one page: a half page or so of text followed by a multiple-choice question. Each choice sent the student to a different page with an appropriate message. For incorrect choices the page explained why the choice was incorrect and sent the learner back to pick another choice (or to a remedial loop). Correct choices typically repeated the answer chosen ("You said, . . . You are right!"), and presented the next chunk of information. Norman Crowder argued for and promoted branching programs (Crowder, 1960).

Programmed instruction, both linear and branching (though mostly linear), found its way into all sectors of society in the early 1960s. It appeared to be the instructional innovation of the decade. The military, business and industry, and education all taught with it.

The Military. Programmed instruction represented an ideal teaching technology for the military as it needed to effectively and efficiently train new recruits, and concurrently it maintained a budget large enough to permit development of programs and machines. The U.S. Air Force alone spent over a billion dollars for formal and specialized courses during the fiscal year of 1961 (Eckstrand, Rockaway, Kopstein, & Morgan, 1962, p. 78). As early as the 1950s, the military looked into feedback devices of the Pressey sort. After Skinner's early papers on programmed instruction, the military got interested in machines that could present material using techniques of successive approximation. In the fall of 1961, the Air Force conducted in-house training courses on programmed instruction. By January 1963 about 350 programmed instruction writers had been trained in three pro- gramming techniques: linear, branching, and mathetics (Garner, 1966, pp. 52-53). (Mathetics was a backward chaining approach promoted by Gilbert, 1962, similar to Skinner's in that the last step in a complex sequence was taught first, then the next-to-last, etc.)

The military favored machines over paper and pencil forms of program- ming, probably because of the difficulty of looking ahead at answers when using a machine. It also turned away from branching programs, relying instead on placement tests to determine the level at which recruits should work. In general, the military used multiple-choice rather than constructed responding—again perhaps because machine implementation was easier with that mode of responding. By 1965, Major Marvin R. Roever reported at the National Society for Programmed Instruction convention that in the Air Force "linear constructed response programs no longer seemed justifiable, and that branching sequences were now used only for remediation and for adjunctive purposes" (Garner, 1966, p. 53).

Business. The business sector became heavily involved in programmed instruction. Several large corporations (AT&T, IBM, Sperry Rand, and Kodak, to name a few) adopted programmed instruction for training new employees. Responding to this demand as well as that from the military, a number of entrepreneurs started firms to produce programmed materials, primarily in paper and pencil formats. Two examples are Teaching Machines, Inc., founded, as previously mentioned, by Lloyd Homme; and Basic Systems, founded by Francis Mechner and David Padwa. These entrepreneurial efforts flourished.

Basic Systems expanded within six years from two to one hundred and thirty employees, largely due to negotiating a major deal with Meredith Corporation. The company hired Columbia Ph.D.'s trained in the basic analysis of behavior by Fred Keller and W.N. Schoenfeld. It also hired staff from the Center for Programmed Instruction at Columbia University. Working at odd hours, in jeans and t-shirts, with an excitement and tension similar to that surrounding the design and birth of the DEC computer described in Kidder's *Soul of a New Machine* (1981), the rapidly increasing staff of Basic Systems produced an amazing number of programs. In 1966, Xerox bought the company and turned it into a division that operated in to the 1980s (Cook, 1984).

In addition to the large corporations using programmed instruction in their training, and the small entrepreneurial firms producing PI for them and the educational market, most of the major publishing houses jumped on the PI bandwagon when it appeared to be picking up speed and profits. Publishers, however, were leery of machines. They did not want to depend on the popularity of a particular machine, and produced instead programmed instruction in book form (Walther, 1961).

A *Programmed Instruction Guide* published by Entelek—another of the small entrepreneurial companies—listed in 1968 over 450 companies publishing programmed instruction materials. Figure 1.4 shows the growth of commercially available programs. From only a handful in 1960, the number of programs increases exponentially to over two thousand in 1968, the last year for which figures are available.

FIGURE 1.4

The Growth of Commercially Available Programs in Print

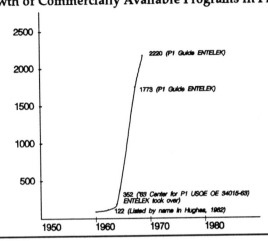

Education. Programmed instruction also entered traditional education. Many programs produced were for elementary and secondary school topics, and such classics, as the Programmed Reading Series published by McGraw-Hill, and Basic Mathematics published by Addison-Wesley, were widely used (O'Malley, 1963; Sullivan, 1969; [see Figure 1.3]).

A survey carried out in New York in 1963 by the Center for Programmed Instruction showed eleven percent of the almost two thousand schools that responded using programmed instruction for part of their instruction (Garner, 1966, p. 35).

Research in programmed instruction flourished in colleges and universities in the 1960s. A 1964 survey of 967 randomly selected institutions of higher education disclosed that 49% of them had conducted research in programmed instruction, and 98% of those planned to continue. Of the rest, 78% planned to start research in the area (Garner, 1966).

By the mid sixties, programmed instruction was well established as a specialized field of instructional technology. The National Society for Programmed Instruction (NSPI) (organized in 1963) flourished and was publishing its own journal. Garner (1966, pp. 56-57) mentions that another journal, *Programmed Instruction*, was in volume V by 1965. Within a few years, there were a dozen societies worldwide, similar to NSPI. Centers for

Programmed Instruction had opened at Harvard, Columbia, and the University of Michigan. It appeared as if the programmed instruction movement was going to remake the field of education, and teaching machines would be the tool of the future in every classroom. They would be. But in a guise that no one had anticipated.

Denouement. The teaching machine and programmed instruction movement reached its peak in the United States in the late sixties. The 1968 Entelek *Programmed Instruction Guide* optimistically begins, "Programmed instruction is here to stay." That was the last of those guides. New books published on programmed instruction reached a crest in the early sixties, maintained their surge for a few years, then ebbed to an occasional one or two per year. The very name, "programmed instruction," lost its appeal. A hint appeared as early as 1962: In a later printing, Mager dropped the word "programmed" from the title of his book, *Preparing Objectives for Programmed Instruction* (1961). Eighteen years later, even its earliest enthusiasts expressed their distaste for the term: in December, 1980, NSPI stood for the National Society for Programmed Instruction; in January, 1981, it became the National Society for Performance and Instruction.

ﺬﻪ

Current Status

The teaching machine and programmed instruction movement seems to have halted. The centers for programmed instruction at Columbia, Harvard, and Michigan universities are closed. There are no extant programmed instruction journals. Mechanical teaching machines no longer roll off assembly lines. Programmed texts no longer crowd shelves in school libraries and college bookstores. Conference announcements no longer herald the latest gathering of PI aficionados. It appears that programmed instruction has died.

Or has it? Certainly not many promote the name or tout the technique. It would be hard to find anyone specifically teaching what they would call "programmed instruction." But all of the principles and procedures are alive, some thriving in different forms, most continuing in subdued but persistent ways.

Diffusion in Education

The original programmed instruction effort diffused throughout education. Programmed instruction characteristics became a part of the conventional wisdom regarding any type of instruction, or melded into other types of instructional endeavors that are flourishing.

Many behaviorally-oriented instructional innovations that presently thrive carry one or more features originating in programmed instruction. A high frequency of responding, measurement of rate, emphasis on antecedent stimulus control in conjunction with consequences, specificity of teaching objectives in behavioral terms, criteria for progress based on high mastery, students going at their own pace, and last and possibly most important, cybernetic feedback—the control of the instructional designer by the student's interaction with the stimulus dimensions of the programmed material; one or more of these characteristics dominate ongoing teaching techniques such as Precision Teaching, Direct Instruction, the Personalized System of Instruction, and Cybernetic Instruction. Precision Teaching, for example, stresses the importance of a high rate of responding and its direct measurement. (Ogden Lindsley, the originator of Precision Teaching, was both student and colleague of Skinner.) Direct Instruction imparts special status to antecedent stimulus control. The Personalized System of Instruction (PSI) features criterion mastery and individual student pacing. (Fred Keller, the originator of PSI and long-time friend of Skinner's, was an early advocate of programmed instruction, and with W.N. Schoenfeld produced many of the leaders in the programmed instruction field in the sixties.) Cybernetic Instruction bases all features of any instructional system on the control of the teacher through changes in the reciprocal interaction between student and instructional system (Vargas and Fraley, 1975).

Within given instructional domains, some of the specific techniques Skinner recommended in his analysis of verbal behavior, and applied to programmed instruction, were adopted as standard procedures. In special education, for example, teachers and aides routinely teach with techniques of prompting, priming, probing, fading, and vanishing. Music education makes use of much instructional craft drawn from programmed instruction especially for work in music therapy (Greer, 1980).

Overall, traditional education adopted one feature of programmed instruction—behavioral objectives (called a variety of names, most often performance objectives); and promoted another—immediate reinforcement (though as "feedback"). Behavioral objectives specified the terminal topographies for which instruction was programmed. After a period of controversy over their usefulness, they settled into establishment practice. They form the linchpin for accountability schemes. Some states, such as California, legally require them, and so does at least one federal law, Public Law 94-142. A corollary of behavioral objectives—competency testing—has also become part of mainstream practices. An increasing number of states require mastery tests to ensure that students have reached objectives, not just spent time in classrooms. Many educators also advocate "immediate reinforcement." Their use of the term often differs considerably from Skinner's, for example, calling test grades returned the next period or even the next day "immediate reinforcement" when they are neither immediate nor necessarily reinforcing. But the fact that mainstream educators use the term at all shows the lasting influence of features coming from programmed instruction.

Lastly, the huge current that was programmed instruction split into trickles here and there, some of them sufficiently like the parent stream to say they continued it. Several of the individuals from Basic Systems in the sixties continue to work in instruction either as consultants in programmed instruction, or as founders of small but successful publishing companies that produce programmed instruction for the medical or educational markets. In industry, programmed instruction continues to be a major mode of training. The military also continues to use programmed instruction in its training.

Failure of Programmed Instruction as a Movement

Despite success in influencing traditional education and the success of the programmed instruction efforts that continue, no instructional thrust is broad enough and distinctive enough to be called programmed instruction. The fervor of the sixties is gone. The term "programmed instruction" fell out of favor. "Teaching machine" is even said pejoratively. The programmed instruction movement as a movement failed. Why? Speculation centers on several reasons.

Inadequacy? Perhaps programmed instruction ceased to interest educators because it did not work—or at least worked no better than cheaper alternative techniques. This accusation constitutes the gist of what many critics said and still say. A number of studies appeared to back up the critics.

Selection I

In reviewing research in 1969, Zoll examined 13 studies comparing programmed instruction in mathematics to traditional instruction. Three showed programmed instruction to be superior, three found traditional instruction better, and the remaining seven showed no difference (Zoll, 1969). Many studies showed success, however, sometimes great success, or at worst no difference. In a review of effectual alternatives to traditional instruction, Jamison, Suppes, and Wells (1974) summarized surveys of the effectiveness of programmed instruction, as well as a number of individual studies. The latest survey on which they reported, one by Lange in 1972, reviewed 112 comparative studies. Forty-one percent found PI to be superior, 49% showed no difference, and only 10% found traditional methods to surpass programmed instruction. Proponents and critics hurled the results of studies back and forth at each other.

The contradiction and ambiguity of results clears up easily if one considers the "programmed instruction" studied and compared. Much of what antagonists and proponents called programmed instruction was that in name only. Studies comparing traditional instruction with programmed instruction used a variety of commercially and locally produced programs. Eager to share in the fall-out from enthusiasm over a new technique, many designers produced programs that ignored the careful sequencing, attention to contingencies, tryout, and revision required by the technology. These products bore only a formal, even superficial, resemblance to the original programs. No agency or professional group exerted any quality control over what was called programmed instruction and many inferior "programs" were marketed. (The current software market in computers displays the same symptoms; J.S. Vargas, 1986.) Had authors met even one of the basic requirements of programmed instruction—extensive field testing and revision—their programs would have resulted in more effective teaching than the alternative techniques to which they were compared.

Hostility? Another reason given for the lack of success of programmed instruction is rejection or downright hostility, often expressed by the education establishment. There were, and continue to be, attacks on programmed instruction's putative dehumanizing and trivial qualities. These attacks primarily emphasize that programmed instruction, regardless of its effectiveness, does not address what is important in education—a grasp of the subject matter beyond rote learning and the teaching of thinking, especially creative thinking. This distress with programmed instruction seems to stem from a misunderstanding of the technology and the science from which it derives. Only ignorance of the technology prevents employing it for *any* educational goal. If an educator desires to teach thinking, then educators must render that objective into what students are to do. Once they do that, a program can be written to accomplish it.

How much weight should be given to such "hostility" is hard to say. One would think that the demonstrated effectiveness of many programmed materials would outweigh lambastic fulminations. Unfortunately that is not always the case. Even recently, the two behavioral Head Start programs found most effective in extensive and long-term evaluations have not received the endorsement of education writers, and have had a hard time getting the resources that their success would deserve (Gersten, Carnine, & White, 1984; Watkins, 1988). And despite the occasional laudatory article (Weinstock, 1984) in establishment journals such as *Phi Delta Kappan*, praising the instructional results achieved with programmed curricula, such efforts continue to be honored more by neglect than by practice.

Ignorance? The failure of many individual programs to teach well resulted from knowing too little or nothing of the experimental analysis of behavior and the conceptual framework—verbal behavior—from which programmed instruction originated. Basic terms derived from experimental work were misunderstood and thus the phenomena they described unknown. For example "reinforcers" and "reinforcement" were said not to work when students failed to work hard. Lacking a background in the experimental analysis of behavior presented a situation equivalent to that of engineering a bridge while misunderstanding physics; it might still be done but the bridge's collapse should not be blamed on the misunderstood science.

Cooke, 1984, documents in detail how preservice education textbooks continue to maintain inaccurate and distorted accounts of programmed instruction. For example (p. 208),

> Although they [Beilher and Snowman] state that programmed instruction 'can be effective with some types of material and some types of students' [p. 168], 'it is not practical for several reasons. Skinner failed to take into account significant differences between rats, pigeons, and younger and older human beings when he developed programmed instruction' [p. 173]. Beilher and Snowman see one of these differences as the effectiveness of immediate

> *reinforcement. Immediate reinforcement may work with animals because 'they are unable to store and process information in sophisticated ways. But older students, who are able to memorize all kinds of information . . . may find that a response-feedback, response-feedback routine becomes tedious, annoying or unnerving' [p. 172].*

But, Cooke goes on to say,

> *Any poorly designed material, programmed or not, will very likely become tedious or annoying. This has nothing to do with human susceptibility to reinforcement or to the "storing or processing" differences in organisms; it has to do with the quality of the program (p. 208).*

Unfamiliarity with Skinner's analysis of verbal behavior from which early techniques such as prompting, etc., were derived and later improvements could develop, also fueled the failure of programmed instruction. Without understanding the subtle stimulus controls over verbal behavior and the manner in which these operated, many "programmers" depended on hand-me-down notions of program design, for example, simply imitating the small step format of instructional design. But there is a world of difference between two frames that look similar, as Donald Cook (1983) has pointed out. Frame A in Figure 1.5 will bring a student under stimulus control of critical features of diagonal, whereas Frame B, which looks very similar, will not.

Economics? The effort to provide a mechanical device to present programmed instruction encountered a stiff stumbling block: lack of profit. Enough programs needed to be available so that school systems would find it useful to buy teaching machines for classroom use. Publishers were reluctant to invest the time and capital to produce programs for machines when popularity of the program or of a particular machine was in question. Further reluctance accrued where the same textual material would be used over and over again by different students instead of a school district having to buy one copy per student (Walther, 1961).

An institutional factor also intruded: School systems assessed their costs by number of students taught rather than degree of repertoire changed. The lecture method, and variants of it, is the cheapest teaching technology possible. Any effort to consider individual differences considerably in-

FIGURE 1.5

A Comparison of Frames with Appropriate and Inappropriate Stimulus Control (from Cook, 1984)

A straight line connecting opposite corners of a quadrilateral is called a diagonal.

In the figure at the right, which is the diagonal?

AB, CD, BD, AC, BC, DA

A To complete this frame, a student must respond to the figure and to the definition of a diagonal.

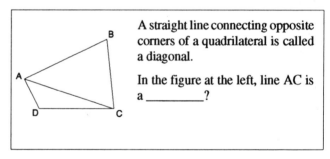

A straight line connecting opposite corners of a quadrilateral is called a diagonal.

In the figure at the left, line AC is a _____?

B This frame, which looks similar, will not teach as effectively as Frame A. Here, the student needs only to copy the word in capitals. He or she does not need to attend to either the definition of diagonals or to the figure.

creases the cost of instruction. Programmed instruction, when properly designed, will work only by considering the specific repertoire and "motivators" of each individual student. Programmed instruction is more expensive than the lecture method if judged only by the cost per student without considering effectiveness. Until schools look at what their dollars buy in terms of student gains in performance, there will be no cost advantage in using more effective technologies (E.A. Vargas, 1980).

The Delivery Device? Perhaps the primary reason for the failure of programmed instruction stemmed from the lack of availability of a delivery tool to present, maintain, and evaluate the arrangements that sophisticated shaping requires. The engineering technology lagged behind the science. Even in a one-to-one situation, for some objectives a human teacher is not up to the job. As Skinner pointed out,

> *In the experimental study of learning it has been found that the contingencies of reinforcement which are most efficient in controlling the organism cannot be arranged through the personal mediation of the experimenter. An organism is affected by subtle details of contingencies which are beyond the capacity of the human organism to arrange. Mechanical and electrical devices must be used . . . Now, the human organism is, if anything, more sensitive to precise contingencies than the other organisms we have studied. We have every reason to expect, therefore, that the most effective control of human learning will require instrumental aid (Skinner, 1968, pp. 21-22).*

Unfortunately, mechanical machines could only in part live up to this requirement, primarily because the mechanical machine could not meet the critical characteristic of precise contingencies: altering the program to adjust it in detail to the varying repertoires and needs between students and for each student between teaching occasions.

Most early programmed instruction was formatted into paper and pencil texts. The mechanical teaching machine maintained true contingencies, such as preventing students from peeking at the answers, but still could not achieve the most important one. The machine available to programmed instruction designers could not meet the basic aim of programmed instruction: individualization of instruction. For example, no mechanical machine could vary sequencing or frame size or require additional practice in response to a wide range of student answers, nor alter, depending on student characteristics, stimulus controls on either side of the action. Further, one of the critical features of proper programming, the *composing* of a response rather than selecting from a set of alternatives, remained insolvable with mechanical devices since they could not evaluate a constructed response

(Cook, 1984). No delivery device, including machines, exploited the technology inherent in the science. (For a summary of principles of programmed instruction, see E.A. Vargas & J.S. Vargas, 1991.)

ॐ

Predictions and Prescriptions

In 1913, Edison, enthusiastic over his new movie projector, predicted a revolution in education: "Books will be obsolete. Scholars will soon be instructed through the eye. It is possible to teach every branch of human knowledge with the motion picture. Our school system will be completely changed in 10 years" (quoted in Griffin, 1983, p. 96). In the early 1960s similar claims were made for educational television. Both of these early innovations, however, only presented material. They did not satisfy even the rudiments for effective instruction. They did not require active responding by students, nor provide feedback for learner responses, nor adjust to students' progress. Students can (and frequently do) sleep through movies or television programs. As an instructional technique, simply presenting material fails (and is bound to fail) for the vast majority of students.

Predictions

A Proper Machine. In the 1980s, however, technology contributed microcomputers to the educational scene. The computer supplies the demands of programmed instruction better than either mechanical devices or paper and pencil ever could. Programmed instruction demands a dynamic interaction between the actions of an individual and the tasks subsequently presented—an interplay with at least as much flexibility, subtlety, and timing precision as that required for shaping the behavior of infrahuman organisms. The contingencies must require the student to discriminate among subtle features, and consequences must depend upon the student's progress in acquiring the repertoire desired. Unlike booklet programmed instruction and even Skinner's disk model of the teaching machine, the microcomputer possesses the speed and flexibility to maintain real contingencies. It can accept and evaluate constructed responses and can adjust what the student is asked to do next as a result of that student's progress.

Many educational programs have been written for microcomputers. In general, however, the instructional design prevalent in computer instruction ignores or overlooks the prior work in programmed instruction. Current instructional formats on computers demonstrate little influence from programmed instruction. The three most prevalent types of instructional formats consist of drill-and-practice, simulation, and tutorial.

Drill-and-practice programs present problems for students to solve and give immediate feedback to students. Like Pressey's machines, the computer presents the problems in random order, and like Pressey's material, drill-and-practice programs usually are quite effective at increasing student performance. They do not, however, shape behavior. They only increase speed and/or accuracy on a repertoire already in place.

Simulations also require a high frequency of student responding. In a simulation, the student responds and the computer imitates the natural consequences of the student's actions. So, for example, in a sophisticated flight simulator, the student operates plane controls, and the top of the computer screen shows the resulting "view" out the windshield as well as giving the resulting speed and altitude, etc., on the dials represented at the bottom of the screen. Simulations duplicate an actual situation well enough so that they lower the cost or danger of training in that situation. Simulations, however, do not shape behavior expeditiously. Instead, they throw students into a trial and error learning experience, usually with a high error rate initially. For those students who persist, simulations can be very effective learning tools. But unless students obtain some success early on, they are likely to give up. More seriously, many of the skills students need to learn (such as reading and solving algebraic equations) do not lend themselves to a simulation format.

For most instructional objectives, tutorials provide the ideal teaching format. Instructional designers can design them to teach a new repertoire by shaping it one step at a time with a minimum of errors. To do so well, the tutorial program must take into account the characteristics of the student's repertoire. With a good tutorial program, the computer could be the ideal teaching machine.

With the potential the computer provides, it is discouraging to see tutorials that violate every principle of instructional design. One would expect tutorials—programs designed for initial teaching of a skill—to follow the procedures developed so effectively during the sixties. No so. Many tutorials assume that a student learns by reading what is on the screen without requiring any response to it, in spite of Doran and Holland's (1971) research which shows that students not only do *not* learn what they do not need for responding—they do not even read it. One PLATO algebra program, for example, consists of a dozen screens of explanations and examples worked for the student before requiring a single response other than "Press the space bar to continue." To press the space bar requires no discrimination on the student's part that involves the subject matter. One could progress through much of the program while concentrating on something else entirely. Instructional design that barely requires active responding poses a futile hope for more sophisticated programming features of prompting, probing, fading, and vanishing.

Not all tutorials are poorly designed. But the vast majority of instructional designers either do not know, or if acquainted with seem not to understand, behaviorological principles, and thus fall back on a present-and-test format when writing tutorials. (The so-called teaching of skills to pass the Scholastic Aptitude Test presents a good example of this [see Stables, 1985].) Thus shaping, with all of the accompanying techniques outlined in *Verbal Behavior*, remains foreign to most microcomputer tutorials.

The Near Future—Some Similarity to the Past. It seems reasonable to predict that the course of programmed instruction with computers as teaching machines will follow the history of programmed instruction in general. Many products will continue to come into the market that fail to use principles of prompting, probing, fading, and vanishing, but that superficially copy the programmed instruction format by breaking information into "screens" (instead of frames). Some good programs will also appear, and some of these will become popular and will be widely used for many years. But the many "tutorials" that present and test instead of teach, will discourage teachers and parents alike, and the term "tutorial" like "programmed instruction" may fall into disfavor. As with the original programmed instruction movement, the military and business communities, where instructional effectiveness means the saving of large amounts of money, will adopt programmed instruction with computers as teaching machines. Companies designing products for the military and for industry will increasingly demand instructional designers with behavioral backgrounds, and many excellent products will be designed and widely used.

School administrators often encourage teachers to try something new, but this jawboning often results in nothing but vacuous merit awards since evaluators do not look at behavior change (what students learned) to evaluate success. In looking through literature on programmed instruction and on computer-assisted instruction, one finds many reports claiming how well some new method of instruction worked—but the results are most commonly reported in teacher and student opinions (occasionally using questionnaires)—rather than in an increase in performance of the users. Under such contingencies, it is *newness*, not *effectiveness*, that gains attention for the teacher willing to try out new procedures.

The public also evaluates by popularity—how well students *like* material or how many other school districts employ a particular series of lessons. Few look at how well the materials accomplish the basic missions of the school. Under these circumstances, one would predict flashy computer programs to gain approval, with little regard for how they fit into existing curricula. Computers are being used for "computer literacy" rather than for teaching those basic skills that students are widely shown to lack.

The Far Future—Organizational Impact on the Schools. Eventually, however, schools will have to look at student achievement. When they do, they will inevitably use computers as teaching machines for basic and advanced skills. Learning centers will group many machines and subjects together. Students will go to those centers initially for remedial instruction, but eventually for mainline instruction in skills such as reading and mathematics. The role of the teacher in these centers and in the basic classroom will change. Machines will take over much of the task of presenting new material and correcting assigned exercises. They will also keep track of student progress, and will help the teacher match learning activities to each student's proficiency level and recent progress. The teacher, freed of the tedium of correcting papers and clerical and record-keeping tasks, will be able to spend more time in activities unsuitable for the computer such as small group discussions, group activities, and projects. The teacher will also gather more information about each student, and thus will be able to diagnose learning problems and to work individually with students not progressing well with the currently available computer programs. In general, then, programmed instruction on computers will filter eventually into the traditional education scene. To help it filter more rapidly, and to arrive more intact, several suggestions are in order.

Prescriptions

The original program designers built programmed instruction upon the experimental analysis of behavior and radical behaviorism, or behaviorology, as the link between the laboratory science and its philosophy is currently called (E.A. Vargas, 1991). For any applied technology to succeed, practitioners must firmly ground their techniques in the basic principles of its science. Prescription One, then, is to engineer from the science, to design materials by following the basic principles that work. From this recommendation other prescriptions follow: Two, evaluate materials from their effect on student behavior change; Three, design sequences according to principles derived from a behaviorological analysis of verbal behavior; and Four, teach teachers so they too become behavioral engineers.

Engineer from Science. An applied field builds upon a scientific foundation. In behaviorology, the keystone of that foundation lies in the functional relationships between actions and stimuli. These relationships occur in a set of contingent interactions between antecedent stimuli, current actions, and postcedent stimuli. When instructional designers ignore those relationships—responding to formal properties of printed material rather than to the functional controls over the student—they lose the advantage of the technology they choose. Like a building built to look like the Taj Mahal, but without the physics of stresses and strains, a movement built on superficial resemblance to programmed instruction is bound to collapse.

Evaluate from Student Behavior. Unlike buildings and bridges, where success and failure are conspicuous, almost everyone judges the success of instructional materials on everything but its behavioral effectiveness. No one would dream of evaluating a bridge solely on its looks, but many publishing houses judge materials by how well teachers like them, without considering whether or not students learned anything through their use. For example, in a survey of checklists for evaluating software, Della Lana (1984) found that a majority of those checklists could be filled out without ever having a student go through the lessons. They included items such as "Are the screen layouts clear and uncluttered," but without any consideration of how students reacted to those screen layouts. But the criterion of proper screen layouts follows from the effectiveness of stimulus control over the student's behavior. One needs only to ask the question, "How well do the screen layouts work?" How a teacher appraises a screen may depart radically from how students react to it. Too many designers obviously judge screens of lecture material and preworked examples on appearance rather than effectiveness.

Design from Verbal Behavior. Most of what is taught in schools consists of verbal behavior. Instructional designers therefore should become sensitive to the subtleties and varieties of control over verbal behavior. Skinner's thorough analysis in *Verbal Behavior* (1957) considers not only dozens of possible sources of control over large word and sentence groups, but also makes one aware of control over parts of sentences and words, or over features not usually considered in an analysis of language, (including the layout and typesetting features of lessons [J.S. Vargas, 1984]). Just as learning the names of various species of bees helps to distinguish between bees, learning names for different sources of control over what we say or write helps distinguish functional relationships previously unnoted. This places the instructional programmer in a better position to use effectively those sources of control in designing instruction.

Teach the Teachers. Finally, teachers themselves should receive basic training in behavior engineering and in the science underlying their profession. We require medical doctors to be well versed about anatomy and physiology. We do not consider those with good physiques or excellent health to be automatically qualified to fix the bodies and health of others. But many make analogous suggestions about those who would teach. Political leaders and public commentators on education seriously propose abandoning education in how to teach, and instead, taking those expert in whatever they know and having them present it.

The argument against the training of teachers reflects the weakness of the training in pedagogy, expertise in how to shape others to predesignated objectives. Colleges of education attend to pedagogy but obviously inadequately. Teachers engineer behavior. They must design the conditions under which a person's repertoire changes in a specified direction. Society may designate terminal repertoires but teachers produce them, or should. Faulty teacher training persists and substantiates the attack on the irrelevancy of teacher training, because colleges of education do not define their mission as producing behavior engineers, and thus ignore a thorough grounding in the basic foundations necessary for behavior engineering—behavior science, specifically the experimental analysis of behavior and its accompanying selectionist philosophy.

Mechanical, aeronautical, chemical, and other kinds of engineers in the physical sciences would know physics only in the most haphazard and narrow way if they encountered the basic science of physics only in bits and pieces in their engineering courses. They would never understand why certain events in their engineering discipline occur as they do. Their training would handicap them for systematically designing new endeavors. Their procedures would consist of compiled rules-of-thumb. Others untrained in engineering procedures would on occasion, perhaps even often, be as successful as they. Academically, questions would rise as to whether such a craft-like discipline, fit perhaps for the training of technicians, belonged in a university. Politically, given the large number of failures, the issue would be raised as to whether such a professional discipline merited public support.

The description above fits professional education much too well. Yet any solution that proposes or discusses dispensing with professional educators is unrealistic. The nature of the human organism demands that someone teach others. In any large, complex society whose economy proliferates forms of expertise with which few are acquainted, that "someone" cannot be a parent, even if available. In a society with millions of young students, teachers will number in the hundreds of thousands. Eventually, those teachers must be produced and organized on a systematic basis.

The difficulty with teaching lies in the general ignorance of the science dealing with its subject matter—human behavior. Not until this century could there be said to be a science of much merit. The science yet tells us little on how to handle many complex human problems, but it tells us more than we knew before. Certainly what there is of that science should be well learned to take advantage of it.

References

Angell, G.W. & Troyer, M.E. (1960). A new self-scoring device for improving instruction. In A.A. Lumsdaine & R. Glaser (Eds.), *Teaching machines and programmed instruction: A source book.* Washington, DC: Department of Audio-visual Instruction, National Education Association.

Bernstein, J. (1981). *The analytical engine.* New York: William Morrow.

Cook, D.L. (1983, October). CBT's feet of clay: Questioning the information transmission model. *Data Training.*

Cook, D.L. (1984). Personal communication.

Cooke, N.L. (1984). Misrepresentations of the behavior model in preservice teacher education textbooks. In W.L. Heward, T.E. Heron, D.S. Hill, & J. Trap-Porter (Eds.), *Focus on behavior analysis in education.* Columbus, OH: Charles E. Merrill.

Crowder, N.A. (1960). Automatic tutoring by intrinsic programming. In A.A. Lumsdaine & R. Glaser (Eds.), *Teaching machines and programmed instruction: A source book* (pp. 286-298). Washington, DC: Department of Audio-visual Instruction, National Education Association.

Della Lana, C.M. (1984). *The use of response rate in the evaluation of instructional software.* Unpublished master's thesis, West Virginia University, Morgantown, WV.

Doran, J. & Holland, J.G. (1971). Eye movements as a function of response contingencies measured by blackout technique. *Journal of Applied Behavior Analysis, 4,* 11-17.

Eckstrand, G.A., Rockaway, M.R., Kopstein, F.F., & Morgan, R.L. (1962). Teaching machines in the modern military organization. In S. Margulies & L.D. Eigen (Eds.), *Applied programmed instruction.* New York: John Wiley and Sons.

Entelek, Inc. (1968). *Programmed instruction guide.* Newburyport, MA: Author.

Galanter, E.H. (Ed.). (1959). *Automatic teaching: The state of the art.* New York: John Wiley and Sons.

Garner, W.L. (1966). *Programmed instruction.* New York: The Center for Applied Research in Education.

Gersten, R., Carnine, D.W., & White, W.A.T. (1984). The pursuit of clarity: direct instruction and applied behavior analysis. In W.L. Heward, T.E. Heron, D.S. Hill, & J. Trap-Porter (Eds.), *Focus on behavior analysis in education.* Columbus, OH: Charles E. Merrill.

Gilbert, T.F. (1962). *Journal of Mathetics, 1,* No. 1.

Greer, R.D. (1980). *Design for music learning.* New York: Teachers' College Press.

Griffin, W.H. (1983). Can educational technology have any significant input on education? *Technological Horizons in Education Journal, November 1,* p. 96.

Herrnstein, R. (Speaker). (1984). After banquet address: Remarks at B. F. Skinner's 80th birthday celebration (cassette recording). The Harvard Club, Harvard University, Cambridge, MA.

Holland, J.G. (1976). Reflections on the beginnings of behavior analysis in education. In L.E. Fraley & E.A. Vargas (Eds.), *Behavior research and technology in higher education.* Reedsville, WV: Society for the Behavioral Analysis of Culture.

Holland, J.G. & Kemp, F.D. (1965). A measure of programming in teaching machine material. *Journal of Educational Psychology, 56,* 264-269.

Holland, J.G. & Skinner, B.F. (1961). *The analysis of behavior.* New York: McGraw-Hill.

Hughes, J.L. (1962). *Programmed instruction for schools and industry.* Chicago: SRA.

Jamison, D., Suppes, P., & Wells, S. (1974). The effectiveness of alternative instructional media: A survey. *Review of Educational Research, 44,* No. 1, 1-68.

Kidder, T. (1981). *The soul of a new machine.* New York: Avon Books.

Selection I

Lumsdaine, A.A. & Glaser, R. (Eds.). (1960). *Teaching machines and programmed instruction: A source book*. Washington, DC: Department of Audio-visual Instruction, National Education Association.

Mager, R. (1961). *Preparing objectives for programmed instruction*. San Francisco, CA: Fearon Publishers.

Mellan, I. (1960). Teaching and educational inventions. In A.A. Lumsdaine & R. Glaser (Eds.), *Teaching machines and programmed instruction: A source book*. Washington, DC: Department of Audio-visual Instruction, National Education Association.

O'Malley, R.H. (1963). *Basic mathematics—A problem solving approach*. (Programmed Text). Menlo Park, CA: Addison-Wesley Publishing Company.

Peterson, J.C. (1960). The value of guidance in reading for information. In A.A. Lumsdaine and R. Glaser (Eds.), *Teaching machines and programmed instruction: A source book*. Washington, DC: Department of Audio-visual Instruction, National Education Association.

Porter, D. (1960). A critical review of a portion of the literature on teaching devices. In A.A. Lumsdaine & R. Glaser (Eds.), *Teaching machines and programmed instruction: A source book*. Washington, DC: Department of Audio-visual Instruction, National Education Association.

Pressey, S.L. (1926, March 20). A simple apparatus which gives tests and scores—And teaches. *School and Society*, Vol. XXXIII, No. 586. (Reprinted in A.A. Lumsdaine & R. Glaser [Eds.], *Teaching machines and programmed instruction: A source book*. Washington DC: Department of Audio-visual Instruction, National Education Association.)

Pressey, S.L. (1950). Development and appraisal of devices providing immediate automatic scoring of objective tests and concomitant self-instruction. *The Journal of Psychology, 29*, 412-447.

Skinner, B.F. (1954). The science of learning and the art of teaching. *Harvard Educational Review, 24*, No. 2, 86-97. (Also published as chapter 2 in Skinner, B. F. [1968]. *The technology of teaching*. New York: Appleton-Century-Crofts.)

Skinner, B.F. (1957). *Verbal behavior.* New York: Appleton-Century-Crofts.

Skinner, B.F. (1968). *The technology of teaching.* New York: Appleton-Century-Crofts.

Skinner, B.F. (1983). *A matter of consequences.* New York: Alfred A. Knopf.

Stables, B. (1985). SAT packages–An update. *Creative Computing, 11*, 86-89.

Vargas, E.A. (1980). Instructional innovation in the university: Requirements for a more certain future. In L.E. Fraley (Ed.), *Behavioral analyses of issues in higher education* (pp. 107-120). Reedsville, WV: Society of the Behavioral Analysis of Culture.

Vargas, E.A. (1991). Behaviorology: Its paradigm. In Waris Ishoq (Ed.), *Human behavior in today's world* (pp. 138-147). New York: Praeger.

Vargas, E.A. & Fraley, L.E. (1975). Cybernetic instruction. In J.M. Johnston (Ed.), *Research and technology in college and university teaching.* Gainesville, FL: University of Florida, Department of Psychology.

Vargas, E.A. & Vargas, J.S. (1991). Programmed instruction: What it is and how to do it. *Journal of Behavioral Education, 1*, 235-252.

Vargas, J.S. (1984). What are your excercises teaching? An analysis of stimulus control in instructional materials. In W.L. Heward, T.E. Heron, D.S. Hill, & J. Trap-Porter (Eds), *Focus on behavior analysis in education* (pp. 126-141). Columbus, OH: Charles E. Merrill.

Vargas, J.S. (1986). Instructional design flaws in computer-assisted instruction. In *Phi Delta Kappan, 67*, No. 10, 738-744.

Walther, C.R. (1961). *Programmed education: A final report to the president.* Internal document prepared for Appleton-Century-Crofts.

Watkins, C.L. (1988). Project follow through: A story of the identification and neglect of effective instruction. *Youth Policy, 10,* No. 7, 7-11.

Weinstock, R. (1984). A title I tale: High reading/math gains at low cost in Kansas City, Kansas. *Phi Delta Kappan, 65,* No. 9, May.

Zoll, E. J. (1969). Research in programmed instruction in mathematics. *The Mathematics Teacher, 62,* February, 103-109.

Direct Instruction:
A Twenty Year Review

Wesley C. Becker, University of Oregon

irect Instruction (DI) grew out of the studies of Carl Bereiter and Siegfried Engelmann at the University of Illinois in the early 1960s. Their empirical approach to problems of instruction were later merged with behavioral analysis through contact with Wesley Becker and Douglas Carnine. Today Direct Instruction stands as a systematic approach to the design and delivery of a range of procedures for building and maintaining basic cognitive skills.

The original version of this chapter contained 20 pages of references. Because of restrictions on the length of the chapter, most references were eliminated. To obtain a full set of DI references, send $2.00 to W. C. Becker, School of Psychology, EDUC, University of Oregon, Eugene OR, 97403.

The central visible features of DI instruction are small-group instruction, with frequent responding by the students, as teachers and aides follow scripts in an active, participation-oriented classroom. Underlying the visible features is a procedural structure built around the rule "Teach more in less time." Procedures are favored which reduce wasted time and hasten the teaching of given objectives. Some procedures help to increase student contact time with adults (aides, small-group teaching, tight scheduling). Some procedures help to increase the effective use of that time (scripted presentation of pretested lessons which focus on general-case teaching, teacher training on program-relevant skills, and monitoring with criterion-referenced tests).

At the core of the model are a set of principles and assumptions which provide the basis for specific program details. We appeal to modern behavior theory for principles to guide teaching strategies and to set constraints in the design of a program. Most distinctive in DI, however, is a focus on the logical analysis of knowledge sets and teaching examples.

In developing this chapter, I will begin with an overview of the more unique aspects of DI. With these underpinnings we can then look back and see where they came from, and examine the research support of their effectiveness.

The Design of Direct Instruction Programs

To understand what is involved in the design of instruction for cognitive learning, it is necessary to make three analyses. First, the ANALYSIS OF BEHAVIOR seeks empirically-based principles that provide the basis for teaching any task. How to motivate and get attention, how to present examples, how to secure student responses, and how to reinforce and correct student response. Second, the ANALYSIS OF COMMUNICATIONS used in teaching seeks principles for the logical design of sequences so that they will effectively transmit knowledge. This analysis focuses on the ways in which sets of stimuli are the same and how they are different (i.e., what discriminations must be taught). Third, the ANALYSIS OF KNOWLEDGE SYSTEMS is concerned with identifying samenesses across apparently different pieces of knowledge.

DI design strategies are presented in detail in the book, *Theory of Instruction,* by Engelmann and Carnine (1982). The design strategies are also covered specifically for reading in *Direct Instruction Reading* by Carnine and Silbert (1979) and for math in *Direct Instruction Mathematics* by Silbert, Carnine, and Stein (1981).

Cognitive Knowledge Forms

The analysis of the structure of knowledge forms underlies Engelmann and Carnine's theory of instruction. This analysis has two goals: (1) the identification of types of structures whose members can be taught with a common strategy, and (2) the identification of samenesses across apparently different knowledge forms. The first analysis leads to efficiency in the design of teaching sequences. The second analysis provides the basis for generalization of what is taught across as broad as possible a set of examples. Before illustrating these ideas, let us examine Engelmann's taxonomy of cognitive knowledge structures (see Figure 2.1 from Engelmann & Carnine, 1982, p. 19).

There are three major knowledge forms: BASIC FORMS or sensory feature concepts, JOINING FORMS which relate basic forms logically or empirically, and COMPLEX FORMS which are comprised of problem-solving routines (chains) and communications about events (sets of facts).

Basic forms are subdivided into single-dimension (or single-feature) concepts and multiple-feature concepts. The latter are nouns or objects concepts (e.g., *ball, tree, car*) and the former are comparatives (*hotter, steeper*) and noncomparatives (*red, rough, under, inside of*). As I will demonstrate, very similar strategies can be used to teach all single-dimension concepts through examples. Nouns on the other hand require a slightly different strategy because of their multiple features and the broad range of their negative instances.

Joining forms include logical transformations and empirical facts which relate basic forms. Given that the student knows how to use singular forms of nouns (ball, house, cup), a transformation rule can be applied to cover plural usage ("This is one ball," "These are two balls," etc.). Transformations take several forms. Differences in form imply different teaching requirements.

FIGURE 2.1

A Taxonomy of Cognitive Knowledge Forms

A.   Basic Forms (Sensory-feature Concepts)

    1.   Comparatives (single-dimension concepts)

    2.   Noncomparatives (single-dimension concepts)

    3.   Nouns (multiple-dimension concepts)

B.   Joining Forms (Relations Between Sensory-feature Concepts)

    1.   Response Transformations

    2.   Correlated Features Relationship (Facts)

        a.   Concrete example → give feature

        b.   Label a set → give feature

        c.   Name substitution (synonym)

        d.   Given a class, tie to higher-order class

C.   Complex Forms

    1.   Communications About Events (fact systems)

    2.   Cognitive Problem-solving Routines (chains)

Facts can take four logical forms (see Figure 2.1). All facts name at least two concepts to be discriminated, e.g., "hotter objects—expand," "ducks—fly south in the winter." Some symbolic facts imply transformations, e.g., "The first digit of a two digit number tells how many 10's you have." Once again, differences in the substructures of classes of facts imply differences in teaching programs.

Problem-solving routines differ greatly in their structures, but a common strategy can be used in designing such routines. In a condensed form the steps are:

1. Specify the range of examples for which the routine will work.

2. Make up a descriptive rule that tells exactly what the learner must do to attack every example within that range. (The same rule must hold for all examples.)

3. Design a task that tests each component discrimination mentioned in the descriptive rule.

4. Construct a chain composed of the tasks that test the component skills or the "steps" in the routine (Engelmann & Carnine, 1982, p. 195).

A simple example of this can be found in teaching fractions. The examples include fractions greater than 1, less than 1, and equal to 1, within the learner's counting range. (Many current textbooks start out with fractions all less than 1 and with only 1 in the numerator). The descriptive rule is "The bottom number tells us how many parts in one whole and the top number tells us how many parts we have." An initial task for the interpretation of fractions would be a series of circles to be divided into parts and filled in to illustrate the fraction. The component steps to be followed in doing this task would be the routine.

Communications about events are sets of facts. Whether we are talking about historical events, kinds of clouds, or the human circulatory system, we are dealing with sets of facts which can be related in some way. Because of the memory demands imposed by learning systems of facts, it is typically helpful to use visual representations of sets of related facts and teaching formats that readily reinforce a lot of practice (such as game formats).

Problem-solving routines and fact systems will be illustrated later.

Introduction to Program Design Strategies

One goal in classifying cognitive knowledge forms is to provide a basis for designing teaching strategies that can be used again and again for similar forms of knowledge. This point will be illustrated shortly with a sequence for the initial teaching of a single-dimension concept.

Some principles that guide design:

1. It is impossible to teach a concept with a single example, since any instance of a concept must be an instance of many concepts. Thus, *we need a set of positive examples.*

2. We want the teaching sequence to produce a generalization so that new examples not used in the teaching will be responded to correctly. Thus, *there must be a structural basis for this generalization in the sameness of our positive examples.*

3. It is impossible to teach a concept using only positive examples, since a group of concept instances can be instances of many concepts. Thus, we also *need a set of negative examples.*

4. A sameness across positive and negative examples rules out a possible interpretation. Thus, for the initial teaching of a concept, *we can minimize the number of examples needed by using a common setup,* where the positive and negative examples share the greatest possible number of features.

5. To show a range of positive features, such as redness, sample that range using the sameness principle: *Juxtapose examples that are as different as possible* (within the context of the setup) *and indicate that they are the same.*

6. Show the limits of a concept using a difference principle: *Juxtapose examples that are minimally different and give them different labels.*

7. After teaching a concept, *test with new examples* to see if it has been learned.

8. Finally, *vary the setup* to show what is irrelevant and to expand the range of applications.

(The design sequence that follows assumes the learner has been taught the logical operations of interpolation and extrapolation. *Interpolation* occurs when after being shown a range of examples of a concept, the student treats examples falling within that range as concept instances. *Extrapolation* occurs when after being shown the boundaries of a concept by minimally different examples, any example more different is treated as a not-instance.)

Selection II

An 11-step sequence that can be used in the initial teaching and testing of most any single-dimension basic concept will be illustrated. First the setup for presenting all 11 examples is designed. For example, to teach the concept OVER, the setup might be a table and a ball (a real table and ball):

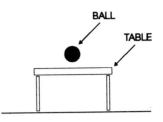

The first two examples are two negatives, with the second example designed to be minimally different from example 3.

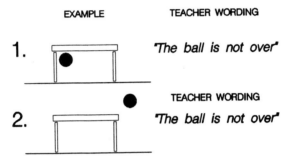

	EXAMPLE	TEACHER WORDING
1.		*"The ball is not over"*
2.		*"The ball is not over"*

Next, show three positives which illustrate the possible range of positive examples, ending with a positive that is minimally different from a negative:

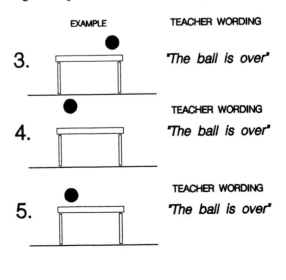

	EXAMPLE	TEACHER WORDING
3.		*"The ball is over"*
4.		*"The ball is over"*
5.		*"The ball is over"*

Next, show six random positive and negative examples (except that the first one is a minimally different from example 5 and test the students.

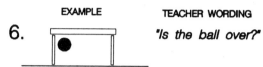

Finally, change the setup and vary the irrelevant features. Take a variety of objects and ask, for example: "Is the ball over the chair?" "Is the pen over the table?" "Is the cup over the saucer?"

This strategy can be applied to a wide number of single-dimension concepts, both comparatives (such as *taller, farther*) and noncomparatives (such as *tall* and *far*). In the case of comparatives, however, a starting point is used to compare the first example with (see Figure 2.2), otherwise the logic of the sequence is the same. Similar strategies are applicable to noun concepts. Since nouns have many features, however, there are no precise minimum differences between instances and not-instance. Also, one is constrained to using negative examples that are in the student's repertoire. Finally, since the names of the negatives have already been taught, they are used in their identification.

Continuous conversion. An additional principle in presenting examples for initial teaching is: Where possible, directly change positive examples into negative examples, and vice versa. In the 11-step sequence above, the negative example of *over* would be converted to a positive example by a simple movement. Since everything is kept the same except the position (difference principle), this helps the learner focus on the critical features of *over*.

Teaching Sets of Related Concepts

Learning does not occur in isolation from other learning. If an addition strategy is learned, it must be discriminated from a subtraction strategy. If the sound for the symbol *m* is learned, it must be discriminated from the symbol and sound for the letter *n*. The concept *on* has to be discriminated from *over*; the concept *pony* from *horse* or *dog*. All knowledge and skills that we learn share some properties with other things we learn. These samenesses provide a basis for overgeneralization of a concept to inappropriate instances. In the paired-associates verbal learning literature, these

FIGURE 2.2

Examples and Teacher Wording

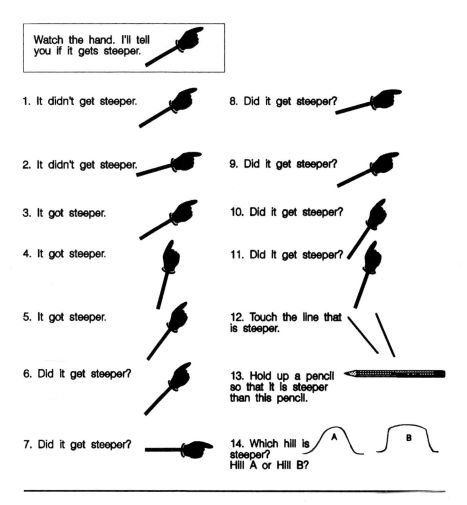

Watch the hand. I'll tell you if it gets steeper.

1. It didn't get steeper.

2. It didn't get steeper.

3. It got steeper.

4. It got steeper.

5. It got steeper.

6. Did it get steeper?

7. Did it get steeper?

8. Did it get steeper?

9. Did it get steeper?

10. Did it get steeper?

11. Did it get steeper?

12. Touch the line that is steeper.

13. Hold up a pencil so that it is steeper than this pencil.

14. Which hill is steeper? Hill A or Hill B?

ideas are reflected in the concepts of *proactive* and *retroactive inhibition*— the effect of prior learning on new learning (proactive) and new learning on prior learning (retroactive). The problem can be approached logically, rather than empirically. The instructional designer can predict where such "interference" will occur on the basis of *samenesses across concepts* and minimum differences between concepts. In remedial reading, for example, *can* and *cane*, or *bit* and *bite*, or *them* and *then* are likely to be confused. Very likely, there is no inhibition process going on, but just a *lack of appropriate discrimination training*. Similarly, as discussed later, there appears to be no process of stimulus generalization, as many theorists have assumed, but just the absence of discrimination training (Honig & Urcuioli, 1981).

Thus, in teaching sets of related concepts (or operations, or strategies, or symbols, etc.), we follow principles to permit successively more precise discriminations among members as the set builds. Some of these principles are:

1. **Cumulatively** introduce new members to a set. Start with two, then three, then four, etc., bringing each subset to criterion before introducing another member.

2. Separate highly similar members as far as possible in the set. In teaching sounds, *b* and *d* would be separated in time (but how far depends on competing priorities, such as frequency of use in making words).

3. As a set gets over eight to ten members, cumulative review would be restricted to: (a) newest members, (b) old members most like new members, and (c) members which tryouts show to cause the most errors.

General-case Teaching

General cases include the learning of concepts, operations, transformations, rules, problem-solving strategies, etc. When teaching a general case, the teacher presents some of the possible examples in a learning objective and the student becomes able to do *any example* in that set. A *general case* set is to be contrasted with an *independent member* (IM) set, wherein each and every set member must be taught (sometimes called rote learning). For some skills, whether a rote skill is learned or a general-case skill *depends on the teaching method*. For example, in the United States, 75 to 85% of the reading textbooks teach beginning reading by the sight-word method (Flesch, 1981). Sight words are members of an IM set. Learning one word does not help you with others. *DISTAR Reading* and the new *Reading Mastery*, on the other hand, use a systematic phonic method. A general-case problem-solving strategy is used for decoding words. The students are taught 40 sounds, blending skills (say the sounds slowly and hook them together), and say-it-fast skills. With these skills, they can read any of more than 10,000 regular-sound words. In the same time as it might take to teach basic phonic skills, one might be able to teach 80 to 100 sight words. But the student who learned the sight words would only know the words taught. There is no general-case learning inherent in the method. In DI Follow Through, low income children starting in kindergarten came out of third grade with reading skills at the 5.2 grade level. DI Follow Through students were more than a year ahead of *average children* and two years ahead of typical disadvantaged children in decoding skills. That result was most likely a product of general-case teaching.

Consider another example from math. Beginning addition can be taught as a set of facts,

$$S = 5$$
$$\underline{+3}$$
$$R = 8$$

or as a generalizable problem-solving skill. To do the latter, first teach these component preskills:

1. Equality rule: "As many as I have on this side of the equal sign, I have to have on the other side."

2. Symbol identification of numbers.

3. Counting-to-a-number up to 20.

4. Making sets of lines for numbers, using counting-to-a-number as the strategy.

We are now ready for the problem-solving strategy.

Figure 2.3 gives a problem-solving strategy for regular addition problems. After teaching five to eight problems using this strategy, the students should be able to do the rest the first time they are presented. Later on, they will drill on addition facts, but even then they would have a strategy for testing whether a given fact answer is correct or not.

The same component skills used to solve regular addition problems can be applied to algebra addition problems and subtraction problems. The initial analysis of the range of related examples planned for this. Algebra addition problems take this form:

$$5 + \square = 8$$

To solve these kinds of problems the student will learn one new component skill, namely, counting-from-a-number-to-a-number. "We are going to count from five to eight, get it going, fiiiiiive, 6, 7, 8 (students make three lines under the box as they count). "How many did we plus?" "Three." "So what's the answer?" "Three." This skill also gives the students a fast way to do regular addition problems—count from the first number as many as the second number stands for.

To solve subtraction problems, including negative numbers, it is only necessary to teach that the minus sign means "take away" and how to minus count by making little minus signs to cross out plus counters. If there are more negative counters than positive counters, a negative number is implied. For example:

$$3 \quad - 5 = -2$$
$$/\!/\!/ - -$$

One goal in the analysis of knowledge is to find common structures across broad sets of problems, so that common strategies can be used to solve them. The addition and subtraction strategies given above illustrate this idea. Each of the problems in Figure 2.4 can also be solved within a common generalized strategy. I won't go into all the needed subskills, but I will illustrate the general idea.

FIGURE 2.3

Adding Five Plus Three

$$5 + 3 = \square$$

TEACHER	LEARNER
1. Read it.	Five plus three equals how many?
2. Which side do we start counting on?	(Points to left side.)
3. Why?	Because there is an unknown on that side.
4. What does this tell us to do? (points to 5)	Make 5 lines.
5. Do it.	$5 + 3 = \square$ /////
6. What does this tell us to do? (points to 3)	Make 3 lines.
7. Do it.	$5 \quad + 3 = \square$ ///// ///
8. How many on this side of the equal?	Eight.
9. So how many must go on the other side?	Eight.
10. Do it.	(Learner makes lines and writes the answer.) $5 \quad + 3 = \boxed{8}$ ///// ///
11. Read the problem and the answer	Five plus three equals eight.

FIGURE 2.4

Sample Story Problems

1. Four cows eat 3 tons of hay. How many cows would be needed to eat 5 tons?

2. Jim typed 7 pages in 4 hours. How many pages did he type per hour?

3. What is the speed of a plane that covers 50 kilometers in 8 minutes?

4. It takes 4 workers 7 hours to paint 5 houses. How many houses can 5 workers paint in 9 hours?

5. $3B = 7$. What is B equal to?

6. 5 percent of what number equals 7?

In systematic steps, the students are taught to convert each problem to an equivalent-fraction statement which they then solve for the unknown. They are first taught how to change any number into any other number. "I want to change 3 to 5."

$$3(\quad) = 5$$

"I don't know how to change 3 into 5, but I know how to change three into 1, so if I have 1 on this side, I can multiply by 5 to make the sides equal."

$$3\left(\frac{1}{3} \times \frac{5}{1}\right) = 5 \qquad 3\left(\frac{5}{3}\right) = 5$$

Next, an equivalent fraction STRATEGY is taught to solve the problems:

1. In the first problem, we are talking about cows and tons. So these are noted first. Then the equation is completed.

$$\frac{cows \;\; 4 \;\; \rightarrow}{tons \;\; 3 \;\; \rightarrow} = \frac{\_}{5}$$

Arrows point toward the unknown.

The student starts the solution on the bottom because there is no unknown there.

$$3\left(\frac{5}{3}\right) = 5$$

"If I multiply by $\frac{5}{3}$ on the bottom to change 3 into 5, I must do the same on the top."

$$4\left(\frac{5}{3}\right) = \frac{20}{3} \quad \textit{Gives the answer.}$$

2. The pages per hour problem uses the same strategy, except we teach that *per* means per "one" something. So:

$$\frac{pages}{hours} \; \frac{7}{4} \overset{\rightarrow}{\rightarrow} = \frac{-}{1}$$

3. By learning to identify the rate unit in problem 3 (kilometers per one minute), it can be written as:

$$\frac{K}{M} \; \frac{50}{8} \overset{\rightarrow}{\rightarrow} = \frac{-}{1}$$

4. By learning to identify the product of the work in problem 4, it is solved. The product (*houses*) goes on top, the work (*hours* x *workers*) on the bottom (or vice versa).

$$\frac{houses}{hours \; x \; workers} \; \frac{5}{7 \, x \, 4} \overset{\rightarrow}{\rightarrow} = \frac{}{9 \, x \, 5}$$

5. To do problem 5, the student simply learns that B is the same as the parentheses.

$$3B = 7 \textit{ is the same as } 3 (\quad) = 7$$

6. Finally, the percent problem is solved by knowing that 5 percent of something is five-hundredths ($\frac{5}{100}$) of something. So:

$$\frac{5}{100} \, N = 7$$

Additional Principles

Some additional principles for designing problem-solving routines are:
(1) teach component skills before using them in a problem-solving routine;
(2) make all steps overt first, later fade the steps so that they become covert;
(3) present examples first in a simplified context, later use more complex
contexts.

Fact Systems

A final illustration of DI teaching strategies will focus on fact systems.
A lot of what children learn in grades four, five, six, and later, are facts about
our history, the world, our government, and nature. By organizing related
facts into graphic presentations which show the relations of the facts to each
other, learning and retention can be facilitated. Figure 2.5 (from Engelmann
& Carnine, 1982, p. 26) shows some facts related to factories. A teacher
script would go long with such charts to guide the presentation. After group
exposure and verbal practice on the facts, the students work with a chart just
like that in Figure 2.5, but without the words, and play a game filling in the
facts. This helps to motivate the practice needed for mastery.

In the past 17 years, these ideas have been used to build 49 year-long
scripted-program sequences, including the nine original DISTAR programs
(and their revisions), *Corrective Spelling Through Morphographs*, five
levels of *Mastery Spelling*, six levels of *Reading Mastery*, a series of *Math
Modules* covering grades 3 to 6 (and remedial classes in grades 7-9), *I Love
Library Books, Expressive Writing, Your World of Facts* (1 and 2), *Cursive
Writing*, six *Corrective Reading* programs, and a home reading program
called *Teach Your Child to Read in 100 Easy Lessons*.

FIGURE 2.5

Group Chart

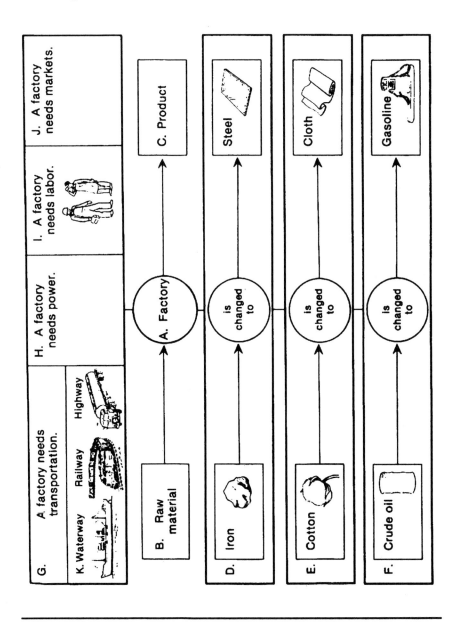

ЄⱭ

Some Historical Background

Siegfried Engelmann

In its current form, Direct Instruction is primarily the product of the efforts of one man, Siegfried Engelmann, although many others have aided him. Engelmann's involvement with education began in 1960 when he and his wife had children and felt the need to teach them basic cognitive skills. This led to the book *Give Your Child a Superior Mind* (Engelmann & Engelmann, 1966). In this book, which reflects Engelmann's thinking from the early sixties, one can find many of the ideas that currently distinguish DI from other educational approaches. *The environment is the teacher . . . The physical environment is a most consistent and persistent teacher of motor skills . . . The active intervention of people in the social environment is essential to learning verbal cognitive skills.* In reviewing early studies on the effects of environmental enrichment on intellectual development, Engelmann points out a correlation between the degree of active parent instruction and estimated IQ's of such famous persons as Pascal, Goethe, and John Stuart Mill. Engelmann was fascinated with J.S. Mill. He had studied Mill's works as an undergraduate philosophy major at Illinois. Engelmann writes:

> *From Mill's account you receive the picture of a boy—not a machine—who learned Greek at 3 and Latin at 8. Granted his performance is good, but notice the charac- teristics of this environment, evident from Mill's quote. The environment works throughout the child's walking hours; it takes pains to ensure that the child has learned his lessons; it carefully reduces the possibility of mistakes; it establishes a clear pattern for using what is learned; it forces the child when necessary; it establishes firm models for him to follow. This is an environment that will succeed with any healthy infant" (Engelmann & Engelmann, 1966, p. 35).*

Although Engelmann had read books on learning theory and he re- spected the importance of reinforcement in learning, he was not, and is not, a Skinnerian. But it is also clear that, like Skinner, he knew the importance of dealing with *the observables* demonstrated to control learning outcomes. As with Skinner, the teacher was viewed as a behavioral engineer. He understood that the learning process involved taking "one step at a time." He understood that important learning involves "rules" (they need not be verbally coded, but it helps when they are). Rules reflect what is common to different examples of the same thing. He understood that generalization to new examples involves identifying the samenesses that are common to the teaching examples. He understood that *the child doesn't merely "learn," but learns specific facts and relations.*

In his presentations to parents on how to present examples to teach samenesses, one can see the rudiments of *Theory of Instruction.* "The presentation is designed to isolate the concept from irrelevant aspects of the situation." Negative examples are selected to help rule out misinterpretations.

Now, let us for a moment jump forward to 1980 when Engelmann was completing *Theory of Instruction.* After developing this massive tome with Doug Carnine (the manuscript was over 900 pages), Engelmann examined the philosophic underpinnings of his work. Clearly, he saw himself aligned with the pragmatic aspects of behaviorism. He learned a lot of formal and self-taught behavior theory through teaching children and contacts with Doug Carnine and myself.

Engelmann writes: "there is nothing wrong with behaviorism as far as it goes"; but to Engelmann, it just does not go far enough. With its laboratory origins in animal research, it has relied too heavily on the empirical analysis of behavior and neglected the importance of logical analysis of stimuli and, more generally, knowledge. According to Engelmann, the goal of instructional design is to present a minimum sequence of examples that will ensure that the learner learns what the teacher intends to be learned. In pursuing his philosophic underpinnings, Engelmann returns to John Stuart Mill and compares Mill's principles (canons) for knowing about causes (Mill, J. S., 1950, 1844) with his own principles for the efficient design of instruction. Mill's principles of Agreement, of Difference, Method of Residues, and Concomitant Variation are shown to parallel Engelmann's principles for showing a sameness, a difference, a transformation sequence, and correlated features or facts.

Engelmann notes that Mill's work could have been taken as a basis for a theory of instruction for 140 years, but it was not. Engelmann also notes that he did not refer to Mill's work in producing his theory of instruction. He noted the similarities after the fact. Good logic, apparently, will stand the test of time.

Engelmann's *sameness principle* states:

> *To show samenesses across examples, juxtapose examples that are greatly different and indicate that the examples have the same label (Engelmann & Carnine, 1982, p. 39).*

Mill's *principle of agreement* (restated to enhance clarity) states: "If examples are different except for a common feature, and if the outcome is the same for all instances, the only possible cause of the outcome is the common feature" (p. 367). In modern behavioral research this principle is called *replication* across differences in subjects, places, and time.

Engelmann's *difference principle* states:

> *To show differences between examples, juxtapose examples that are minimally different and treat the examples differently (p. 39). If positive and negative examples of a concept are the same in all ways but one, that difference must pertain to a critical concept feature.*

Mill's *principle of difference* (again restated) states: "If the positive and negative examples of a given outcome are the same in all features but one, the single feature must be essential to the outcome" (p. 39). Mill's principle of difference when applied to behavioral research means simply that to show a causal variable, *change only one thing* in changing experimental conditions.

Thus, the logic for knowing about causes in basic research is closely related to the logic for learning from examples, and provides, in part, a basis for the efficient design of instruction.

Bereiter, Becker & Carnine

In the interest of space, I must skip the contributions of Carl Bereiter, Douglas Carnine, and myself. But I must mention the Bereiter-Engelmann Preschool. In the fall of 1964, Bereiter decided to give up studies of individual preschool children because he found that no special strategies were emerging. Instead, it appears that whatever he chose to teach could be taught. The problem became one of deciding what to teach and developing a program to teach it (Bereiter, 1967). Engelmann joined with Bereiter in 1964 to help develop the preschool with financing from the Carnegie Foundation.

Twelve low income children who spent two years in the preschool (three hours a day) averaged a 26 point gain in Binet IQ (from 95 to 121) and performed at mid-second grade in reading and math at the end of preschool. These promising results led to Engelmann being asked in 1967 to participate in a nationwide experiment to "see what works" in teaching economically disadvantaged children in kindergarten through third grade. This experiment became known as the Follow Through Project, a sequel to efforts in Head Start.

Before the start of Follow Through in late 1967, Bereiter left Illinois to take a position at the Ontario Institute for Studies in Education. Since Engelmann did not have a Ph.D. and a faculty appointment, he needed a faculty member to serve as sponsor for the Carnegie grant. I agreed to fill this role. When the opportunity to join the Follow Through Project arose in December, 1967, I became an active participant with Engelmann. Douglas Carnine, who had been an undergraduate National Science Foundation Fellow in Psychology with me, joined with Engelmann about this time to work on the *DISTAR Arithmetic* series.

ta

Research Background of Direct Instruction

There are four kinds of research findings which can be viewed as supporting DI: (1) basic behavioral research, (2) studies of effective teaching practices, (3) studies of the outcomes of DI instruction, and (4) studies of design principles and specific DI teaching practices. Space restrictions require me to restrict this review primarily to a brief coverage of the last two areas.

It should be noted first, however, that *DI was not developed on the basis of any of these research findings,* except perhaps in a general way from behavior theory. Rather, it grew initially from logical analyses of what was to be taught and how to teach it. The analyses were then used to generate lesson scripts which were tested to see if they were efficient. The ultimate test was whether the procedures produced the learning intended. This day-by-day field testing and the analysis of errors provided was the real research basis for DI. Again, there is a parallel to Skinner's career. Skinner is often quoted as saying, "Let the pigeons teach you." Engelmann let the children teach him.

૨ુ

Outcome Research on Direct Instruction

Research on Effective Teaching Practices

Recent research on effective teaching practices has served to confirm the value of the basic structure of Direct Instruction practices. Since the early 1970s a number of investigators including Bloom, Brophy, Evertson, Fisher, Good, Kounin, Stallings, etc., have correlationally and experimentally related observed teaching practices to student outcomes. Rosenshine has written a number of summaries of these studies (Rosenshine, 1976; Rosenshine & Berliner, 1978; Rosenshine, 1980). He believes that the term *Direct Instruction* best describes the positive outcomes. Rosenshine's direct instruction refers to teaching activities focused on academic matters where goals are clear to the student, time allocated for instruction is sufficient and continuous, content covered is extensive, student performance is monitored, the majority of questions have a clear cut right or wrong answer, produce many correct responses, and feedback to students is immediate and academically-oriented. The teacher controls the instructional goals, chooses tasks appropriate for the student's level, and paces the teaching. Interaction is structured, but lively and fun, not authoritarian.

This body of research is quite consistent with what we know about effective learning conditions from behavior theory—get attention, present instruction, get lots of student responding, monitor the responding, reinforce and correct, etc. This research is important to DI because it helped to legitimize our basic classroom structure which has been thought by some to be inappropriate for teaching children since it was not self-directed, individualized, nor focused on affective outcomes.

Head Start and Follow Through

As a planned-variation field experiment, Follow Through began in 1968 and ended in 1976. As a service program it still continues. By 1970, the DI Model was responsible for 9,000 children each year, in kindergarten through third grade, in 20 communities all over the U.S. The ethnic groups involved included Native Americans, Hispanics, urban and rural Blacks, and rural Whites. By 1970, 20 different educational models were working in 170 communities, with a total of 75,000 children each year. This was the largest educational experiment ever undertaken. While there have been attacks on the statistical analyses (e.g., House, Glass, McLean & Walker, 1978), there is much agreement that the DI Model performed the best of any (Bereiter & Kurland, 1981; Stebbins, St. Pierre, Proper, Anderson & Cerva, 1977; Wisler, Burns, Iwamoto, 1978).

The DI Model in Follow Through was evaluated using the children who started in 1970 and 1971. The Model was also evaluated in Head Start in three communities for 1969, 1970, and 1971. The Head Start evaluation compared eight models and showed that the DI Model and the Kansas Behavior Analysis Model had the most positive achievement outcomes (Weisberg, 1974).

The data in the Abt Report (Stebbins, et al., 1977) show the DI Model to have more significant positive outcomes than any other model on *basic skill measures* (Word Knowledge, Spelling, Math Computation, and Language), *comprehension measures* (Reading Comprehension, Math Concepts, Math Problem Solving), and the *affective measures* (Self-esteem and Locus of Control). In terms of normative levels of performance on the Metropolitan Achievement Test (MAT) at the end of third grade, DI students who started Follow Through in kindergarten performed the highest of the nine major sponsors on Total Reading, Total Mathematics, Spelling, and Language. Most important is the fact that the students were performing at or near the 50th percentile on all academic measures. This provides a strong demonstration that compensatory education can work.

Figure 2.6 shows the normative performance using our own data on close to 3,000 children from 13 communities over six starting years (Becker & Carnine, 1980). Our own data on the MAT are nearly identical to those independently collected as part of the national evaluation. In addition, our own data show disadvantaged children reading on the Wide Range Achievement Test at the 82nd percentile (5.2 grade equivalents at the end of third

FIGURE 2.6

Norm-referenced Gains on the Wide Range (Pre K to Post 3) and Post 3 Performance on the Metropolitan for K Starting, Low Income, E-B Model Follow Through Students.

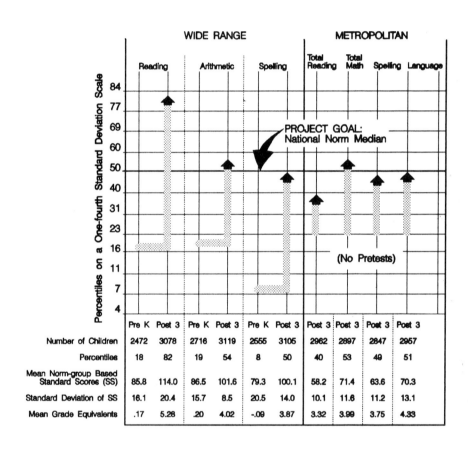

| | WIDE RANGE | | | METROPOLITAN | | | |
	Reading	Arithmetic	Spelling	Total Reading	Total Math	Spelling	Language
	Pre K Post 3	Pre K Post 3	Pre K Post 3	Post 3	Post 3	Post 3	Post 3
Number of Children	2472 3078	2716 3119	2555 3105	2962	2897	2847	2957
Percentiles	18 82	19 54	8 50	40	53	49	51
Mean Norm-group Based Standard Scores (SS)	85.8 114.0	86.5 101.6	79.3 100.1	58.2	71.4	63.6	70.3
Standard Deviation of SS	16.1 20.4	15.7 8.5	20.5 14.0	10.1	11.6	11.2	13.1
Mean Grade Equivalents	.17 5.28	.20 4.02	-.09 3.87	3.32	3.99	3.75	4.33

grade). The Wide Range assesses the children's ability to decode (oral word reading), while the Metropolitan assesses reading comprehension. Clearly, disadvantaged children do not have to fail in school.

Our own data also show that it was better to start formal teaching in kindergarten (five-year olds) than first grade (six-year olds). A clear advantage of about .7 grade equivalents was present at the end of third grade. IQ gains were found averaging 7 points overall, and 18 points for children starting with IQ's under 80 (mean IQ of 72; the 18 point gain is adjusted for regression artifact) (Becker & Engelmann, 1978).

An analysis of achievement gains by IQ levels of the children shows that lower IQ students start lower in reading and math and end up lower, but *gain as much* on almost every measure (Gersten, Becker, Heiry, & White, 1984). Lower IQ children can be taught.

Follow-up studies in 5th and 6th grade showed that the DI children were significantly better in reading and math on 50% of the comparisons made, but there was some loss against national norms (in reading comprehension and math, but not decoding) probably due to the inadequacies of the programs after the children left Follow Through (Becker & Gersten, 1982).

We have recently examined the first high school graduates (18-year olds) in several communities. Results show that there were fewer retentions, fewer dropouts, and more high school graduates among the DI Follow Through students than non-Follow Through comparison students.

The hardest task faced in Follow Through was building reading comprehension skills (Becker, 1977). I believe this was because of the vocabulary learning load faced by children growing up in homes where the adult caretakers were not well educated and/or did not speak English well. In homes with reasonably educated parents, children are constantly learning new words. This is less likely to occur in homes of the disadvantaged. Much school learning *assumes* knowledge of vocabulary.

The Australian Studies

Since 1972, Alex Maggs and his students have conducted more than 30 studies of the effectiveness of DI programs on a variety of normal and special populations. Their studies have included eight of the nine DISTAR programs, two *Corrective Reading Programs*, and *Morphographic Spell-*

ing. In addition to this work at Macquarie University (Sydney), there has been a long series of studies with Down's Syndrome children by Clumes-Ross and his wife, and students at the Preston Institute in Melbourne. These Australian studies are summarized in Lockery and Maggs (1982).

One study was carried out by Maggs and Morath (1976) with 28 moderately and severely retarded children who had been institutionalized at least five years. The children were randomly assigned to either a *DISTAR Language I* group using behavioral teaching techniques or to a *Peabody Language Kit* group. Instruction was provided for one hour a day over two calendar years. Independent testers (blind to groups) tested the children before and after the two years of instruction. The results are summarized in Table 2.1.

The results show the DISTAR group did better on all measures of cognitive functioning. The last line in Table 2.1 (Omega Squared) shows the percent of variance attributable to experimental treatments. These are powerful effects. The IQ gains show that the *DISTAR Language I* group

TABLE 2.1

Mean Gain Scores on Six Tests

GROUP		Basic Concept Inventory	Reynell Verbal Comprehension in Mental Age Months	Stanford-Binet IQ in Mental Age Months	Sereatim (Total Score)	Class Inclusion (Total Score)	Matrix (Total Score)
Distar (N=14)	Mean	12.0	17.1	22.5	2.9	2.2	2.1
	Standard Deviation	3.6	6.9	5.2	1.5	1.0	1.4
Peabody Group	Mean	3.1	6.0	7.5	1.1	.6	.4
	Standard Deviation	3.8	4.1	6.4	1.1	.8	1.0
Significance of Difference		.01	.01	.01	.01	.01	.01
Omega Squared		60%	57%	47%	41%	31%	28%

gained 22.5 months in 24 months, while the *Peabody Language Kit* group gained only 7.5 months in 24 months. The DISTAR group gained at almost a normal rate. The Peabody group gained at the rate to be expected from those with an average IQ in the low 30's (which is where the children started).

In a study by Booth, Hewitt, Jenkins, and Maggs (1979), 12 moderately retarded children with IQ's averaging about 40 were followed for five years. *DISTAR Language I* was started the first year and *Reading I* was added after *Language I* was completed (18 months later). The children were in beginning *Reading III* when tested. While there was no pretest on reading, the children were reading at the early-third-grade level on posttest. Their mean IQ's had risen from 41.9 to 50.6 (p<.001) (Gersten & Maggs, 1982).

Lockery and Maggs conclude their review by indicating that DI has changed approaches to teaching both retarded and normal children in Australia and that the work strongly supports the related findings in the United States.

Studies with Bilingual Students

Four of our Follow Through sites (E. Las Vegas, NM, Dimmitt, TX, Uvalde, TX, and San Diego, CA) had high percentages of Spanish speaking students. Our approach in these settings was first to get English speech and reading strong, and then add oral Spanish, followed by reading in Spanish. This approach was quite successful in reducing the typical "Texmex" confusions of many bilingual settings.

A recent study from the Marina Del Mar school in Monterey, CA, (Gersten, Brockway & Henares, 1983), gives further support to the use of *DISTAR Reading* and *Language* programs, as well as the *Corrective Reading Programs*, in bilingual settings.

Chris van Rensburg (1982) did an experimental comparison of DISTAR with two other programs in South Africa using random assignment to groups of all children in first grade in five schools. The children were from India and bilingual, and the schools had a history of high failure rates. The DISTAR students achieved significantly higher scores on all tests (decoding, comprehension, spelling, and writing).

Structured-immersion approaches (as the DI program is) have been found superior to traditional bilingual approaches in studies by Lambert and Tucker (1972) and Barik, Swain and Nwanunobi (1977).

Weisberg's Preschool Studies

Paul Weisberg (1984) has run a preschool for poverty-level students since 1970 at the University of Alabama. From the beginning, he was concerned with reading skills. At first, his staff focused on the traditional "readiness" skills—

> *going to the book area, holding a book right side-up, turning the pages properly, looking at pictures and discussing them, listening to stories and learning about a plot, and so on. We soon discovered that reading did not magically evolve from these 'prereading' activities. . . .*
>
> *We subsequently adopted a whole-word, meaning-emphasis approach which incorporated many basal reader methods . . . a recognition vocabulary of 40 to 60 words was possible, but only for the highest performers . . . However, caught without reliable prompts (pictures, redundant syntactic and semantic sentences), guessing often became the children's major word-attach strategy. . . . They had trouble with similar words such as in-on, no-not, run-ran, as-ask. . . . When reading simple sentences, they readily substituted boat for ship, cat for kitten, water for wet, and so on.*

Weisberg goes on to describe the other problems his students had in learning basic concepts. He needed something better.

> *In mid 1975, we observed a DISTAR Reading I program in a rural, all-Black school. The teacher's training consisted of a weekend workshop. Her pacing was marginal and she spoke in a monotone, hardly ever challenging the children. We worried about all those signals and drills and teaching from scripted material. Yet, the children didn't seem to mind and, to our astonishment, they energetically and carefully sounded out each word (Weisberg, 1984, pp. 1-2).*

About this time, Weisberg was also impressed by a movie of the kids from the Bereiter-Engelmann Preschool and by some early data on DI in Follow Through (Becker, Engelmann, & Thomas, 1975). In 1976, Paul and his wife Roberta spent their sabbatical year at the University of Oregon learning about and teaching DISTAR. Upon returning to Alabama, the preschool was converted to DI methods (and subsequently, Roberta introduced DISTAR into several schools in Tuscaloosa).

The data collected in the next seven years is truly remarkable. Paul's teachers (three per class) had their poverty-level children *all day* in a *full-year* program (not half-day for nine months). He used the continuous progress tests developed by Becker and Engelmann for Follow Through to monitor student and teacher progress. His data shows scores on these tests ranged from 85% correct (unfamiliar word reading) to 97% correct (sound identification). During 1980, he gathered comparative data on similar children from a Head Start preschool, the University Home Economics preschool, and entering kindergarten and first grade children in local schools who had not had preschool. These comparison groups did not differ from each other on the achievement tests and therefore were combined by age groups (K Starting Age and 1st Starting Age). Four-year olds after one year are called K Starting Age by Weisberg and after two years, 1st Starting Age. Weisberg carefully documents the entry comparability of his groups and their skill deficits. On the Slosson Intelligence Test over the past four years, 58 students in his preschool had averaged IQ's of 87, with only 19% higher than 100.

Figure 2.7 shows outcomes on the Wide Range Achievement Test (WRAT). The DI-trained 1st Starting Aged group was consistently above the 98th percentile (3.4 grade equivalents) (two standard deviations above the National average)! Those with two years of DI (N = 31) averaged 3.8 grade equivalents. The K Aged students averaged between the 77th and 98th percentile across program years. In comparison to prior studies of children with two years of DISTAR in preschool, these are the highest performances yet obtained. The Bereiter-Engelmann Preschool children reached 2.6 grade equivalents (G.E.) in their second group and Anderson (1971) reached 2.6 G.E. with slightly above average children. The added time in Weisberg's preschool was obviously used to advantage. Children staying for two years typically completed *Level II Reading* and *Language*, and at least half of *Arithmetic II*. Those staying one year complete *Level I Reading* and *Language* and three-fourths of *Arithmetic I*.

FIGURE 2.7

WRAT reading across program years. Data are plotted in equal percentile units on a .25 standard deviation scale.

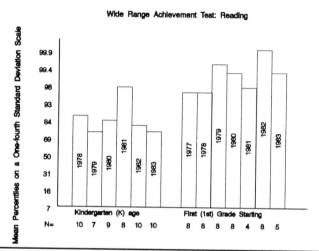

Wide Range Achievement Test: Reading

A subskill analysis of the WRAT shows where the performance differences come from. On the subskills *irrelevant* to reading (Labeling Two Letters in Name, Letter Matching, and Letter Naming) DI and non-DI groups are comparable. But on Word Reading, the DI students excelled (K Starting Age: DI = 9.1, non-DI = .2; 1st Starting Age: DI = 28.4, non-DI = 2.2 on number of words read).

Comprehension skills were tested using end of first grade tests. The Gates-MacGinitie Test (Primary A, Form 2) was used in 1977, and the Metropolitan Achievement Test (MAT) (Primary Level) thereafter. Median Grade Equivalents across program years on the MAT for 1st Starting Aged children were:

- Word Knowledge 2.1
- Word Analysis 3.0
- Reading Sentences and Stories 2.4
- Total Reading 2.2
- Non-DI groups performed at a chance-level.

A comparison of 1st Starting Age children with one ($\underline{N}$ = 12) versus two years ($\underline{N}$ = 31) years of DI, show mean Total Reading grade equivalent scores to be 1.5 and 2.4, respectively. Weisberg concludes by pointing out that two years of DISTAR are needed to be truly functional readers.

This study is truly a remarkable demonstration of what can be done in teaching poverty-level children.

Other DISTAR Studies

It would be impossible to cover all of the studies of DI programs that have occurred in the past 15 years. The best we can do is to mention a few of the better ones. Early summaries of over 25 studies, mostly norm-referenced, can be found in Gordon (1971) and Kim, Berger & Krotochvil (1972). Studies by Richard and Marilyn Crozier (1974) demonstrated the effectiveness of DISTAR programs with educable mentally retarded children in the Edmonton Public schools. Anthony Branwhite (1982) compared the use of DISTAR for remedial reading students in England. The same teacher taught both programs. After 11 weeks, the conventional remedial program group had gained six months and the DISTAR group had gained 12 months.

L'E. Stein and Goldman (1980) compared the effectiveness of *DISTAR Reading* and the Palo Alto Reading Program, another phonics based program. The students were six-to-eight-year-olds with reading problems, but had average IQ's, and were said to have "minimal brain dysfunction." Posttesting on the Peabody Individualized Achievement Test (PIAT) nine months later, the DISTAR group had gained 15 months and the Palo Alto group seven months. Differences were present for both decoding and comprehension.

Engelmann and Carnine (1976) studied the progress of 28 *middle-class* second graders who had been in DISTAR in first grade (the top half of the total first grade). Two low performing children were also added in the group. University students in DI training taught reading and math to the groups 30 minutes a day, and were supervised by an excellent teacher and a University DI supervisor.

On the Stanford Achievement Test Total Reading (comprehension), the 30 students averaged 4.6 grade equivalents (only two students were below 2.7, the two low performers added to the class were at 2.6). On the Wide

Range (decoding) the class averaged 5.1 grade equivalents. On Total Math (Stanford) they averaged 3.4 grade equivalents, and on SAT Science (which is much of the subject matter of the *Reading III* program), they averaged 4.0. A questionnaire for the students showed very positive attitudes about reading and self.

Like behavior analysis and other innovations in education, the DI approach has often been attacked as being inconsistent with humanistic and other philosophies of education. From our experiences in Follow Through, we knew that for 99 out of 100 teachers, the feelings of philosophic clash disappeared in three to six months as the teachers gained competence, and especially as they saw children learning who had failed with other methods. Serving as an independent contractor, Cronin (1980) documented through interviews these kinds of attitude changes in one of our bilingual Follow Through sites. "Although there were several Cohort I and limited-first-year teachers whose 'holistic' educational philosophy had initially clashed with what they had perceived as DISTAR's less 'humanistic' approach to teaching, all of these teachers now found DISTAR to be compatible with their educational philosophy" (p. 23).

About half of the teachers cited the dramatic changes in progress by their kindergarten and first grade students as the basis for change in attitude. Many reported that Black and Chicano students were performing at levels they had thought impossible after ten years of teaching experience. One "teacher stressed the importance of teaching DISTAR before an accurate appraisal of its underlying philosophy could be made" (Cronin, 1980, p. 23).

Studies with Other Programs

Corrective Reading and *Morphographic Spelling* have also been evaluated. Earlier versions of each consisted of one program; latter versions expanded the number of levels and goals involved. Most (but not all) of the research is on the earlier programs. In general, two months or more gain for each month of instruction has been typically found using a variety of tests.

Selection II

&

Studies of Design Principles and Specific Teaching Practices

Chapters 29 and 30 of *Theory of Instruction* (Engelmann & Carnine, 1982) summarize many of the specific studies of DI theories and practices. Many of these studies are also reviewed in Becker and Carnine (1980) and Weisberg, Packer, and Weisberg (1981). I will highlight a few of the studies to illustrate their character.

Positive Examples Only

Negative examples are necessary to rule out the misinterpretations possible from use of only positive examples. This assumption was tested by Williams and Carnine (1981). A hypothetical concept "Gerbie" (angles between 0 and 110 degrees) was taught to 28 subjects. Half received 12 positive examples and the other half eight positives and four negatives. The transfer test included both positives and negatives. The positive-only group scored 50% and the positives-plus-negatives group scored 88%.

Sameness Principle

The sameness principle states: "Show the range of positive examples by juxtaposing widely differing examples and labeling them in the same way." Forty-seven students with knowledge of fractions, but not decimals, were given the same number of examples of how to convert fractions of 100 into decimals. The numerator for Group One was always 2 digits, for Group Two it was 1, 2, or 3 digits. Tests included all three types. Group Two scored 80% and Group One scored 36% (Carnine, 1980a).

Sprague and Horner (1981) tested the sameness principle using vending machines and severely retarded high school students. Ten different varieties of machines were collected. Training on one machine or on three highly similar machines did not lead to generalization to the other. Training on three machines which sampled the range of discriminations and responses to be made led to generalization. A parallel study (Horner & McDonald, 1981) was carried out in a sheltered workshop. Severely retarded high school students were to attach 20 different kinds of biaxle capacitors to circuit boards. Training on one example led to no transfer. Training on three instances selected to sample the range produced generalized performance.

An Irrelevant Sameness

Flanders (1978) followed the procedure used by Guess (1969) to teach a generalized use of *plurals* to low performers. Two samenesses in the teaching procedure followed by Guess were hypothesized to cause misrules to be learned. The examples in one group *always* had *one* object and the other had *two*. The group of two was always of the same class and label. Flanders found that when child was presented these groups—(1) dog, dog; and (2) dog, dog, dog—the child tended to respond to the smaller group as singular. When tested with (1) dog; and (2) dog, cat—the second group was called plural (either "dogs" or "cats"). A corrected teaching sequence, eliminating the inappropriate samenesses, led to correct responding on appropriate test trials.

Many others have studied the effects of irrelevant samenesses in learning discriminations. The results clearly follow the rule, "If it is logically possible, mislearning will occur."

Minimum-difference Principle

A negative example rules out the maximum number of possible interpretations when it is least different from some positive example. Carnine (1980a) used examples like those in Figure 2.8 (from Becker & Carnine, 1980, p. 454) to teach *on* to five groups of 13 preschoolers. After a fixed set of demonstrations, they were tested on transfer items. There was a linear trend going from 10.2 correct for A to 5.0 for E (positives only).

Granzin and Carnine (1977) taught a multiple-feature (conjunctive) concept to 44 first graders. The same examples were used for two groups. In Group One, minimally different examples were juxtaposed. In Group Two, maximally different examples were juxtaposed. Group One required 17.4 average trials to reach criterion, Group Two required 29.9 trials. A second study by Granzin and Carnine (1977) produced similar results with both disjunctive and conjunctive concepts.

FIGURE 2.8

Teaching "On"

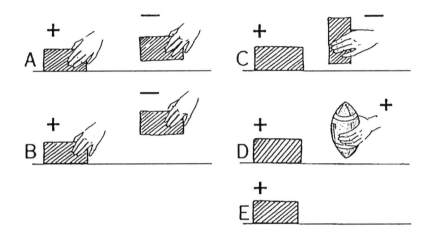

Continuous Conversion

If a positive example can be converted directly into a negative (such as holding a pencil vertically and saying "vertical" and moving it slightly and saying "not vertical"), everything is kept the same except a critical feature, which is thus isolated. Gersten, White, Falco, and Carnine (1982) compared continuous and noncontinuous conversion. The concepts *convex (nonconvex)* and *diagonal (nondiagonal)* were taught to 40 preschoolers and a group of disabled students. In each study the same example sequences were used. The continuous conversion group reached criterion significantly sooner in each case. For example, for the preschoolers on *diagonal* the difference was 20.6 to 56.4 average trials.

The Setup Principle

Keeping the setup of initial teaching the same permits the use of continuous conversion and therefore can be maximally efficient in isolating critical concept features. The samenesses in going from a positive to a negative (or the reverse) eliminate possible critical features. Carnine (1980b) compared his procedure with one proposed by Tennyson, Woolley, and Merrill (1972). They proposed changing the setup after every second example. Carnine used the Tennyson, et al., procedure and two comparison procedures: (1) same setup with continuous conversion; and (2) same setup without continuous conversion. The concept taught was *90 degrees (non-90 degrees)*. The same examples were used for (2) as (1), but were on cards. Following initial training, all students were brought to criterion on a transfer set with none of the irrelevant features the same as those used in the training examples. Trials to criterion with continuous conversion and same setup were 10.6. For the noncontinuous conversion same setup, it took 15.8 trials, and paired trials setup 26 trials. The trend was significant.

In a related study, Williams and Carnine (1981) found that keeping the teacher wording the same (as recommended in designing a setup) led to faster acquisition (half the trials) of a discrimination than when wording was varied. The varied wording was like this: "Is there a blurp on this page?" "Do you see a blurp?" "Is there a blurp here?"

Other Studies

A host of additional studies support many design principles for teaching rules, the use of transformation structures to help teach addition facts, the use of visual displays in teaching fact systems, and the design of cognitive operations (Engelmann & Carnine, 1982, chap. 29).

Finally, important aspects of teacher behavior such as pacing, signals, praise, and corrections are supported by several studies.

ٿ

The Future

Direct Instruction has come a long way in the 20 years or so of its existence. Engelmann-designed programs are taught to at least five million children in regular and remedial programs around the English speaking world. In the past two years while working for UNESCO, Alex Maggs introduced DI methods into special education programs in seven African countries (Kenya, Tanzania, Malawi, Zimbabwe, Swaziland, Mauritania, and Botswana). There are adaptations of DI programs operating in at least a half a dozen non-English speaking countries. An Association for Direct Instruction (P.O. Box 10252, Eugene, OR, 97440) was formed in 1981 which has about 1,000 members. The Association provides training on DI methods, runs a state-financed preschool for developmentally retarded children, markets books in the area, and publishes a quarterly journal on DI research and methods.

The developing computer revolution in education promises to expand the influence of DI technology immensely. Engelmann and Carnine have already developed authoring languages for programmers and teachers. Demonstration programs are available using DI programming strategies in tutorials (concept and strategy teaching), drill and practice, and simulations. Like other DI programs, they include instructional feedback on errors, provide cumulative review, and various kinds of reinforcement, as well as following basic DI analysis and sequencing strategies. Carnine is also developing DI applications on a microcomputer-based network capable of monitoring responses from 32 students with one microcomputer. Applications of this system (called Teacher Net) in teaching, testing, giving the teacher feedback, and teacher training on critical teaching behaviors have already been demonstrated. Classroom demonstrations are now being evaluated.

The most ambitious future application of DI technology is to high school and community college programs in math and science. Alan Hofmeister (Utah State) has helped to put together private development funds aimed at producing at least 50 videodisks to cover the essentials of high school math, biological science, and physical science. The videodisk programs are being designed, scripted, prototyped, and field tested by Engelmann and a staff supervised by him. They will be put on professional quality videotape by a staff in Utah and tested again, and finally go on disks to be marketed by Systems Impact, Inc. (Eugene, OR).

As I look to the future, the most pressing need I see is for the development of more persons with Engelmann's analytical skills and knowledge of programming strategies to apply his methods to other areas of human competence.

References

Anderson, B.E. (1971). *An evaluative study—Teaching three- and four-year olds in a structured education program.* Unpublished master's thesis, University of Utah, Salt Lake City, UT.

Barik, H.C., Swain, M., & Nwanunobi, E.A. (1977). English-French bilingual education: The Elgin study through grade five. *Canadian Modern Language Review, 33,* 459-475.

Becker, W.C. (1977). Teaching reading and language to the disadvantaged—What we have learned from field research. *Harvard Educational Review, 47,* 518-543.

Becker, W.C. & Carnine, D.W. (1980). Direct Instruction: An effective approach to educational intervention with the disadvantaged and low performers. In B.B. Lahey & A.K. Kazdin (Eds.), *Advances in clinical and child psychology* (Vol. 3). New York: Plenum.

Becker, W.C. & Engelmann, S. (1978). *Analysis of achievement data on six cohorts of low income children from 20 school districts in the University of Oregon Direct Instruction Follow Through Model* (Technical Report No. 78-1). Eugene, OR: University of Oregon Follow Through Project.

Becker, W.C., Engelmann, S., & Thomas, D.R. (1975). *Teaching 2: Cognitive learning and instruction.* Chicago: Science Research Associates.

Becker, W.C. & Gersten, R.A. (1982). Follow-up of Follow Through: The later effects of the Direct Instruction Model on children in fifth and sixth grades. *American Educational Research Journal, 19,* 75-92.

Bereiter, C. (1967). *Acceleration of intellectual development in early childhood* (Final Report Project No. OE4-10-008). Urbana, IL: College of Education, University of Illinois.

Bereiter, C. & Kurland, M. (1981). A constructive look at Follow Through Results. *Interchange, 12,* 1-22.

Booth, A., Hewitt, D., Jenkins, W., & Maggs, A. (1979). Making retarded children literate: A five year study. *Australian Journal of Mental Retardation, 5,* 257-260.

Branwhite, A.B. (1982). The singer or the song? Does the program make a difference with a good teacher? *Direct Instruction News, 1* (2), 6-7.

Carnine, D.W. (1980a). Relationships between stimulus variation and the formation of misconceptions. *Journal of Educational Research, 72,* 106-110.

Carnine, D.W. (1980b). Three procedures for presenting minimally different positive and negative instances. *Journal of Educational Psychology, 72,* 452-456.

Carnine, D.W. & Silbert, J. (1979). *Direct instruction reading.* Columbus, OH: Charles E. Merrill.

Cronin, D.P. (1980). *San Diego implementation study, year 2: Instructional staff interviews.* Los Altos, CA: John A. Emmrick & Associates.

Crozier, M. (1974, September). *An attempt to accelerate low-achieving elementary students using the DISTAR Instructional System.* Report to the Edmonton Public School System.

Crozier, R. (1974, September). *Some effects of Direct Instruction on the academic performance of educable mentally retarded students.* Report to the Edmonton Public School System.

Engelmann, S. & Carnine, D.W. (1976). A structural program's effect on the attitudes and achievement of average and above-average second graders. In W.C. Becker & S. Engelmann (Eds.), *Technical Report No. 76-1, Appendix B: Formative research studies.* Eugene, OR: University of Oregon Follow Through Project.

Engelmann, S. & Carnine, D.W. (1982). *Theory of Instruction: Principles and applications.* New York: Irvington. Revised edition (1991), Eugene, OR: ADI press.

Engelmann, S. & Engelmann, T. (1966). *Give your child a superior mind.* New York: Simon and Schuster.

Flanders, J.A. (1978). *Teaching receptive and expressive usage of plurals to a language delayed mentally retarded child.* Unpublished master's thesis, College of Education, University of Oregon, Eugene, OR.

Flesch, R. (1981). *Why Johnny still can't read.* New York: Harper & Row.

Gersten, R.M., Becker, W.C., Heiry, T.J., & White, W.A.T. (1984). Entry IQ and yearly academic growth of children in direct instruction programs: A longitudinal study of low SES children. *Educational Evaluation and Policy Analysis, 6,* 109-121.

Gersten, R.M., Brockway, M.A., & Henares, N. (1983). The Monterey DI program for students with limited English (ESL). *Association for Direct Instruction News, 2*(4), 8-9.

Gersten, R.M. & Maggs, A. (1982). Five year longitudinal study of cognitive development of moderately retarded children in a direct instruction program. *Analysis and Intervention in Developmental Disabilities, 2,* 329-343.

Gersten, R.M., White W.A.T., Falco, R., & Carnine, D.W. (1982). Enhancing attention of handicapped and non-handicapped students through a dynamic presentation of instructional stimuli. *Analysis and Intervention in Developmental Disabilities, 2,* 305-317.

Gordon, M.B. (Ed.). (1971). *Distar Instructional System. Summaries of case studies on the effectiveness of the Distar Instructional System.* Chicago, IL: Science Research Associates.

Granzin, A.C. & Carnine, D.W. (1977). Child performance on discrimination tasks: Effects of amount of stimulus variation. *Journal of Experimental Child Psychology, 24,* 332-342.

Guess, D. (1969). A functional analysis of receptive language and productive speech: Acquisition of the plural morpheme. *Journal of Applied Behavior Analysis, 2,* 55-64.

Honig, W.K. & Urcuioli, P.J. (1981). The legacy of Guttman and Kalish (1956): 25 years of research on stimulus generalization. *Journal of the Experimental Analysis of Behavior, 36,* 405-445.

Horner, R. & McDonald, R. (1981). *A comparison of the effectiveness of single instance training versus general case training on the acquisition of a generalizable vocational skill by four severely handicapped high school students.* Unpublished Manuscript. Eugene, OR: Specialized Training Program, University of Oregon.

House, E.R., Glass, G.V., McLean, L.D., & Walker, D.F. (1978). No simple answer: Critique of the follow through evaluation. *Harvard Educational Review, 48,* 128-160.

Kim, Y., Berger, B.J., & Kratochvil, D.W. (1972). *Distar Instructional System* (Product Development Report No. 14). Palo Alto, CA: American Institute for Research.

Lambert, W.E. & Tucker, G.R. (1972). *Bilingual education of children: The St. Lambert experience.* Rowley, MA: Newburg House.

L'E. Stein, C. & Goldman, J. (1980). Beginning reading instruction for children with minimal brain dysfunction. *Journal of Learning Disabilities, 13,* 219-222.

Lockery, M. & Maggs, A. (1982). Direct Instruction research in Australia: A ten-year analysis. *Educational Psychology, 2,* 263-288.

Maggs, A. & Morath, P. (1976). Effects of direct verbal instruction on intellectual development of institutionalized moderately retarded children: A two year study. *The Journal of Special Education, 10,* 357-364.

Mill, J.S. (1950). *John Stuart Mill's philosophy of scientific method.* E. Nagel (Ed.) New York: Hafner Publishing Company. (First published as *A system of logic,* in 1844.)

Rosenshine, B.V. (1976). Classroom instruction. In N.L. Gage (Ed.), *The psychology of teaching methods.* Seventy-fifth yearbook of the National Society for the Study of Education. Chicago: University of Chicago Press.

Rosenshine, B.V. (1979, April). *Direct instruction for skill mastery.* Paper presented to the School of Education, University of Wisconsin at Milwaukee, WI.

Rosenshine, B.V. & Berliner, D.C. (1978). Academic engaged time. *British Journal of Teacher Education, 4,* 3-16.

Silbert, J., Carnine, D.W., & Stein, M. (1981). *Direct instruction mathematics.* Columbus, Ohio: Charles E. Merrill.

Sprague, J. & Horner, R. (1981). *Vending machine use: An analysis of stimulus features and the application of a general case programming strategy to induce generalization to a full range of examples by severely handicapped students.* Unpublished manuscript, Specialized Training Program, University of Oregon, Eugene, OR.

Stebbins, L., St. Pierre, R.G., Proper, E.C., Anderson, R.B., & Cerva, T.R. (1977). *Education as experimentation: A planned variation model (Vol. IV).* Cambridge, MA: Abt Associates.

Tennyson, R.D., Woolley, R.R., & Merrill, M.D. (1972). Exemplar and nonexemplar variables which produce correct classification behavior and specified classification errors. *Journal of Educational Psychology, 63,* 144-162.

Van Rensburg, C. (1982). Comparative Distar results from five South Afrikaans schools. *Association for Direct Instruction News, 1*(4), 4.

Weisberg, H.I. (1974). *Short-term cognitive effects of Head Start programs: A report on the third year of planned variation—1971-72.* Cambridge, MA: Huron Institute.

Weisberg, P. (1984). Reading instruction for poverty-level preschoolers. *Association for Direct Instruction News, 3,*(2), 1, 16-19.

Weisberg, P., Packer, R.A., & Weisberg, R.S. (1981). Academic training. In J.L. Matson & J.R. McCartney (Eds.), *Handbook of behavior modification with the mentally retarded.* New York: Plenum.

Williams, P. & Carnine, D.W. (1981). Relationship between range of examples and instructions and attention in concept attainment. *Journal of Educational Research, 74,* 144-148.

Wisler, C.E., Burns, G.P., & Iwamoto, D. (1978). Follow Through redux: A response to the critique by House, Glass, McLean, & Walker. *Harvard Educational Review, 48,* 171-185.

Precision Teaching

Richard P. West and K. Richard Young
Utah State University

olving the problems of the human condition and improving the quality of life are viewed by our Western culture as the logical results of rational inquiry and an application of the scientific method (Ehrenfeld, 1978). We are led to believe that our educational community holds the answers to life's problems, but educators are not generally known for their analytic approach to instruction nor are they regarded as enthusiastic consumers of the fruits of the scientific method. The field of education continues to cry out for more empirical, objective evaluation and research by those working in the front lines of the educational enterprise (Barlow, Hayes, & Nelson, 1984), but many of the field's practitioners are ill-prepared to take advantage of the information they seek.

In education, as in other "helping" disciplines, there is a developing trend toward better documentation of the efforts of its practitioners and the impact of those efforts on the performance of individuals served by the practitioners. In other words, what are educators doing and are they able to help students learn important information and skills? Consumers of educational services (students and parents) are anxious for educators to be accountable for what they accomplish or fail to accomplish, and many educators are willing to learn about more effective methods of instruction. Barlow, Hayes, & Nelson (1984) argue that members of the helping professions are obligated to

> *become active participants in determining the efficiency and effectiveness of their treatments in a manner that will be readily apparent to those who seek this information, such as consumer groups and government and third-party agencies. In other words, [they] should become, at least, evaluators of their own work and preferably researchers providing new data to the professional community interested in behavior change (p. 21).*

But Barlow, et al., recognize that a true integration of research and practice has not "occurred due to the almost universally acknowledged inadequacies of [traditional] research methodology to address issues important to practice" (p. 23).

Based upon the methods of operant conditioning and experimental analysis of behavior developed in the laboratory, Precision Teaching offers educators an alternative to traditional research methods and helps them to become "scientists-practitioners" (Barlow, et al., 1984). Using the procedures of Precision Teaching, educators become students "of the pupil's behavior, carefully analyzing how the behavior changes from day to day and adjusting the instructional plan as necessary to facilitate continued learning" (White, 1986). Precision Teaching is not so much a method of instruction as it is a precise and systematic method of evaluating instructional tactics and curricula. In naming this approach, Ogden Lindsley, the originator of Precision Teaching, noted that "what was really new in [the] procedure was precision, [so] we decided to use that as an adjective in front of whatever it was one was doing; hence, in our case, 'Precision Teaching'" (Lindsley, 1972, p. 9). Lindsley, who was a student of B. F. Skinner, built Precision Teaching around a framework of operant conditioning and the methods of experimental analysis of behavior developed by Skinner. This framework consisted of seven basic elements: (1) the principle that the student knows best; (2) the use of "rate of response" as a universal measure of behavior; (3) a standard chart display used to study performance patterns; (4) an emphasis on the direct measurement of behavior and continuous monitoring; (5) the use of descriptive and functional definitions of behavior and processes; (6) an emphasis on building behavior rather than eliminating it; and (7) an analytic investigation of the impact of environmental influences on individual behavior (Lindsley, 1972).

ॐ

The Student Knows Best

Skinner defined "behavior" as "what an organism is *doing*—or more accurately what it is observed by another organism to be doing" (1938, p. 6). Behavior analysts observe the behavior of organisms and interpret the influences that affect its performance. According to Lindsley (1972), Skinner said the rat knows best because it was the rat's behavior he was observing and studying. Therefore, the impact of a variety of influences is readily observed in what the rat does—the rat's behavior. In fact, in his classic work *The Behavior of Organisms* (1938), Skinner based his explanation of behavior upon the "permanent first-hand accounts" of behavior produced by the uniform displacement of a writing point on a slow-moving record each time the organism closed a mercury switch by moving a lever. The first-hand accounts were photographic reproductions of records made directly by the rats themselves.

Using Precision Teaching, the student "tells" the teacher how effective the instructional program is by reflecting the impact of instruction in his or her behavior. When a desired behavior occurs more frequently following instruction, the teacher knows the instructional program is appropriate. Likewise, when an instructional program fails to produce an increase in the behavior it is designed to affect, the teacher is likely to judge the program ineffective and will change or discard it. But the value of a given instructional tactic is always based upon what the student "knows" and "tells" through a study of his or her behavior, even though this interpretation may run counter to conventional wisdom or published research reports. The student knows best.

ɜ▲

Rate of Response:
A Universal Measure of Behavior

Any of a variety of dimensions of performance can be used to measure behavior: form or topography, latency, intensity or force, and duration—the so-called static properties of the reflex[1] (Skinner, 1938). Skinner preferred the use of rate of response regarding it as the "main datum to be measured in the study of the dynamic laws of an operant" (1938, p. 58). He defined rate of response as "the length of time elapsing between a response and the response immediately preceding it" (p. 58). Lindsley and others (Johnston & Pennypacker, 1980; White, 1986) have chosen to substitute "frequency" for "rate" because many people do not interpret rate to mean "behaviors divided by unit of time," but think of rate in the sense of a "rating scale" or "How do you rate?" More important than the term is the concept of measuring a behavior by the dimensional quantity of "occurrences in time."

Focusing attention on the rate of classroom behaviors is foreign to most educators; they are generally more concerned about measures of accuracy alone, e.g., the number of arithmetic problems answered correctly or the percent of words spelled correctly. A typical teacher might be interested to know that Student A was able to correctly answer only five of 25 questions on a quiz given at the beginning of the term, but today the same student answered 23 of the questions correctly. The student's performance has obviously improved; he or she can now correctly answer considerably more questions. The accuracy of the student's performance has improved.

Measuring Behavior is an Essential Activity in the Evaluation of Teaching

Student learning is the objective of teaching; therefore, the measurement of learning is an important activity for the educator who is a scientist-practitioner. A common notion of teacher effectiveness "refers to the ability

---

1 Skinner uses the term "reflex" to represent the relation between the part of the environment called the "stimulus" and the correlated part of the organism's behavior (response). He first uses this term when describing respondent behavior, or behavior that is elicited by the environment. He then introduces operant behavior explaining that "operants" are not elicited, but rather emitted by the organism. He then states "the term reflex will be used to include both respondent and operant even though in its original meaning it applied to respondents only" (1938, pp. 20-21).

of a classroom teacher to produce higher-than-predicted gains on standardized achievement tests" (Good, 1979, p. 53). According to this paradigm, "a teacher is *effective* if, within the time period studied, students, *averaged* over the *whole class*, answered *more* questions *correctly* on *multiple-choice standardized achievement tests* than expected, based on the pretest performance" (Shavelson, Webb, & Burstein, 1986, p. 52). The use of standardized achievement tests is the industry standard in education. But, as Shavelson, Webb, & Burstein (1986) point out, this approach has the following properties that may render it inappropriate for many applications, particularly those in which a teacher is interested in making his or her instruction more effective for a particular student:

1. Effectiveness assumes commonality of curriculum goals, objectives, and content coverage across classrooms because one standardized achievement test is used to judge the effectiveness in all classrooms.

2. Effectiveness is strictly summative in its measurement of subject matter knowledge. It is not what students know or don't know that matters, but the accumulated quantity of their knowledge in comparison with students in other classrooms.

3. Performance on the effectiveness measure is equated with knowledge or skill in subject matter. There is no notion of "less than best effort," guessing, partial knowledge, or test-taking skill.

4. Effectiveness is strictly aggregative across students within a classroom. Operationally, regardless of how student performance is distributed within the classroom, the class average is chosen to represent class performance (p. 52).

Standardized achievement tests may be used in education for broad evaluations of a district's educational offerings or for placement decisions in special programs, but they are rarely used by teachers either in an evaluation of their instruction or for other purposes. In fact, according to research conducted by Stan Deno and his associates from the University of Minnesota, "teachers do not use formally developed and commercially available tests, nor do they develop their own carefully structured inventories. Instead, teacher preference is to use informal observations based on their interactions with students as the data source. Unfortunately, the reliability and validity of this source is at best unknown and at worst inadequate" (Deno, 1985. See also Fuchs & Deno, 1981; Fuchs, Wesson, Tindal, Mirkin, & Deno, 1981; Jenkins & Pany, 1978; Salmon-Cox, 1981). In other words, teachers are likely to guess about the effectiveness of their instruction based upon their interpretations of the performance of their students. Occasionally, they may hastily construct a quiz to probe the performance of their students. But as with teacher judgment, the reliability and validity of the information resulting from this practice are also suspect. The problem with standardized achievement tests is not the standardization *per se*, but the standardization of ineffective practices. Informal measurement procedures aren't always improved either just by standardizing them; they must be replaced by more effective and appropriate procedures, and then standardized.

Learning can be defined as a change in performance, or a change in the occurrence of behavior (Skinner, 1950); therefore, measuring behavior at a minimum of two points in time is necessary to evaluate learning. Comparing the measurements of behavior before and after instruction tells the teacher how much the student has learned (or at least, how much change has taken place in the behavior of interest) and gives the teacher an idea of the effect instruction has had on the behavior. Of course, the teacher could measure various properties of behavior, e.g., magnitude, latency, duration, but the rate of the behavior may be as practical as any and it is capable of greater measurement sensitivity than most. Studying the rate of behavior also permits the teacher to evaluate *automaticity*, "the student's ability to maintain correct and fluid display of knowledge *under varying conditions*" (Howell & Morehead, 1987, p. 34). In an article concerning automaticity, Benjamin Bloom (1986) wrote: "The mastery of any skill—whether a routine daily task or a highly refined talent—depends on the ability to perform it unconsciously with speed and accuracy while consciously carrying on other brain functions." Bloom's explanation is not based upon an empirical analysis of "consciousness," but on his interpretation that expert or competent performance of any skill or task begins with an emphasis on accuracy of performance but develops as the emphasis shifts to fluency or automaticity. In other words, competent performers are generally those whose performance is marked by fluent responding. In reading, for example, Deno (1985) discovered that oral reading rate was an effective discriminator of reading proficiency, at least in the elementary school years. Samuels (1979) claims that fluent readers are more efficient and effective in their use of word attack skills than are beginning readers. In his research of the instructional tactic he calls "repeated readings," Samuels discovered that

> *as reading speed increased, word recognition errors decreased. As the student continued to use this technique, the initial speed of reading each new selection was faster than initial speed on the previous selection. Also, the number of rereadings required to reach the criterion reading speed decreased as the student continued the technique (p. 404).*

Furthermore, he learned that when accuracy was overemphasized, fluency was slower to develop. Other researchers have noted that speed of responding is a characteristic that discriminates capable from less capable performers. And while it is true that the desirability of response speed is probably related to the nature of the response, most educational tasks are viewed more favorably when they are performed fluently. Denekla and Bowen (1973) state that many "developmental dyslexics" are quite slow in their visual-verbal processing, a characteristic noted by other investigators as well (Denekla & Rudell, 1974; Mattis, French, & Rapin, 1973; and Spring & Capps, 1974). Perfitti, Finger, and Hogaboam (1977) found that skilled readers were faster in naming words than less-skilled readers, and Biemiller (1978) and Singer (1970) have presented evidence that speed of identification is positively correlated with reading comprehension measures. Although automaticity is gradually receiving more attention in education (Bloom, 1986), educators continue to be more interested in measures of learning that do not permit the analysis and study of automaticity.

We say that learning has occurred when something is done that could not be or was not done before under similar circumstances, *or* that something can now be done better than it was done before. Better, but in what way is the performance better: accuracy, fluency, or a combination of accuracy and fluency, perhaps? Generally speaking, educators emphasize accuracy when they are concerned with learning. The quality of an answer to a question, or the correctness of a response receives more attention. At the beginning of the term, for example, Ernst was able to correctly answer only five of 50 math problems. Today, he answered 45 of the problems correctly. Obviously, Ernst's performance has improved and he has learned something, but what has he learned, and how much has he learned? We may say that Ernst answered only 10% of the problems correctly at the beginning of the term and he can now answer 90% of the problems correctly. That's an improvement of 80% in the accuracy of Ernst's performance. However, let us now suppose that Ernst required 50 minutes to answer the five problems correctly at the beginning of the term, and he now needs only ten minutes to answer 45 of the 50 problems correctly. He has improved not only in accuracy but also in fluency, or in the rate of responding. His performance is much more efficient now than in the past. At the beginning of the term, Ernst answered five problems correctly in fifty minutes, or .1 (one-tenth of a) correct answer per minute (5 answers/50 minutes). At the close of the term, he answered 45 problems in only ten minutes, a rate of 4.5 correct answers per minute. Over the course of the term, Ernst's rate of correct (or accurate) performance has improved by 45 times (X45).

There is powerful logic in the argument for using rate as a measure of performance, and therefore, learning, but the logic is not obvious because educators are generally unaware of certain facts. Common sense tells us that how quickly firefighters put on their uniforms is as important as the accuracy of their performance.

> *If two firefighters both put on their uniforms with 100% accuracy, but one does it in one minute and the other does it in ten minutes, which one do you want working in your neighborhood? . . . Rate also seems related to generalization in that it is hard to assemble tasks into more complex responses if you are slow at all the pieces. If we encouraged our students to disregard any of the other dimensions (like height or width), they would leave school and walk into walls. Similarly, students who are not prepared to work within certain time constraints will not be able to function in the real world. Slower workers are thought to be less proficient workers—and it's true because rate is a proficiency dimension just like accuracy (Howell & Morehead, 1987, p. 87).*

By combining measures of rate and accuracy, we have a more complete picture of learning than with either measure alone. The addition of rate enables us to detect improvement that might not be detected when accuracy is the only dimension of performance that is investigated. This concept is reflected in the following example in which the performance of two students is compared. Both students have been given ten algebra problems to solve and both students have correctly solved two of them. Therefore, both students have achieved accuracy scores of 20%. If accuracy were the only consideration, these two students would be treated the same and many teachers would fail to detect some important differences in their perform- ance. Ortiz, however, solved the problems in two minutes, while John required twenty minutes to solve them. Obviously, Ortiz is more capable at solving these algebra problems than is John. Ortiz has learned more than John or at least has learned some things better.

Now, let us assume that the algebra teacher gives each student a little more instruction in solving these problems. If the teacher attended only to the accuracy of responding, no improvement in either student's perform- ance could be detected until one more problem could be solved correctly. Nothing less than an improvement of 10% could ever be detected. On the other hand, when the teacher also looks at the rate of correct responses, even slight improvements are noticeable. When John is able to solve the problems in less time, even though he solves no more problems, we can say that he has learned something, and when he attains the rate of one correct solution per minute, his performance will be comparable to Ortiz's.

The Relationship Between Rate of Response and Maintenance and Generalization of Responding

In the previous section, we included a quotation from Howell & Morehead (1987) wherein they explained that rate seems to be related to generalization because "it is hard to assemble tasks into more complex responses if you are slow at all the pieces." While they use the term *generalization*, the phenomenon they describe is probably not generaliza- tion at all, but an example of a chain of responses possibly affected by response shaping. Keller and Schoenfeld (1950) describe two types of generalization. The first is noted when "the reinforcement of a response in the presence of one stimulus will strengthen it in the presence of other stimuli when these have properties in common with the first" (p. 168). Therefore, as Stokes and Baer (1977) explain, "newly taught responses [could] be controlled not only by the stimuli of the teaching program, but by others somewhat resembling those stimuli" (p. 349). The second form of generalization mentioned by Keller and Schoenfeld is also known by the term "response induction." This form is seen when the "strengthening of one response may bring about a strengthening of certain others" (p. 168). A particular form of response generalization or induction, in which responses are emitted that are similar in form (topography) to a trained response, is referred to by Keller and Schoenfeld as *transfer of training*. In instances where transfer of training is claimed, untrained responses seem to emerge or occur as the result of somewhat less training than was required in the original training setting (Stokes & Baer, 1977). Presenting a complete taxonomy of generalization is beyond the scope of this work, and it is an activity fraught with complexity and controversy. We have chosen to adopt a more pragmatic notion of generalization on the order of a proposition offered by Stokes and Baer (1977). According to them, generalization is the "occurrence of relevant behavior under different, nontraining conditions (i.e., across subjects, settings, people, behaviors, and/or time) without the scheduling of the same events in those conditions as had been scheduled in the training conditions" (p. 350). Stimulus and response generalization, including topographical response induction (also known as transfer of training), and maintenance of responding over time, will all be referred to as generalization in this paper.

In a study by Jenkins, Barksdale, and Clinton (1978), fourth- and fifth-grade students in a language arts class were differentially rewarded on the basis of correct answers to comprehension questions and oral reading rates. Each day, the students read aloud two new selections from their reading books. They were encouraged to read the selections as quickly as possible and their performance was reinforced with small amounts of money; faster rates produced more money. After they had read the passages, the students were given a set of questions to answer that tested their comprehension of the reading selection. In addition to learning that rate measures could be used successfully in the classroom, the investigators discovered that increased reading rate was associated with slight improvements in comprehension, however both were affected by the presentation of monetary reinforcements. Generalization of comprehension gains was also assessed; generalization across settings and across time (maintenance). The reinforcement contingencies were installed in a special education classroom while generalization of comprehension skills and reading rate in regular classrooms was assessed. No contingencies were in place in the regular classrooms and no training or encouragement was offered. Comprehension improved in the remedial setting (special education) but failed to improve in the regular classroom. However, the improvements achieved in comprehension in the remedial setting were maintained even after reinforcement of comprehension had been absent for over eight weeks.

Rate of response has been shown to be related to generalization in other research as well. Samuels (1979) and Chomsky (1978) noted transfer of training effects in their research of repeated readings. This teaching method "consists of rereading a short, meaningful passage several times until a satisfactory level of fluency is reached. Then the procedure is repeated with a new passage" (Samuels, 1979, p. 404. See also Lapardo & Sadow, 1982; Moyer, 1982; Rashotte & Torgesen, 1985). In her research, Chomsky noted that repeated readings were successful in producing greater reading fluency and that successive stories required fewer listings to reach fluency (1978). Samuels (1979) recorded a similar phenomenon, known to many precision teachers as *steeper slopes* and *rising bottoms*. Figure 3.1 displays a student's progress in reading rate (word recognition) on five passages using the method of repeated readings. According to Samuels,

> *As reading speed increased, word recognition errors decreased. As the student continued to use this technique, the initial speed of reading each new selection was faster than initial speed on the previous selection. Also, the number of rereadings required to reach the criterion reading speed decreased as the student continued this technique. The fact that starting rates were faster with each new selection and fewer rereadings were necessary to reach goals indicates transfer of training and a general improvement in reading fluency (1979, p. 404).*

The *steeper slopes* phenomenon in Precision Teaching refers to the increasingly steeper slopes of the lines created by individual data points on a graph for successive instructional targets, where each point represents one day's reading score. When fewer scores are needed to reach a criterion, the slope of each line will generally be steeper. Such is the case in Figure 3.1. The phenomenon of *rising bottoms* can also be seen in this figure. It is the result of increasingly higher initial performance scores for each reading. Both steeper slopes and rising bottoms are indicators of transfer of training and are commonly seen in educational programs where students are required to perform critical skills fluently.

FIGURE 3.1

Scores from Daily Timings of Oral Reading, Reflecting the Phenomena of Steeper Slopes and Rising Bottoms

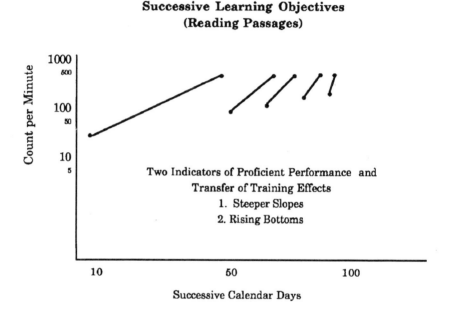

Successive Learning Objectives
(Reading Passages)

Two Indicators of Proficient Performance and
Transfer of Training Effects
1. Steeper Slopes
2. Rising Bottoms

Williams, Brown, and Certo (1976) offered their recommendations for the necessary components of instructional programs for persons with disabilities. According to Williams, et al., persons with disabilities must be able to perform tasks at rates that are appropriate for the situation and accepted by the community; otherwise, their ability to compete with and be accepted by others may be seriously restricted. The ability simply to perform a skill correctly is not sufficient; an individual must develop fluency in the performance of the skill (Young, West, Howard, & Whitney, 1986). An investigation by Young, et al. (1986) demonstrated the effect of developing fluency on generalization of performance (across settings, trainers, and time). Two preschool boys with moderate retardation, frequent noncompliant behavior, extremely limited communication skills, and poorly developed self-help skills, were taught three dressing skills: (1) putting on a pullover shirt, (2) taking off a pullover shirt, and (3) putting on pants. The skills were taught one at a time, using the whole task training method (Spooner, Weber, & Spooner, 1984). In this method, the trainer elicited a complete chain of responses (each skill was broken into its component steps) during each trial, beginning with the first step and continuing through all the responses in the chain. Physical, verbal, and gestural prompts were used as needed, but were gradually withdrawn as responses were performed independently. As soon as the children consistently responded correctly without prompts, the teacher instituted training to improve fluency (the rate of performing the sequence of steps comprising each dressing skill). Fluency training consisted of identifying the responses in the chain where the children were having the most difficulty and providing repeated practice on that response. The whole task training procedure proved to be effective in producing consistently correct performance of the skills, but the skills failed to be performed in settings other than the original setting in which training had occurred and in the presence of persons other than the trainer (e.g., classroom aides and graduate assistants). Once fluency training was instituted and response rates approached the rates representing the performance of peers who had no disabilities and who were judged to be proficient in these dressing skills, the students' performance increased in the generalization conditions. Both children's performance of the skills at school four weeks following training consistently exceeded standards for accuracy and fluency, and parents reported that their sons continued to dress themselves at home.

Young, West, and Crawford (1985) studied the effects of fluency on the retention of word recognition and comprehension skills by students with severe and multiple disabilities (moderate to severe mental retardation and profound hearing impairments). In two separate studies, students were taught to fluently perform reading tasks (oral reading, i.e., look at words and make the appropriate manual communication signs, and matching exercises to demonstrate comprehension). Data collected four months after the completion of training indicated high levels of retention on all tasks. Performance was not maintained at or near the levels achieved during training on word lists taught to accuracy criteria but not to fluency criteria. Since the students had a history of not retaining information once learned, it was concluded that teaching until the fluency criterion was achieved aided retention.

White and Haring (1976) have emphasized that measures of fluency or rate are as important, if not more important, than the traditional educational measurement of accuracy. They also point out that "fluency seems to be a better indicator of the child's ability to maintain, generalize, and apply a skill outside the classroom" (p. 101). Fluency may not influence the generalization of behavior directly, but indirectly because of increased likelihood that a response may be reinforced (i.e., as the children developed fluency, they dressed independently more often and may have obtained more social reinforcement from parents) and by increasing opportunities to perform the skills in the natural environment (i.e., training sufficient exemplars; Baer, 1981; Stokes & Baer, 1977). Both of these factors may have contributed to increased generalization and maintenance.

Other Benefits of Increasing the Rate of Academic Responding

In addition to the benefits that have been mentioned of increasing the rate of academic responding, other benefits have also been noted in the research literature. In a study conducted by West and Sloane (1986), five students characterized as being very disruptive in their elementary school classrooms were presented opportunities to respond to academic tasks at two different rates; one was relatively slow (a new task every sixty seconds) and the other rate was quite fast (a new task every twenty seconds). The responses required by these tasks were appropriate for the students' instructional level, but each response was quite simple and required very little time. The researchers noted that conditions in which response opportunities (and therefore, response rates) were higher were associated with significantly lower rates of disruptive behavior. Based upon an ecobehavioral analysis of classroom environments, Greenwood and his colleagues at the Juniper Gardens Children's Project have discovered an interesting relationship between opportunities to respond and academic achievement. In a series of studies conducted by these researchers (Delquadri, Greenwood, Stretton, & Hall, 1983; Delquadri, Greenwood, Whorton, Carta, & Hall, 1986; Greenwood, Dinwiddie, Terry, Wade, Stanley, Thibadeau, & Delquadri, 1984; Stanley & Greenwood, 1983) the use of classwide peer tutoring (a system that allows all students in a classroom to read orally to a peer tutor for at least ten minutes each day) produced student gains in reading behavior during instruction (tutoring sessions) and in oral passage reading assessed by the teacher. The peer tutoring sessions were designed to increase each student's opportunity to respond to critical academic tasks rather than to sit passively, perhaps even quietly, in a classroom, but without interacting overtly with curriculum or instructional materials. According to Greenwood, Delquadri, & Hall (1984), "tactics that establish high rates of correct academic responding over periods of instruction by the most students are those providing the greater opportunity [to respond]" (p. 65). Thus, high rate (fluent) responding is named as a contributor to gains in academic performance.

ᴕ

Standardized Graphic Display

According to Johnston and Pennypacker (1980), a "quantitative summarization [of data] should occur concurrently with the creation of visual displays that pictorially amplify the information emerging from the quantification" (p. 330). The spatial arrangement of the representations (dots, lines, and other symbols) of the data describe the relations that exist among the variables included in an investigation. Most graphic displays also permit a study of the temporal aspects of the data. Parsonson and Baer (1978) promote a systematic analysis of graphic data as an important element in the scientific process.

> *The close and continuing data contact that results from graphic analysis allows for diversity in research endeavor. Both Skinner (1956) and Sidman (1960) appreciate the value of indulging one's curiosity as part of the scientific enterprise. Skinner's unformalized principles of scientific practice reflect the fact that important scientific advances are not always the product of an intentional search. Close, ongoing contact with data allows those events and results that arouse interest and curiosity to be noticed and subsequently investigated systematically. Thus experimental designs and forms of data analysis that do not isolate researchers from direct, continuing contact with their subject matter, or smooth out interesting variations in performance, may broaden the scope of scientific discovery (p. 109).*

Precision teachers recognize the value of displaying data from their periodic performance probes and studying the displays to find ways of improving their instruction. Changes in performance can be studied more easily when scores are plotted on a graph and inspected visually, especially when many performance scores are obtained for each of several students. Graphs enable the inspection and comparison of many data points without having to sort through pages and pages of tabularized data and raw performance scores. However, not all graphic displays are created equal and some thought should be given to the type of display used for a given situation. Graphs and charts have proliferated in psychology and education; each one is designed for a particular purpose and is suited to display a particular set of data. Tailoring a display to fit an array of data seems sensible enough, after all, each data set may cover a different range of values and contain a unique frequency distribution. The scales affixed to the axes should be determined only after the range and distribution have been established and investigated.

Earlier in this chapter we discussed our concerns with the standardized approach to educational assessment. One of the arguments against this approach was based on the fact that many standardized tests fail to assess the skills that may have been acquired by each student, or that had been taught to the students by the teacher. Only through assessment procedures that are tailored for each classroom can instructional effectiveness be studied appropriately. Furthermore, performance assessments may need to be tailored even more carefully, and fitted precisely to each student, if the resulting data are to be used to design and improve an individualized plan of instruction.

It may seem inconsistent to depart from this philosophical approach of individualization and tailored assessment and adopt a rigid, standardized method of displaying data. Doing so, however, is for several good reasons. Data are, by their nature, already individualized. They are, at least, if they are not grouped and summarized so that the individuality is lost. Once performance data for individual students are grouped together and reduced to a single value, they are no longer useful for instructional planning. The individuality of data is not a function of tailoring scales and displays, but is a quality inherent in the data themselves. Therefore, standardizing a format for displaying data does not eliminate the individual character of the data, it simply standardizes the methods of interpreting them.

The format of the graphic display can exaggerate or obscure quantitative dimensions of the data, thereby confusing the interpretation. For example, data from repeated performance assessments conducted daily over a period of three weeks that show modest change can be displayed in such a way that the change appears to be substantial. This is accomplished by stretching the scale representing the performance scores in relation to the scale that represents time. The opposite can be accomplished by stretching the time scale, usually plotted on the abscissa. A comparison of identical sets of data plotted in Figure 3.2, panels A and B, elaborates this point. When display tactics are tailored to individual data sets, interpretive tactics must also be individualized. This represents a problem inasmuch as we generally fail to recognize the more subtle format changes and therefore, use the same methods to interpret and analyze all graphic displays. Making comparisons and interpretations across a variety of graphs or charts, each one employing a different scale, is a little like comparing prices of items in a grocery store where each item is priced in a different currency. It is possible to convert each price to some common currency, but it would require considerable effort to do so. Adopting a standard format and scale for graphic displays permits us to make consistent and reliable interpretations of instructional effectiveness.

A graph with a standard scale along which response measures can be plotted seems like a good idea, but like so many good ideas, many teachers consider it to be impractical. How can one scale accommodate performance scores that may vary tremendously in value? A percentage scale would be a solution to this problem, for virtually any score can be converted into a percentage of "total response" or "opportunities." But we've already discussed the disadvantages of percentage scores. A better solution to the problem of creating a scale that spans a wide range of performance values, without requiring excessive space, is a ratio or logarithmic scale. An example of a graph with a logarithmic scale on the ordinate is presented in Figure 3.3. This graph is referred to as the standard celeration chart because the logarithmic scale and other aspects of the chart are standardized. The scale emcompasses essentially all performance values of probable interest to educators.

FIGURE 3.2

Data Plots That Emphasize Accomplishment (A) and Time (B)

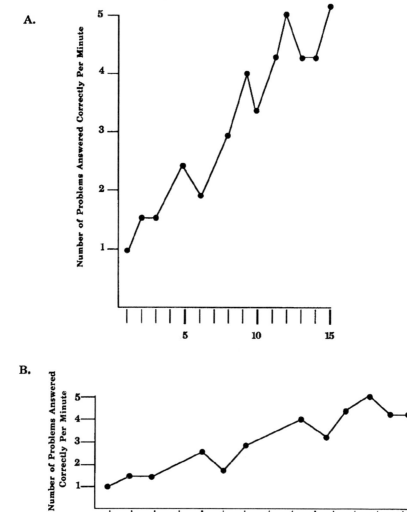

FIGURE 3.3

Standard Celeration Chart

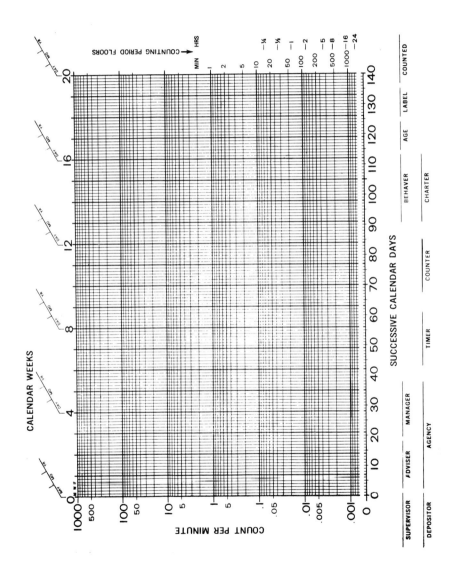

The logarithmic scale is important for reasons other than its ability to display widely varying scores. It also enables the teacher to study a picture of learning that can be more easily interpreted. When the scores from repeated measures of performance are plotted on the more typical "equal interval" or "arithmetic" scale, learning (represented by a line or function which "best fits" the data) is found to accelerate. In other words, a curve with an ever-steeper slope is created. When data are plotted on the standard celeration chart, learning is generally represented by a straight or nearly straight line. The value of the slope of the line which best fits the distribution of values plotted on the logarithmic scale is thought of as an "index of learning." The steeper the slope, the faster the learning is; the flatter the slope, the slower the learning is.

Because learning (change in performance scores) appears to grow like compound interest, or by multiplying, it is analogous to acceleration. Change is measured in terms of responses per minute per week. Theoretically, the change in performance scores can be in either direction, up or down, meaning that performance scores can either increase or decrease. "Celeration," the root of acceleration, has come to mean learning, with "ac-celeration" or "times (X) celeration" representing "up learning" or an increase in performance scores, while "de-celeration" means that scores are declining in value.

The index of learning, or celeration, which is represented by the slope of the line best fitting the performance scores can be estimated with a simple calculation. Data are generally obtained from daily timings; therefore, the most representative score from the week would probably be the median or mode of the five daily scores. The celeration score (which is always 1.0 or greater) can be thought of as a factor by which the most representative score from the five scores in the first week is either multiplied or divided to obtain the most representative score in the second week. Thus, if the median of the scores in week 10 is 40 correct responses per minute, and the median of the scores in week 11 (the next week) is 50 correct responses, the celeration score is X1.25 or 25% improvement, because 40 responses X1.25 = 50 responses.

The logarithmic scale employed by the standard celeration chart is also useful in studying the variability of scores, or relative change in the values (as opposed to absolute change). Equal units of change (distances) on the logarithmic scale correspond to equal ratios, so that differing distances on the scale will be proportional to differing ratios. Figure 3.4 compares two simple, but identical, data sets, one plotted according to an arithmetic or equal interval scale (Panel A), and the other according to a ratio scale (Panel B). Note that the scores plotted on the equal interval scale in sets (A) and (B) vary in identical proportions, yet the absolute score differences vary unequally. The equivalence of the relative changes in the scores in sets (A) and (B) can be seen clearly when plotted on the logarithmic scale. Learning, by our definition, is a change in the relative values of repeated performance measures and it is more appropriately studied when displayed on a logarithmic scale which permits the inspection of relative changes.

FIGURE 3.4

Arithmetic (A) and Ratio (B) Scales

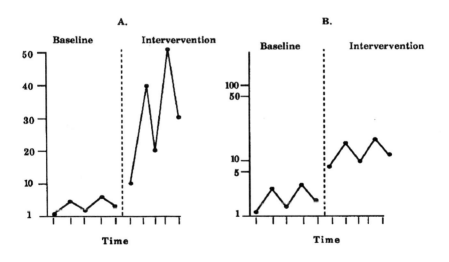

≈

Direct Measurement and Continuous Monitoring

The first issue we must consider in a discussion of measuring of learning is what is the phenomenon we are planning to quantify? What is learning? Is learning the same as knowing? Defining these terms is prerequisite to a discussion of how learning ought to be quantified. While they are not the same, "learning" and "knowing" are certainly related. However, one appears to be an outcome, while the other is a process. "Learning" is the process of acquiring knowledge; "knowing" is the outcome or result of the process of learning. When we measure learning, are we really measuring "learning" or "knowing"?

We may think of learning as a continuous process, much the same way a motion picture gives a continuous study of an event or events. Assessing a student's performance is like examining a single frame from the motion picture. At a certain point in time, the student did "this-and-so," or the student knew "X." Knowledge, in this sense, is a static property, something that is inferred by the student's performance on a particular occasion, under particular circumstances. Learning, on the other hand, requires more than a single instance of measurement. In fact, the more instances of measurement we have to inspect, the more accurate and representative will be our interpretation of learning. If we can study many frames from our motion picture, we will know much more and have a much better idea of the continuous process the motion picture represents (West, Young, & Spooner, 1990). However, just as one frame in a motion picture differs little from frames that are adjacent to it, we don't need to measure "knowing" constantly in order to detect significant changes in what is "known." Nevertheless, just as it is difficult to determine the story reflected in a motion picture if we see only the first and last frames, measurement must be frequent enough to permit an inspection of the process of "coming to know" or learning. Therefore, measurement of learning should be frequent enough to detect changes in "knowing," and it should relate to specific skills the instructor considers to be important, presumably those which are the objects of instruction. Generally speaking, each student's performance should be assessed at least once during each instructional session or class period. Changes in the student's performance from one assessment to the next may be thought of as "learning." More will be said later about the importance of measuring performance frequently, even daily if possible.

Daily Timings

The argument for assessing performance frequently has already been presented. The question of how frequently performance should be assessed remains. We have found that most academic skills of interest to teachers may improve slightly in a single day's time. Therefore, we recommend that timed observations of performance be conducted each day, or four to five times per week. The more frequently assessments are made, the more often decisions can be made about the effectiveness of instruction. A minimum of three data points (resulting from three assessments) is generally required before a picture of learning emerges. If performance assessments were conducted only once per week, three weeks or more would be required before teaching effectiveness could be evaluated. Too much valuable instructional time may be lost when assessments are as infrequent as this.

Each daily timing should (1) be essentially the same from day to day; (2) be free from constraints that inhibit responding; (3) provide sufficient opportunities to respond; and (4) provide time for repeated occurrences of the response. The conditions under which the timings are presented should remain essentially the same from one day to the next. This consistent format reduces the possibility that a detected change in performance is the result of a change in the assessment environment, rather than a change in the performance ability of the student. One can imagine how different a student's score may appear if a different set of arithmetic problems is presented each day, especially if a significantly easier set is accidentally presented. A comparison of the scores across the several days, for the purpose of studying how much learning has occurred, would be inappropriate. Any change in performance would most likely by the result of the different sets of problems, and not "learning."

The best situation for assessment is one that allows free responding, where the student is not hindered by physical constraints (e.g., prompting, or pacing that is too slow) that might inhibit the ease and quickness (fluency) with which the student responds. If prompts or other constraints are necessary, White and Haring (1976) have pointed out that "they should remain consistent each time an assessment is made." For example, if a teacher presents words to a student using flashcards, the pace at which they are presented should be consistent across all assessment trials and fast enough that improvement is not constrained. However, a better method of assessment would be to have the words typed on a sheet of paper so that the student's fluency would not be hindered by the teacher's presentation rate.

To establish an accurate measure of a student's ability to respond fluently, the assessment situation should always provide more opportunities for student responding than can probably be used in the time allowed. Otherwise, the student stops responding because he runs out of opportunities to respond even though additional time may still be available. White and Haring (1976) presented the following example:

> . . . if we give a child a reading passage with 50 words one day and 75 words the next, the child has more opportunities to show his reading skill on the second day. If a child reads all 50 words on the first day and all 75 words on the second day, we would have no way of knowing whether or not he improved. Perhaps he was just as fluent on the first day, but simply did not have the opportunity to show us (p. 49).

The amount of time allotted for responding should remain the same each time the same skill is assessed. The time should be long enough to provide ample opportunity for the student to make repeated responses but not so much time to run out of opportunities to respond, or to allow fatigue or other factors to influence performance.

ॐ

Descriptive and Functional Definitions

There are several important factors that must be considered when selecting the targets of instruction. These skills, or responses, must be described in such a way that it will be obvious to any who may observe the student's performance that the skill was or was not displayed. A music teacher may desire that each student improve in his or her appreciation of good music; an English teacher may expect each of her students to write thoughtful compositions; and a history teacher may hope that every student will understand the philosophical forces that contributed to the development of the U.S. Constitution. These are all worthy objectives, but will the teachers detect when the students have accomplished them? How will the teacher, or any of the students, know when they reach *"appreciation* of *good* music"? Too many terms are open to different interpretations. What does the teacher mean by "thoughtful compositions"? How can a student demonstrate "understanding"? The particular behaviors, from which the objectives are inferred, must be stated clearly and explicitly. Terms that represent action are clearer and can usually be included in these descriptions, because they are more objective, and communicate with greater precision. Thus, a student will *"write* the answers to math problems," *"state* the four principal political parties that existed in the 1820s," *"name* the instruments heard in a musical selection," or *"name* the appropriate correlational procedure when one data set is composed of nominal data and the other set contains ratio data."

Instructional targets or *pinpoints* should be repeatable, and each instance of the pinpoint should be of roughly the same duration. Only when the "pinpointed" responses are repeatable, can the present approach to measuring learning be applied. One may not decide upon a career, get married, or make a million dollars often enough to see a change in performance. However, many repeatable behaviors are tremendously important in the classroom, and can be selected as instructional targets or pinpoints. It is also important that each instance of the pinpoint be of similar duration. It would be inappropriate to mix simple add fact problems with more complicated long division problems and state simply that the goal is for the student to answer forty problems in a minute. Each problem represents a substantially different effort; they are obviously not equivalent in any sense. Measuring a change in performance rate where the units are of different sizes is analogous to measuring distances with a rubber ruler. Each response unit must be of approximately the same size.

It is necessary to have a representative sample of each type of response during each observation period. We have found that about twenty instances of behavior are needed to assure representativeness. In other words, each time the skill is assessed, enough time should be allowed for about twenty instances of the pinpoint to be performed. This means that at least twenty math problems, or twenty spelling words should be presented.

ॐ

An Emphasis
On Building Behavior

Skinner has written on several occasions concerning the importance of making schools pleasant places for students and teachers (1968, 1969a, 1969b). Skinner credits Jean Jacque Rousseau, whose writings inspired the French revolution, as the one who initiated a revolution of comparable magnitude in education. Rousseau was interested in abolishing the punitive methods of his time. Much of our current educational practice can be characterized by terms that would have been familiar to Rousseau. "In spite of all our efforts, it is still true that students learn mainly to avoid the consequences of not learning" (Skinner, 1968). But "we are in the process of rejecting methods which have long dominated the field, in which students study primarily to avoid punishment and which impose upon the teacher the necessity of maintaining a sustained threat" (Skinner, 1968). Historically, education "...made an honest effort to dispense with punishment, but it never found the alternatives it needed. Effective alternatives are now available" (Skinner, 1969a).

Skinner has been critical of the educational community's reliance upon aversive control of students. Writing in *Education*, Skinner explained his concern:

> *Why do students go to school? Why do they behave themselves in class? Why do they study and learn and remember? These are important questions, but they are seldom asked—possibly because we are not proud of the answers. Whether we like it or not, most students still come to school, behave themselves, and study in order to avoid the consequences of not doing so. True, most teachers have abandoned the birch rod (though its return is called for in some quarters), but there are many ingenious, less violent replacements. Violent or not, punitive methods have serious consequences, among them truancy, apathy, resentment, vandalism, and ultimately an anti-intellectualism which includes an unwillingness to support education. These are great problems of the educational establishment, and they*

*can be traced in large part to the techniques of the estab-
lishment itself.*

*Few teachers are happy about punitive methods (most of
them would like to be friends with their students), but
alternatives have seldom proved fruitful. Simply to abandon punishment and allow students to do as they please is
to abandon the goals of education (1969, p. 93).*

Nevertheless, "the aversive techniques of the birch rod or cane are not
likely to reinforce coming to school, and students so treated are likely to
play truant or become dropouts when they can legally do so. Social contingencies are important. A child is more likely to come to school if he gets
along with his peers and his teacher; he is not likely to come if he is
frequently criticized, attacked, or ostracized" (Skinner, 1969a).

From its beginnings with Lindsley at the University of Kansas, Precision Teaching as an approach has focused on positive methods to strengthen
behavior. The emphasis on building fluent performance is designed to help
students to be successful and enjoy school. As their skills improve, their
behavior results in increasingly more reinforcements. Lindsley referred to
this practice as "behavior building" (1972). As an expression of operant
conditioning, Precision Teaching has been used to produce dramatic gains
in the performance of behavior. Lindsley stated that "what made [him] an
early operant conditioner was that only one month after learning the method,
[he] was able to learn from Samson Rat how to teach him to lift over 250%
of his own body weight in only four days of training. Skinner knew this and
used to say, 'The animals make operant conditioners; I don't'" (p. 4).

Haughton (1972) reported the work of colleagues (Ann and Clay
Starlin) which suggested that educationally significant gains were more
likely if emphasis was placed on correct rather than incorrect (oftentimes
called "learning opportunities" by precision teachers) performances.

*Clays' data indicated that when correct oral reading fre-
quencies were less than 50 per minute, emphasis on learning opportunities (such as word substitutions, mis-said
letters, omissions) produced little gain in charted performance. Learning opportunities (or errors) failed to deceler-
ate and correct performance failed to accelerate.
However, if we concentrated on accelerating correct*

*words to at least 50 per minute **before** attempting to work
on decelerating learning opportunities, youngsters showed
marked improvement (p. 23).*

ۮ

Analytic Investigation of
Environmental Influences

An ambitious, conscientiously applied program of collecting and displaying performance scores can not ensure that instruction will be effective. This will not occur until the data are regularly inspected and instruction is adjusted according to the analysis. A given instructional strategy is presumed to be effective if the learning slopes (or best fitting lines) are steeper in the desired direction when the strategy is used than when the strategy is not used. When a learning slope is found to be nearly flat or going in the wrong direction (down, for example, in the case of a line representing correct response), different teaching strategies are tried until one is found that reverses the trend, or raises the slope. Decisions to change instruction are made for each student, thus individualizing each instructional program. The rate of a student's response is very sensitive to changes in instruction, so the effects of a new teaching strategy will be immediately obvious.

The effects of instructional techniques may be expressed in other ways as well. In addition to a change in the *rate* of learning (indicated by a change in the slope, or a change in the celeration score), we may note a change in the *level* or in the *variability* of responding. Each type of change may be used to evaluate the quality of instruction, and each type can be analyzed visually. Figure 3.5 shows that the effect of instructional strategy (A) can be seen in a change of the trend, or slope of the "learning" line, changes in the level of responding, and changes in the variability or consistency of responding. Each change may give the teacher clues of even more powerful instructional strategies.

FIGURE 3.5

Visual Analysis of the Effects of Instructional Strategy (A)

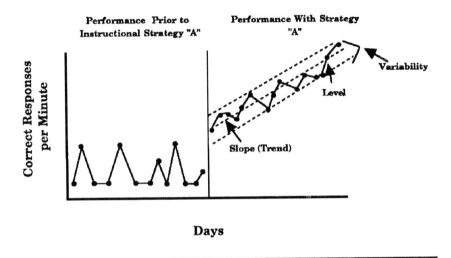

Days

Our research has reliably shown that teachers are more effective if they clearly specify what they want to teach, provide opportunities for their students to learn, frequently measure the performance of critical skills, regularly analyze the performance data, and adjust instruction according to the analysis (Beck, 1981; Beck & Clement, 1976; Burney & Shores, 1979; deAyora, 1988; West, Young, & deAyora, 1988; West, Young, & Spooner, 1990). The picture of learning which results from this type of program is convincing evidence of the teacher's commitment and dedication to a program of effective instruction.

References

Baer, D.M. (1981). *How to plan for generalization.* Lawrence, KS: H & H Enterprises.

Barlow, D.H., Hayes, S.C., & Nelson, R.O. (1984). *The scientist practitioner: Research and accountability in clinical and education settings.* Elmsford, NY: Pergamon Press.

Beck, R. (1981). *Curriculum management through a data base.* Validation Report for ESEA Title IV. Great Falls, MT: Great Falls Public Schools.

Beck, R. & Clement, D. (1976). *Precision teaching in review, 1973-1976.* Great Falls, MT: Great Falls Public Schools.

Biemiller, A. (1978). Relationship between oral reading rates for letters, words, and simple text in the development of reaching achievement. *Reading Research Quarterly, 13,* 223-253.

Bloom, B. (1986). Automaticity: The hands and feet of genius. *Educational Leadership, 43*(5), 70-77.

Burney, J.D. & Shores, R.E. (1979). A study of relationships between instructional planning and pupil behavior. *Journal of Special Education Technology, 2,* 16-25.

Chomsky, C. (1978). When you still can't read in third grade: After decoding, who? In S.J. Samuels (Ed.), *What research has to say about reading instruction.* Newark, DE: International Reading Association.

deAyora, P.A. (1988). *A peer-mediated application of a computer-based instructional decision-making program for improving academic performance.* Unpublished doctoral dissertation, Utah State University, Logan, UT.

Delquadri, J., Greenwood, C.R., Stretton, K., & Hall, R.B. (1983). The peer tutoring spelling game: A classroom procedure for increasing opportunity to respond and spelling performance. *Behavior and Treatment of Children, 6,* 225-239.

Delquadri, J., Greenwood, C.R., Whorton, D., Carta, J., & Hall, R.V. (1986). Classwide peer tutoring. *Exceptional Children, 52,* 535-542.

Denekla, M.B. & Bowen, F.P. (1973). Dyslexia after left occipipitotemporal lobectomy: A case report. *Cortex, September,* 321-332.

Denekla, M.B. & Rudell, R. (1974). Rapid "automatized" naming of pictured objects, colors, letters, and numbers by normal children. *Cortex, June,* 186-202.

Deno, S.L. (1985). Curriculum-based measurement: The emerging alternative. *Exceptional Children, 52*(3), 219-232.

Ehrenfeld, D. (1978). *The arrogance of humanism.* New York: Oxford University Press.

Fuchs, L. & Deno, S. (1981). *A comparison of reading placements based on teacher judgment, standardized testing and curriculum-based assessment* (Research Report No. 56). Minneapolis: University of Minnesota, Institute for Research on Learning Disabilities.

Fuchs, L., Wesson, C., Tindal, G., Mirkin, P., & Deno, S. (1981). *Teacher efficiency in continuous evaluation of IEP goals* (Research Report No. 53). Minneapolis: University of Minnesota, Institute for Research on Learning Disabilities.

Good, T. (1979). Teacher effectiveness in the elementary school: What we know about it now. *Journal of Teacher Education, 30,* 52-64.

Greenwood, C.R., Delquadri, J.C., & Hall, R.V. (1984). Opportunity to respond and student academic performance. In W.L. Heward, T.E. Heron, D.S. Hill, & J. Porter (Eds.), *Behavior analysis in education,* (pp. 58-88). Columbus, OH: Charles E. Merrill.

Greenwood, C.R., Dinwiddie, G., Terry, B., Wade, L., Stanley, S., Thibadeau, S., & Delquadri, J. (1984). Teacher- versus peer-mediated instruction: An eco-behavioral analysis of achievement outcomes. *Journal of Applied Behavior Analysis, 17,* 521-538.

Haughton, E. (1972). Aims—growing and sharing. In J.B. Jordan & L. S. Robbins (Eds.), *Let's try something else kind of thing: Behavioral principles of the exceptional child* (pp. 1-11). Arlington, VA: The Council for Exceptional Children.

Howell, K.W. & Morehead, M.K. (1987). *Curriculum-based evaluation for special and remedial education.* Columbus, OH: Merrill.

Jenkins, J.R., Barksdale, A., & Clinton, L. (1978). Improving reading comprehension and oral reading: Generalization across behaviors, settings, and time. *Journal of Learning Disabilities, 11*(10), 5-15.

Jenkins, J.R. & Pany, D.Z. (1978). Standardized achievement tests: How useful for special education? *Exceptional Children, 44,* 448-453.

Johnston, J.M. & Pennypacker, H.S. (1980). *Strategies and tactics of human behavioral research.* Hillsdale, NJ: Lawrence Erlbaum Associates.

Keller, F.S. & Schoenfeld, W.N. (1950). *Principles of psychology.* New York: Appleton-Century-Crofts.

Lapardo, G. & Sadow, M.W. (1982). Criteria and procedures for the method of repeated readings. *Journal of Reading, 26,* 156-160.

Lindsley, O.R. (1972). From Skinner to precision teaching: The child knows best. In J.B. Jordan & L.S. Robbins (Eds.), *Let's try something else kind of thing: Behavioral principles of the exceptional child* (pp. 1-11). Arlington, VA: The Council for Exceptional Children.

Mattis, S., French, J.H., & Rapin, I. (1973). Dyslexia in children and young adults—Three independent neuropsychological syndromes. *Developmental Medicine, 17,* 150-163.

Moyer, S.B. (1982). Repeated reading. *Journal of Learning Disabilities, 15*(10), 619-623.

Parsonson, B.S. & Baer, D.M. (1978). The analysis and presentation of graphic data. In T.R. Kratochwill (Ed.), *Single subject research: Strategies for evaluating change* (pp. 101-165). New York: Academic Press.

Perfitti, C.A., Finger, E., & Hogaboam, T.W. (1977). Sources of vocalization latency difference between skilled and less-skilled readers. *Journal of Educational Psychology, 70,* 730-739.

Rashotte, C.A. & Torgesen, J.K. (1985). Repeated reading and reading fluency in learning disabled children. *Reading Research Quarterly, 22,* 180-188.

Salmon-Cox, L. (1981). Teachers and standardized achievement tests: What's really happening? *Phi Delta Kappan, 62*(9), 631-634.

Samuels, S.J. (1979). The method of repeated readings. *The Reading Teacher, 32,* 403-408.

Shavelson, R.J., Webb, N.M., & Burstein, L. (1986). Measurement of teaching. In M.C. Wittrock (Ed.), *Handbook of research on teaching* (3rd ed.) (pp. 50-91).

Sidman, M. (1960). *Tactics of scientific research: Evaluating experimental data in psychology.* New York: Basic Books.

Singer, H. (1970). A developmental model for speed of reading in grades three through six. In H. Singer & R. Ruddell (Eds.), *Theoretical models and processes of reading.* Newark, DE: International Reading Association.

Skinner, B.F. (1938). *The behavior of organisms.* Englewood Cliffs, NJ: Prentice-Hall.

Skinner, B.F. (1950). Are theories of learning necessary? In B.F. Skinner (Ed.), *Cumulative record: A selection of papers* (3rd ed.) (pp. 69-100). New York: Appleton-Century-Crofts.

Skinner, B.F. (1956). A case history in scientific method. *American Psychologist, 11,* 221-233.

Skinner, B.F. (1968). *The technology of teaching.* Englewood Cliffs, NJ: Prentice-Hall.

Skinner, B.F. (1969). *Contingencies of reinforcement: A theoretical analysis.* Englewood Cliffs, NJ: Prentice-Hall.

Skinner, B.F. (1969a). Contingency management in the classroom. *Education, 90,* 93-100.

Skinner, B.F. (1969b). *Contingencies of reinforcement: A theoretical analysis.* New York: Appleton-Century-Crofts.

Spooner, F., Weber, L.H., & Spooner, D. (1984). The effects of backward chaining and total task presentation on the acquisition of complex tasks by severely retarded adolescents and adults. *Education and Treatment of Children, 6,* 401-420.

Spring, C. & Capps, C. (1974). Encoding speed, rehearsal, and probed recall of dyslexic boys. *Journal of Educational Psychology, 5,* 780-786.

Stanley, S.O. & Greenwood, C.R. (1983). Assessing opportunity to respond in classroom environments through direct observation: How much opportunity to respond does the minority, disadvantaged student receive in school? *Exceptional Children, 49*, 370-373.

Stokes, T.F. & Baer D.M. (1977). An implicit technology of generalization. *Journal of Applied Behavior Analysis, 10*(2), 349-367.

West, R.P. & Sloane, H.N. (1986). The effects of teacher presentation rate and point delivery rate on classroom disruption, performance accuracy, and response rate. *Behavior Modification, 10*, 267-286.

West, R.P., Young, K.R., & deAyora, P.A. (1988, May). *The effects on academic performance of peer tutors who use precision teaching and computerized decision making.* Paper presented at the 14th Annual Convention of the Association for Behavior Analysis, Philadelphia, PA.

West, R.P., Young, K.R., & Spooner, F. (1990). An introduction to precision teaching: Making instruction effective. *Teaching Exceptional Children, 22*(3), 4-9.

White, O.R. (1986). Precision teaching—Precision learning. *Exceptional Children, 52*(6), 522-534.

White, O.T. & Haring, N.G. (1976). *Exceptional teaching: A multimedia training package.* Columbus, OH: Charles E. Merrill.

Williams, W., Brown, L., & Certo, N. (1976). Basic components of instructional programs. *Theory into Practice, 14*(2), 123-136.

Young, K.R., West, R.P., & Crawford, A. (1985). The acquisition and maintenance of functional reading skills by multiply handicapped deaf students. *Journal of Precision Teaching, 5*, 73-86.

Young, K.R., West, R.P., Howard, V.F., & Whitney, R. (1986). Acquisition, fluency training, generalization, and maintenance of dressing skills of two developmentally disabled children. *Education and Treatment of Children, 9*, 16-29.

Behavior Analysis and Technology in Higher Education

Kenneth E. Lloyd and Margaret E. Lloyd
Drake University and Central Washington University

course organization called Personalized System of Instruction (PSI) presents an opportunity for an applied analysis of behavior in the college classroom (Keller, 1965, 1968). PSI is defined by its five basic characteristics, which are: unit tests, optional lectures, 100% mastery, self (student)-pacing, and undergraduate proctors.

In the original format the course material was divided into many small units, e.g., 30, for studying and testing. A set of questions accompanied each unit; usually these questions appeared, sometimes with new questions, on the unit tests. Class time was used to discuss student questions or for testing, although occasionally lectures were available to, but not required of, those students who had previously completed certain units, and, presumably, could best understand them.

Unit tests were graded pass or fail according to a prespecified criterion (for Keller this was 100%). Failure to answer all questions correctly necessitated remedial work and further attempt(s) to achieve mastery on comparable forms of the test. All students were assumed to be capable of performing the work at the mastery level. Students could differ in the number of retests necessary to complete a unit, but not in the final level of performance on a unit. At the end of the term, students also differed in the number of units they had mastered; this was the basis for the differential assignment of letter grades. Mastery ensures that students know whatever material they have covered. This differs from traditional university testing procedures which allow students to complete assignments inadequately, e.g., a grade of "D" under PSI might indicate a student covered two units perfectly while a "D" in a traditional course means the student covered all units inadequately.

Self-pacing allowed each student to decide when he or she was ready to take a unit test. Only after mastering one unit could a student begin studying the next unit. In a large class, self-pacing necessitated that a testing center be open many hours each week. An instructor and graduate assistant(s) could supervise some of the testing hours, but usually the instructor recruited former-grade students to serve as proctors. Proctors maintained regular office hours, answered questions, administered tests, and provided immediate feedback about test performance to students. The instructor met with the proctors to conduct training sessions and to monitor their proctoring skills.

The PSI course organization shifted the emphasis in teacher-student classtime relations. Students were no longer passive recipients of lectures. Instead they were actively reading and studying. Teachers were no longer primarily lecturers. Instead they devised study questions and objectives; discussed issues raised by students; trained and supervised proctors; gave students feedback on their tests; and managed a complex grading system.

૨▲

Origins

PSI was developed from several sources (Sherman, 1974). Programmed instruction (e.g., Skinner, 1954, 1968) and PSI both emphasize careful task analysis and a concern for terminal performance; both permit self-pacing. However, programmed instruction operates with smaller response units than PSI.

A more distant, but nonetheless important, origin of both PSI and programmed instruction is the laboratory study of behavior known as the experimental analysis of behavior (*Journal of the Experimental Analysis of Behavior*, 1958 to present; Skinner, 1953). This approach is characterized by continuous measures of the behavior of single individuals. The most important variables controlling behavior are the immediate consequences which determine whether the future occurrence of that behavior will be increased (reinforcement) or decreased (extinction). If a desired terminal response is not in the behavioral repertoire of the individual then it may be necessary to reinforce successive approximations of the behavior (shaping) until the target behavior is mastered. Sometimes it may be necessary to restrict the occurrence of a behavior to certain specific circumstances (stimulus control) by means of prompts which are later gradually removed (faded).

Although Keller chose not to describe his educational methods in the language of the experimental analysis of behavior, the influence of this analysis is apparent. The self-pacing of large numbers of unit tests approximates the continuous response measures of the laboratory. Feedback on unit test questions by the instructor or proctors provides immediate consequences for correct or incorrect answers. Study questions as well as proctor questions and suggestions can guide students who lack a particular terminal behavior until they master more appropriate responses (shaping and fading).

૨▲

Variations of PSI

Following Keller's initial reports, several other PSI course descriptions were published. None were exact replications, but all acknowledge Keller as their source. Although several authors have cautioned against altering the five PSI characteristics (Green, 1971; Keller, 1985; Sherman, 1974, pp. 4-5), much variation has occurred. Several variations retained the five original characteristics, but modified one or more of them, e.g., oral interviews were substituted for written answers in unit tests (Ferster, 1968); students chose the number of pages to be covered in a unit test (Born, Gledhill & Davis, 1972; and students were permitted to choose among assignments other than unit tests (Lloyd & Knutzen, 1969). Although a final examination was not considered a basic PSI characteristic, Keller included one; others have omitted them. Review tests have been added during the term (e.g., Semb, 1980) and optional lectures have been omitted (Ferster, 1968).

A more extreme deviation from the PSI format is the omission of some of the five basic characteristics. In a review of 29 PSI studies, 29 were found to use frequent unit tests, 19 used self-pacing, 17 used proctors, 14 used optional lectures, and 11 required 100% mastery (Lloyd, 1978). A subsequent examination of 14 more recent studies revealed similar omissions (Lloyd, 1986). Since these 43 studies include those most often cited to indicate the superiority of PSI over traditional teaching methods (see Comparison Studies below) leaving out some of the defining features is especially serious (Fernald & Jordan, 1991).

In pure or altered form PSI has been used in almost every course in the psychological curriculum as well as in almost all areas of the liberal arts and sciences (Lloyd, 1978, pp, 490-492).

ð

Empirical Evaluations

Unlike many educational systems which come and go with little or no demonstration of their empirical validity, PSI, originating from a research tradition, was immediately evaluated by experiment. One research approach, labeled comparison studies, (e.g., Semb, 1980; Calhoun, 1976) compared the performance of students in a PSI class with those enrolled in a traditional class. Another approach, labeled component analyses, evaluated one or more of the five characteristics. Both approaches have been extensively reviewed (Hursh, 1976; Kulik, Jaksa, & Kulik, 1978; Kulik, Kulik, & Carmichael, 1974; Kulik, Kulik, & Cohen, 1980; Lloyd, 1978;

Robin, 1976; Williams, 1976). For a detailed examination of this research, the reader should consult these sources.

◆

Comparison Studies

An early review of comparison studies concluded that PSI classes outperformed traditionally taught classes on end of term examinations and that student opinion favored PSI (Kulik, et al., 1974). A meta-analysis of 312 studies of the effects of five instructional technologies (PSI, computer-based instruction, Audio-Tutorial, programmed instruction and visual-based instruction) on college teaching (Kulik, et al., 1980; see also Kulik, Kulik, & Bangert-Drowns, 1988; McKeachie, 1990) concluded that PSI outperformed traditional lecture classes by a greater margin than the other four technologies. The meta-analysis included 74 comparisons of PSI classes with traditionally taught classes. These studies differed in experimental designs (e.g., same or different instructor in experimental or control classes); course setting (e.g., science or nonscience discipline); and whether the study had been published. Altogether 14 such "demographic" variables were examined. However, none of the variables pertain to the learning process or to the degree to which the courses contained the variables relevant to the instructional method supposedly being tested. Given the variation of PSI characteristics noted above, the absence in the meta-analysis of a measure of the validity of the independent variable was a critical omission (see Peterson, Homer, & Wonderlich, 1982). Previous reviews have noted that those studies incorporating four or five of the PSI characteristics have the greatest chance of demonstrating differences between PSI and control sections (Lloyd, 1978, 1986).

The most frequent dependent variable employed in the comparison studies was a final examination of up to 100 multiple-choice (m-c) items. In some studies, the study questions and unit tests used in the PSI groups contained m-c items as well. In these studies, the PSI groups either had already answered and received feedback on a subset of the items on the final examination (when they had taken their unit tests earlier) or, at least, they had experience with the style of m-c questions used by that instructor. Those studies which reported using m-c items on both tests and examinations were more likely to demonstrate superiority of PSI classes over control classes (Lloyd, 1978, 1986). Some of PSI's apparent success may be a result of using identical items and/or item formats in unit tests and final examinations.

The mean absolute difference between PSI and traditional lecture classes in final examination scores has been approximately seven multiple-choice items out of 100 (Kulik, et al., 1980; Lloyd, 1978, p. 496; Lloyd, 1986).

> *The educational changes produced by manipulating these PSI features may at first glance seem small. They usually amount to an increment of less than 10% on final examination scores or to less than half of a standard-deviation-unit separation of experimental and control groups. But closer examination should reveal that increases of this magnitude are large enough to have major significance for education. Considering how many courses each student takes, and how many years colleges have been around and will be around, changes of even 1% in educational effectiveness can have major implications for a society (Kulik, et al., 1978, p. 12).*

Two years later the same authors were not so optimistic when writing about all five technologies they had examined.

> *The studies . . . gave us a basically positive picture of instructional technology. . . .*
>
> *It would be foolish, however, to pretend that the effects of educational technology are large ones. Clearly they are not. . . . Teaching technologies have produced positive results, but in a typical class, these results would be barely perceptible to the unaided human eye.*
>
> *It has often been said that instructional technologies have been oversold, and this seems to be the case. . . . Those who judge technology by the standards of its publicity are likely to be disappointed by its actual performance. Those who approach it with more modest expectations are likely to find that technology has something to offer college teachers (Kulik, et al., 1980, p. 204).*

Despite the conclusion that PSI is superior, it is still relevant to ask whether college deans, department heads, and other faculty will be impressed by these differences. It does not seem practical to argue seriously "that an average improvement of seven multiple-choice items should be the basis for reorganizing a university system" (Lloyd, 1978, p. 496).

Ꮠ

Interest in PSI
Research and Teaching

Interest in PSI research, judged by the number of published journal articles and the number of papers and posters presented at professional meetings, is declining (Lamal, 1984). The percent of articles published in *Teaching of Psychology*, which were comparison studies, component analyses or PSI reviews, fell steadily from 8.5% (Volumes 1-4; 1974-77) to 3% (Volumes 15-18; 1988-91). Forty-four posters and papers were presented at the Association for Behavior Analysis from 1976-79, and only eight from 1988-91.

Interest in PSI as a teaching method also seems to be declining. Seventy-three percent of questionnaires sent to 42 senior authors of PSI articles published before 1975, and to 29 senior authors of PSI papers published after 1974 were returned. Half of the respondents still teaching (53%) used PSI as much as ever, 21% used it less, and 26% no longer used it (Lloyd & Lloyd, 1986). Recent users taught 73 courses and used PSI in 22, of which 13 were being taught as potentially publishable experiments.

Data was also obtained from chairpersons of 218 randomly selected psychology departments. Fifty-six percent returned the questionnaire. At least one PSI course had been taught the previous year in 30% of the departments. PSI had not been used the previous year in 70% of the departments. Only 7% of the departments indicated their usage of PSI had increased over the past ten years, while 17% reported a decrease (Lloyd & Lloyd, 1986).

The results of these questionnaires support Keller's description (1985) of the failure of PSI to gain widespread acceptance among working teachers. Several working teachers have cited problems with the PSI components in an anecdotal fashion, for example, the necessity for large numbers of study and test questions may result in "low content levels" (Hobbs, 1987); students find it easy to share the contents of their tests with others who, in a self-paced format, have not yet taken the tests (Rosenkoetter, 1984); and proctors may be shaped by students to accept less than perfect answers (Caldwell, 1985). The respondents to the Lloyd and Lloyd questionnaire consistently stated that the system required considerable labor by the instructor. To add insult to injury, the instructor was likely to be criticized by colleagues and administrators for using PSI.

Although PSI is being used less, some of its features are being incorporated into university instruction. For example, in recent years publishers have added study questions to the supplemental textbook materials they produce. The number of published study questions suggests that students at best buy them; the extent to which they use them is not known.

Recommendation for Researchers

It may be that a change in the direction of PSI research could revitalize its use in the classroom. PSI research has not been a behavioral analysis of university classrooms. Neither within-subject research strategies, such as reversal designs and multiple-baseline designs, nor continuous measures of relevant behaviors (Burt, 1974; Mawhinney, Bostow, Laws, Blumenfield, & Hopkins, 1971) have been used (cf., Fernald & Jordan, 1991).

Perhaps researchers too readily adjusted their designs to fit the established classroom organization. A classroom defines a ready-made group and a final examination defines a ready-made dependent variable within a semester, which defines a ready-made treatment duration. It is also likely that authors who submitted manuscripts to a variety of educational journals encountered editors who emphasized group designs and statistical analyses. The goal of the research has not been to change the behavior of individual students from baseline to some academically more desirable level, but rather to raise the value of the mean score of an experimental class in relation to a comparison class. The result of this goal is the absence of an analysis of the variables accounting for individual differences in response to PSI. Such an analysis might widen the 10% difference between experimental and comparison groups and convince administrators to support PSI.

ᥣ

Recommendations for Teachers

As noted above, PSI is defined by five components. In the research literature the original five features have been subdivided so that seven or eight exist. Major findings for each component are discussed below.

Answering study questions before attempting a unit test helps students pass unit and review tests if the study questions emphasize the issues covered in the unit tests. Unit tests and review tests facilitate performance on final examinations (Kulik, et al, 1978; Semb, Hopkins & Hursh, 1973). Checking written answers to study questions or verbally quizzing students on them improves unit test performance (Peters, 1975) especially when items are similar (Laham & Caldwell, 1979).

Optional lectures neither alter final performance (e.g., Calhoun, 1976; Roberts, Suderman, Suderman, & Semb, 1990) nor reinforce class attendance (Lloyd, Garlington, Lowry, Burgess, Euler, & Knowlton, 1972). From the beginning (e.g., Johnston & O'Neill, 1973), research has supported the mastery criterion even though mastery at less than 100% (e.g., 80% or 90%) is typical (Kulik, et al., 1978; Marholin II, 1976). Students who do not attain mastery on their first attempt are permitted remediation. Although students preferred optional remediation, they performed better when it was required (Sundberg, Malott, Ober, & Wysocki, 1978). Limiting the number of retests (e.g., only two) may improve performance (Barkmeier, Duncan, & Johnston, 1978).

Self-pacing has received as much attention as any of the characteristics. Its presence does not effect student performance (Kulik, et al., 1978; Lloyd, 1978; Roberts & Semb, 1990), but with an absence of assignment deadlines, many students wait until the end of the term to turn in work. The teaching staff must then complete most of its grading responsibilities all at once. Instructors avoid this by introducing various deadlines throughout the term, or by arranging contingencies which encourage students to set and meet their own deadlines (Lloyd & Zylla, 1981; Roberts, Fulton, & Semb, 1988). Although procrastination bothers instructors, students frequently list self-pacing as one of PSI's most desirable features (Kulik, et al., 1978).

Proctors facilitate student interaction with the teaching staff and permit rapid feedback about test scores to students. The extra interaction does not please students particularly, but it does improve their performance; immediate feedback about test performance from proctors or other sources does enhance test scores (Kulik, et al., 1978). Since training proctors to interact objectively with students is complex and time-consuming, many instructors may avoid it (e.g., Robin, 1977; Robin & Cook, 1978; Robin & Heselton, 1977).

In summary, study questions, frequent unit tests, required mastery, and immediate feedback result in improved test performance. Student-pacing pleases students. Nonrequired lectures are an optional characteristic. These recommendations agree with how PSI researchers described the classes they teach: study guides were used by 85%, frequent tests by 94%, mastery by 78%, immediate feedback by 100%, student-pacing and proctors by 76% (Lloyd & Lloyd, 1986).

ò

The Challenges

The challenges facing PSI are twofold. The first is an intellectual challenge: to conduct an analysis of behavior in the college classroom rather than accepting the easier route of using between-groups research designs and statistical analyses. The second is a more practical challenge: to respond to the existing PSI research in a manner more likely to induce support from the existing university environment of colleagues, deans, and administrators. Despite the critical analysis presented above, the instructor who has not tried PSI is undoubtedly missing an exciting educational experience.

References

Barkmeier, D.R., Duncan, P.K., & Johnston, J.M. (1978). Effects of opportunity for retest on study behavior and academic performance. *Journal of Personalized Instruction, 3*, 89-92.

Born, D.G., Gledhill, S.M., & Davis, M.L. (1972). Examination performance in lecture-discussion and personalized instruction courses. *Journal of Applied Behavior Analysis, 5*, 33-43.

Burt, D.W. (1974). Study and test performance of college students on concurrent assignment schedules. In Johnston, J.M. (Ed.), (1974). *Behavior Research and Technology in Higher Education.* Springfield, IL: C.C. Thomas.

Caldwell, E.C. (1985). Dangers of PSI. *Teaching of Psychology, 12*, 9-12.

Calhoun, J.F. (1976). The combination of elements in the personalized system of instruction. *Teaching of Psychology, 3*, 73-76.

Fernald, P.S. & Jordan, E.A. (1991). Programmed instruction versus standard text in introductory psychology. *Teaching of Psychology, 18*, 205-211.

Ferster, C.B. (1968). Individualized instruction in a large introductory psychology course. *Psychological Record, 18*, 521-532.

Green, B.A. (1971). *Is the Keller plan catching on too fast?* Unpublished manuscript. Education Research Center, MA: Institute of Technology.

Hobbs, S.H. (1987). PSI: Use, misuse, and abuse. *Teaching of Psychology, 14*, 106-107.

Hursh, D.E. (1976). Personalized systems of instruction: What do the data indicate? *Journal of Personalized Instruction, 1*, 91-105.

Johnston, J.M. & O'Neill, G. (1973). The analysis of performance criteria defining course grades as a determinant of college student academic performance. *Journal of Applied Behavior Analysis, 6*, 261-268.

Journal of the Experimental Analysis of Behavior. (1958-present). Bloomington, IL: Society for the Experimental Analysis of Behavior.

Keller, F.S. (1965). New reinforcement contingencies in the classroom? *American Psychologist, 20*, 542. Also reprinted in Sherman, J.G. (Ed.). (1974). *Personalized System of Instruction* (chap. 8). Menlo Park, CA: Benjamin.

Keller, F.S. (1968). "Goodbye, teacher...". *Journal of Applied Behavior Analysis, 1*, 79-89.

Keller, F.S. (1985). Lightning strikes twice. *Teaching of Psychology, 12*, 4-8.

Kulik, J.A., Jaksa, P., & Kulik, C.C. (1978). Research on component features of Keller's Personalized System of Instruction. *Journal of Personalized Instruction, 3*, 2-14.

Kulik, J.A., Kulik, C.C., & Bangert-Drowns, R.L. (1988). *Effectiveness of mastery learning programs: A meta-analysis.* Ann Arbor: University of MI, Center for Research on Learning and Teaching.

Kulik, J.A., Kulik, C.C., & Charmichael, K. (1974). The Keller-plan in science teaching. *Science, 188*, 379-383.

Kulik, C.C., Kulik, J.A., & Cohen, P.A. (1980). Instructional technology and college teaching. *Teaching of Psychology, 7*, 199-205.

Laham, S.L. & Caldwell, E.C. (1979). Pre-quiz discussion differentially affects student performance. *Teaching of Psychology, 6*, 213-216.

Lamal, P.A. (1984). Interest in PSI across sixteen years. *Teaching of Psychology, 11*, 237-238.

Lloyd, K.E. (1978). Behavior analysis and technology in higher education. In Catania, A.C. and Brigham, T.A. (Eds.). *Handbook of Applied Behavior Analysis: Social and instructional processes* (pp. 482-521). New York: Irvington Press.

Lloyd, K.E. (1986, May). Updating behavior analysis in higher education. Invited symposium presentation at the meeting of the Association for Behavior Analysis, Milwaukee, WI.

Lloyd, K.E., Garlington, W.K., Lowry, D., Burgess, H., Euler, H.A., & Knowlton, W.R. (1972). A note on some reinforcing properties of university lectures. *Journal of Applied Behavior Analysis, 5*, 151-155.

Lloyd, K.E. & Knutzen, N.J. (1969). A self-paced programmed undergraduate course in the experimental analysis of behavior. *Journal of Applied Behavior Analysis, 2*, 125-133.

Lloyd, M.E. & Lloyd, K.E. (1986). Has lightning struck twice? Use of PSI in college classrooms. *Teaching of Psychology, 13*, 149-151.

Lloyd, M.E. & Zylla, T. (1981). Self-pacing: Helping students establish and fulfill individualized plans for pacing unit tests. *Teaching of Psychology, 3*, 100-103.

Marholin II, D. (1976). The effects of a minimal grade penalty on mastery quiz performance in a modified PSI course. *Journal of Personalized Instruction, 1*, 80-85.

Mawhinney, V.T., Bostow, D.E., Laws, D.R., Blumenfield, G.J., & Hopkins, B.L. (1971). A comparison of students studying behavior produced in daily, weekly, and three-week testing schedules. *Journal of Applied Behavior Analysis, 4*, 257-264.

McKeachie, W.J. (1990). Research on college teaching: The historical background. *Journal of Educational Psychology, 82*, 189-200.

Peters, R.D. (1975). Pre-quiz monitoring of study materials improves performance in two PSI courses. In J.M. Johnston (Ed). *Research and technology in college and university teaching.* Gainesville, FL: Society for Behavioral Technology and Engineering.

Peterson, L., Homer, A.L., & Wonderlich, S.A. (1982). The integrity of independent variables in behavior analysis. *Journal of Applied Behavior Analysis, 15*, 477-492.

Roberts, M.S., Fulton, M., & Semb, G. (1988). Self-pacing in a personalized psychology course: Letting students set the deadlines. *Teaching of Psychology, 15*, 89-92.

Roberts, M.S. & Semb, G.B. (1990). Analysis of the number of student-set deadlines in a personalized psychology course. *Teaching of Psychology, 17*, 170-172.

Roberts, M.S., Suderman, L., Suderman, R., & Semb, G. (1990). Reading ability as a predictor in a behaviorally based psychology course. *Teaching of Psychology, 17*, 173-175.

Robin, A.L. (1976). Behavioral instruction in the college classroom. *Review of Educational Research, 46,* 313-354.

Robin, A.L. (1977). Proctor training: Snapshots, reflections, and suggestions. *Journal of Personalized Instruction, 2,* 216-221.

Robin, A.L. & Cook, D.A. (1978). Training proctors for personalized instruction. *Teaching of Psychology, 5,* 9-13.

Robin, A.L. & Heselton, P. (1977). Proctor training: The effects of a manual versus direct training. *Journal of Personalized Instruction, 2,* 19-24.

Rosenkoetter, J.S. (1984). Teaching psychology to large classes: Videotapes, PSI and lecturing. *Teaching of Psychology, 11,* 85-87.

Semb, G. (1980). PSI versus contingency-managed lecture in student-selected and randomly assigned sections of the same course. *Journal of Personalized Instruction, 4,* 129-135.

Semb, G., Hopkins, B.L., & Hursh, D.E. (1973). The effects of study questions and grades on student test performance in a college course. *Journal of Applied Behavior Analysis, 6,* 631-642.

Sherman, J.G. (Ed.). (1974). *Personalized system of instruction.* Menlo Park, CA: Benjamin.

Skinner, B.F. (1953). *Science and human behavior.* New York: Macmillan.

Skinner, B.F. (1954). The science of learning and the art of teaching. *Harvard Educational Review, 24,* 86-97.

Skinner, B.F. (1968). *The technology of teaching.* New York: Knopf.

Sundberg, C., Malott, R., Ober, B., & Wysocki, T. (1978). An examination of the effects of remediation on student performance in a PSI psychology course. *Journal of Personalized Instruction, 3,* 93-97.

Williams, R.L. (1976). Personalized system of instruction: Future research areas. *Journal of Personalized Instruction, 1,* 106-112.

❦

PART TWO

Designs for Excellence:
Behavioral Training and Programs

Early Childhood and Parent Education

Sidney W. Bijou, The University of Arizona

ducators, developmental psychologists, and the general public as well, all agree that early childhood education and parent education are important aspects of education. There is no similar unambiguous agreement on *how* important they are, hence the reluctance to press for some kind of explicit national policy and program. Since 1965, the United States Government has been providing funds for educating young, socially disadvantaged children (Head Start), and a number of states have made preschool education for developmentally disabled children mandatory. The rationale for supporting preschool education for socially disadvantaged children is that these children would fail in the elementary school grades if they were not given early educational stimulation, whereas the rationale for mandatory education for developmentally disabled young children is that these children, like all children, have a right to the kind of education that would help them develop their full potentialities.

Our contention is straightforward: Early childhood education and parent education are essential to the proper social, emotional, and intellectual development of *all* children in a highly industrialized society; therefore, we need more explicit and vigorous policies to promote them within and outside of the educational establishment.

Psychological development that takes place between two and six years of age has powerful and enduring effects. This is the period in which a child's basic psychological equipment is formed, namely, motor abilities, language style, and social behavior patterns, as well as attitudes, values, and beliefs. Upon these foundations are established the great mass of psychological behaviors that constitute his or her unique individuality, referred to as personality, character, and intelligence.

There are two reasons why behaviors acquired between two to six years have a *lasting influence*. It is during this period that a child learns to adjust to the characteristics of the social environment that has been established by his or her family, relatives, close friends, baby-sitters, and preschool teachers. That is to say, a child's social skills, language style, attitudes, values, and beliefs must conform to the properties of human environment just as his or her biological and physical interactions must conform to natural conditions, or the ecological environment (Bijou, 1980). The second reason as to why early learning is strong is that this learning has little or no competition from previous learning to interfere with its thorough establishment. In other words, early learning is not readily weakened by the retroactive inhibitive effects of prior learning acquired under either natural circumstances (as in exploratory behavior) or contrived arrangements (as in tutoring).

An illustration of the significance of early childhood development is in the domain of personal-social maladjustment. Young children brought to child guidance clinics because of behavior problems such as noncompliance or excessive aggressiveness are generally the victims of parents who either do not know how to handle their children's social and emotional development, or are simply negligent. When young children do not conform to parents' wishes or to social standards, management difficulties arise which are often beyond the ability of parents to handle. If not treated, these early deviances will tend to expand into behavior disorders in middle childhood and beyond. Another illustration of the importance of early development is in intellectual, or cognitive, achievement. Preschool age children deprived, for whatever reason, of ample opportunities to develop positive attitudes and motivation for academic achievement and to acquire foundational skills are often candidates for becoming progressively retarded in the elementary grades, and "dropouts" during the high school years. Relevant to this point are the frequent exhortations by black leaders in the U.S., notably the Reverend Jesse Jackson and best-selling author, Alex Haley, to black parents and children that they value academic achievement at least as much as athletic accomplishments.

Perhaps we can best summarize our view on the significance of early childhood education with the words of an unknown author: "No matter your years, your abode, or your status, you remain in the shadows of your early childhood."

This chapter begins with a brief account of the historical roots of preschool and parent education, focusing on the influences of behaviorally-oriented philosophers, psychologists, and educators. We then assess the current situation, evaluating the impact of the behavioral approach, and finally we describe our projections and concerns for the future.

 za

Historical Background

We shall sketch briefly the origins of early childhood education and parent education by tracing separately the kindergarten, nursery school, and parent education movements. We recognize fully that they are interrelated but believe it is expedient to treat each separately mainly because most of the literature is categorized in this way.

The Kindergarten

It is well known that the original impetus for the establishment of the first kindergarten in Germany in 1837 came from the conviction and fervor of Friedrich Froebel, who was influenced by such educators and philosophers as Comenius, Rousseau, and Pestalozzi. The timing was not accidental; it was coincidental with the beginning of the industrial revolution. Without the change of adult lives from home, farm, shop, and village to mill, mine, factory, and city, a new arrangement for the care of young children would have been unnecessary.

In the United States two decades later, in 1856, in Watertown, Wisconsin, Margarethe Schurz founded the first private kindergarten. It was not until almost two decades after that, in 1873, that Susan Blow established and taught the first public kindergarten in St. Louis, Missouri, and only one year later, the National Education Association created a kindergarten department as part of its organization. Public kindergartens in varying formats proliferated over the next hundred years, winning widespread acceptance.

Initially, kindergartens in this country, as one might have expected, were based largely on the philosophy and pedagogy of Froebel who thought of the child as "the divine unity in God's universe." (Spodek, 1982a). The major vehicles of Froebel's curriculum were "gifts" and "occupations." The gifts were small manipulative materials that included solids (balls, cubes, and blocks), surfaces (squares and triangles), lines, points (metal or paper rings), and reconstructions (softened peas or wax pellets, and sharpened sticks and straws). Among other gifts were songs, games, movement activities, stories, poetry, nature study, and gardening. The occupations were crafts involving solids (clay and woodcarving), surfaces (paperfolding and painting), lines (weaving and drawing) and points (stringing beads and perforating). The teachers, who were mainly young, single women, were instructed to describe and demonstrate the gifts and occupations.

Gradually kindergarten education was transformed, due mainly to the emerging field of child study under G. Stanley Hall and the educational philosophy of John Dewey, founder of the Chicago School of Functional Psychology and leader of the progressive education movement. Hall (1883), who advocated studying children by direct observation and analysis of their productions and by querying teachers through interviews and questionnaires, believed that preschool education should reflect a child's development. He argued that young children need large, bold body movements rather than the sedentary activities of the gifts and occupations advocated by Froebel, and that free play could well serve their growing needs. Without substantiating data, he took the position that the emotional life of a child should be given more attention than his or her intellectual life. Dewey (1900) also called for educational activities that would support continuity in children's development and insisted that school activities should be related to the everyday lives of children. The laboratory school at the

University of Chicago served as a demonstration site for Dewey's point of view.

Dewey's views were elaborated by Patty Hill-Smith (1916) who was instrumental in establishing a model kindergarten at the Horace Mann School of Teachers' College, Columbia University. Experiences in this school were organized around the social and physical sciences, the creative arts, and the "tool" subjects of reading, writing, and arithmetic, the latter presented informally and incidentally. The social science program was designed to help clarify children's social experiences and to provide for their adjustment to social life. The physical sciences were presented to afford opportunities to observe, enjoy, experience, and experiment with nature, and to acquire information. The creative arts, designed to help children develop skills and to enjoy and appreciate art experiences, utilized a wide range of media including language. Interestingly, the method of teaching was related to "habit" training, advocated by John B. Watson and Edward L. Thorndike.

The work of Hall, Dewey, and Patty Hill-Smith led to a thorough and complete reconstruction of the kindergarten during the first third of the twentieth century. Although some Froebelian vestiges, such as circle time, remained, the practices became more reflective of a child's life at home and in the community. By the 1930s, the transformation from the Froebelian kindergarten to the developmental-progressive kindergarten was virtually complete. But in the 1950s, progressivism in its various forms began to fade and the kindergarten began to take on the characteristics of the primary grades. It began to blossom again in the 1960s, apparently as a reaction to the stultifying effects of group, routine teaching. The general classroom atmosphere of that period also came under criticism because teachers were not applying the knowledge about learning that had accumulated through research during the previous two decades (Skinner, 1954).

The Nursery School

Fifty years elapsed between the founding of the first American kindergarten and the first American nursery school, which was established in 1919 (Mayer, 1960). Four years later, the first parent cooperative nursery school was opened. Demonstration nursery schools, in conjunction with research institutes like the Gesell Child Guidance Nursery at Yale University, the Merrill-Palmer Institute in Detroit, Teachers' College of Columbia Univer-

Selection V

sity in New York, and the Child Welfare Station at the University of Iowa, were founded between 1910 and 1930. The movement was accelerated further, thanks to funds from the federal government, during the economic depression in the early 1930s, and during World War II in the 1940s, when many mothers of young children patriotically joined the work force. By the late 1960s there were about 816,000 children in nursery schools on the campuses of colleges and universities, in churches, homes, shopping centers, and civic buildings. Variations in the way these schools were operated and continue to be operated are endless.

Some are commercial; others are nonprofit. Some require professional credentials; others do not. Some are exclusively parent-cooperative ventures, while others may exercise no apparent commitment to parental involvement. Some accommodate three, four, and five-year-olds; others accept four-year-olds only. Some are limited to half-day programs; others include a full day. Some schools convene two or three days a week; others utilize the full five-day week. In short, variation is the rule rather than the exception. Exceptional, however, is the sponsorship of nursery school programs by public school systems. During the 1966-67 school year, nursery programs were mandated by only 148 public school systems as compared to nearly 9,800 which regularly mount kindergarten programs (Ream, 1968).

Perhaps the earliest data-based theory influencing nursery school practices came from the Gesell Child Guidance Nursery at Yale University. Gesell and his colleagues maintained that a child's personality unfolds in a fixed and prescribed manner, parallel to embryological development (Gesell & Thompson, 1934), hence nursery schools should provide opportunities for each infant, toddler, and preschooler to develop according to his or her maturational time table.

Although Gesell's maturational theory simplified the scheduling of daily nursery school activities, it was wholly inadequate in helping teachers deal with problem behaviors such as enuresis, extreme shyness, excessive aggression, and persistent disobedience. Consequently, information on the norms of development had to be augmented with principles of mental hygiene and child psychotherapy.

Gesell's perspective began to lose its influence in the late 1950s and early 1960s with the publication of studies clearly indicating that intelligence, as measured by standardized tests, was not a fixed entity but was a set of behaviors that changed with circumstances. One group of studies, spearheaded by Skeels and his colleagues at the University of Iowa, showed that the IQ's of children born of retarded, institutionalized parents increased when the children were reared under normal family and community conditions (e.g., Skeels & Dye, 1939). This finding was disconcerting not only to personality-unfolding theorists but also to those who claimed that intelligence tests measured innate ability. A second group of studies by J. McV. Hunt (1961) and his students indicated that early social stimulation had positive and lasting effects on a child's later development. They showed that under marginal institutional conditions, a baby's development, particularly language, is indeed retarded but that under conditions approximating family living, with its warm and individualized social relationships, a baby's development tends to approach normalcy. A third group of investigations, centering on the work of Bijou (1959) and his colleagues at the Institute of Child Development, University of Washington, demonstrated that by arranging social conditions in accordance with behavior principles, desirable changes were facilitated in the social, motor, and preacademic behaviors of normal and handicapped children (Harris, Johnston, Kelley, & Wolf, 1964; Birnbrauer & Lawler, 1964; Wolf, Risley, & Mees, 1964).

Gesell's influence was also attenuated by competition from the application of Piaget's developmental theory to nursery school practices (e.g., Forman & Fosmot, 1982).

Nursery school practices for normal children in the 1960s and 1970s took on an eclectic flavor, combining concepts from Gesell, Piaget, Rogers, Freud, and Erikson, whereas for the socially disadvantaged, retarded, and emotionally disturbed children during the same period, practices moved toward the behavioral approach, exemplified by Bijou and Baer (1978) and others.

Parent Education

Before describing the background highlights of parent education, we shall attempt to clarify the meaning of the key terms in this field: parent education, parent counseling, and parent training. Parent education focuses on the application of child development principles to child rearing practices in order to help parents enhance the enjoyment of their children and family relationships, to deal effectively with everyday problem behaviors, and to prevent the development of serious problem behaviors. Parent counseling concentrates on the application of personality-social psychological principles to help parents remediate and improve family relationships and adjustments. Parent training deals with the application of developmental principles to teach parents treatment techniques to ameliorate their children's conduct or developmental problems. Our interest here is limited to parent training.

Parent training for children with conduct problems. The dawn of modern parent training took place in Vienna shortly after the turn of the century and as an incidental part of Freud's clinical practice. Through advice and guidance to a friend, also a physician and parent, Freud (1925) was able to counsel him on helping his son ("Little Hans") to overcome a phobic reaction to horses. Undoubtedly the report of this successful case inspired Anna Freud (1946) and Melanie Kline (1949) to develop treatment techniques for neurotic children (child analysis) in the 1930s and 1940s. The procedures of these clinical pioneers were soon adapted for children with milder behavior problems by Allen (1942), Pearson, (1949) and other psychoanalytically-oriented psychiatrists in the United States and became known as child psychotherapy.

Somewhat later, in the 1950s and 1960s, the introduction and application of learning theory to the treatment of child conduct problems and disorders was introduced. This approach emphasized motivation, functionally defined, systematic and quantifiable record keeping, and active parent involvement. It is this last feature–active parent involvement–that we shall elaborate on. A series of studies including one by Wolf, Risley, and Mees (1964) on the treatment of a young autistic child, demonstrated that including parents in treatment accelerated the therapeutic process. Other studies went one step further and showed that, in certain situations, parents could be trained to be the sole therapists (Hawkins, Peterson, Schweid, & Bijou, 1966).

Since the 1960s, research relating to parent training has increased at a rapid rate. There were studies on the kinds of problem behaviors that could be treated by parents, on the kinds of parents who benefited most from training, on the qualifications of parent trainers, on the effectiveness of various teaching strategies, on the short- and long-range outcome of intervention, and on parental satisfaction with the training procedures and outcomes.

Parent training for children with developmental problems. Since the 1950s there have been sporadic examples of parent training programs for children with physical and psychological handicapping conditions, some conducted in the clinic (center-based), and some in the home (home-based). There have been programs for the blind, such as the one by Fraiberg, Smith, & Adelson (1969), for the deaf, such as the John Tracy Clinic (Horton, 1968), for the mildly retarded with socially disadvantaged backgrounds (Weikert, 1967), and for the emotionally disturbed (Doenberg, Rosen, & Walker, 1968). But the program that stands out in bold relief is the behaviorally-oriented program that is designed for handicapped children, particularly the retarded. This is the Portage Project (Shearer & Shearer, 1972) established with the aid of a grant from the Bureau for the Education of the Handicapped, U.S. Office of Education. In this model, originally developed for families in rural Wisconsin, a specially trained teacher visits the home once a week to train a parent in the specific ways that will enhance the development of his or her handicapped child. The model has been rightly described as practical, cost-effective, and replicable. Since 1971, the Portage staff has worked with over a hundred replication sites in this country and has prepared a Head Start option which deals with areas other than self-care and academic subjects, namely, home management and family problems. This home-based program, equally successful abroad, has been translated into Spanish, French, Japanese, Samoan and 25 other languages, and has served as a basis for center-based as well as home-based programs in Canada, England, Wales, Peru, The Dominican Republic, and Japan (Bijou, 1991). Research conducted by the staffs of the Portage Project and those at the replication sites has shown that (1) the progress of children involved in the Portage Project is far about their mental age scores (Peniston, 1972; Shearer & Shearer, 1976), (2) that trained paraprofessionals perform as well as certified teachers (Shortinghuis & Frohman, 1974) and (3) that parents are well satisfied with their participation in the program and with the progress of their children (Revill & Blunden, 1977).

Selection V

ঽ▲

Current Status

This review of the current status of early childhood education and parent training includes a discussion of contemporary kindergarten and nursery school practices and recent research in early childhood education and parent training.

Kindergarten

As pointed out previously, kindergarten practices have moved away from the developmental model and have edged toward the format typical of the primary grades. The shift is attributed to several notable influences. One was the study increase since 1978 in the number of children entering kindergarten; in 1981, ninety-three percent of the children entering first grade had kindergarten experience (Goodlad, 1984). These large enrollments led the designers of educational programs and materials to view the education of five-year-olds as the beginning point for establishing continuity in the elementary school program, hence they introduced into the kindergarten both the organization and content of the primary grades. Another influence stemmed from the demands of parents, particularly those parents who regarded their children as gifted and believed that the primary-grade format adapted for kindergarten would be more challenging for their offspring. Joining this group were parents who were concerned about their children's future school success, and believed that an earlier start in mastering reading, writing, and arithmetic would ensure better achievement in the elementary grades. A third influence came from the introduction into the kindergarten of standardized achievement tests, a practice which leads teachers to slant their teaching toward enhancing children's test performance. A fourth factor was the inadequate preparation of teachers, despite their certification, to conduct the kindergarten on a development format (Spodek, 1982a). The final influence may well be attributed to a misinterpretation of the developmental literature. Statements by investigators regarding the essential conditions for learning were taken to mean that teaching "tool" subjects should begin in the kindergarten year. For example, some cognitive psychologists have claimed that anything can be taught to any child at any time, and some behavioral psychologists have claimed that any task can be taught effectively by the proper management of motivation and the utilization of empirical learning principles. To say that under the proper circumstances any school subject can be taught does not mean that academic subjects should necessarily be taught as early as possible in the school curriculum. What is important is that each child's developmental needs should determine which and when particular subjects or tasks are taught to him or her.

The present-day school format is mainly one of expediency and is rationalized as being the best way of adapting children to the primary grades and of helping them master the tool subjects. Unfortunately, this view fails to consider that many five-year-olds are still in need of a variety of experiences that will help them round out their basic stage, personality development.

Nursery School

Approximately forty-five percent of the children now entering kindergarten have had some kind of nursery school or day care experience (Goodlad, 1984). Their experiences vary widely. Some preschool practices are based on the Montessori model, some on the open education plan, some on the Piagetian format, and so on. But most are eclectic, their practices taken from the work of Dewey, Erikson, Werner, Gesell, Piaget, and their disciples. The behavioral approach has little influence. It may be manifested occasionally by the method used to train children in self-help skills or in the management of social and emotional problems.

The nursery school of the Bank Street College in New York City was deemed a model contemporary preschool (Franklin & Biber, 1977). Its goal was to foster development in the broadest sense, but particularly with respect to ego-strength, autonomy, and the integration of thought, feeling, and action including self-understanding and empathy for others. The method of teaching was described as "support-guided" play which focuses on helping a child to achieve a positive self-image and a concept of self-direction in learning situations. Motivation for learning was to be derived from the satisfaction of learning, and curriculum implementation took into account the child's learning style, interests, and problems. The initial developmental status of a child and his or her growth was measured by impression, testimony, direct observation, and rating scales.

Because the Bank Street nursery school goals were stated in ambiguous terms and its "support-guided" play method of teaching was not detailed, the effectiveness of such a model in achieving its objectives is difficult to evaluate. Moreover, guidelines were not provided for helping children who are not intrinsically motivated by learning. Finally, assessment of an entering child's learning style, interest and problems, and progress in the program was highly subjective, which created difficulties in determining the appropriateness of tasks or projects for enhancing a child's development, particularly in needed areas. It is abundantly clear that the success of such a program depended largely on the procedures for selecting, training, and supervising the teachers (Evans, 1975).

Research

Research on early childhood education has been active and productive in recent years (e.g., Spodek, 1982b) and behaviorally-oriented investigators have contributed a fair share of the literature. From the methodological perspective they have emphasized single-subject research designs (e.g., Hall & Van Houten, 1983; Kazdin, 1982) for obtaining descriptive and experimental information on individual-environmental interactions in natural and contrived settings.

From a substantive point of view, behavioral psychologists have advanced our knowledge of normal children with respect to preacademic and academic learning (e.g., Etzel, LeBlanc, Schillmoeller, & Stella, 1981), the stimulation of creative behavior in painting, drawing, and block-building (e.g., Goetz, 1982), language (e.g., Garcia, 1982; Whitehurst, Kedesdy, & White, 1982), and social behavior (e.g., Rheingold, 1977). At the same time, the literature on the education and reeducation of developmentally deviant children has been expanding rapidly. Outstanding has been the work at the University of Kansas on a wide range of problem behaviors (e.g., Allen & Goetz, 1982; Goetz & Allen, 1983), at the University of Washington in Seattle on Down's Syndrome babies and children (e.g., Hayden & Haring, 1976), and at the University of California in Los Angeles on autistic children (e.g., Lovaas & Bucher, 1974).

Despite this high productivity, some cognitive child psychologists claim that the behavioral approach is on the decline because it cannot deal with the concepts of curiosity and exploration, cannot explain new findings in animal research, and has not produced anything comparable to Piaget's hypothetical stages of cognitive development or Chomsky's deep (innate) structure. Furthermore, they say that the behavioral approach is not compatible with computer technology as a theoretical model for the functions of the mind, e.g., it is not compatible with the concept of information processing. These criticisms obviously deserve the kind of careful consideration that is beyond the scope of this chapter; nevertheless, a few brief remarks are indicated to show how far from the mark these allegations are.

It is true that the empirical behavioral approach cannot deal with the generally accepted concepts of curiosity and exploration. Such terms, based largely on Berlyne's analysis (1960), present research difficulties because of their vagueness. Such flaws, which are traceable mainly to the use of Hullian hypothetical drives, have led to contradictions in findings on the nature of and conditions for exploratory behavior. A reformulation involving Skinner's three-term-contingency with ecological stimuli, as well as Kantor's setting conditions, has been offered to eliminate these deficiencies and to revitalize this area of study so pivotal to the understanding of development during the early years (Bijou, 1980).

Reacting to the alleged failure of the behavioral approach to account for recent findings in animal research, Skinner (1983) reviewed in detail the kinds of animal behavior, such as auto-shaping and the Garcia Effect, which have been said to be beyond the ken of a behavioral explanation, and concluded that such allegations are without foundation. In the same vein, Morris, Higgins, and Bickel (1982) have questioned the practice of some behaviorists to interpret their experimental findings on animal behavior in terms of cognitive constructs.

The final criticism that behaviorists have not produced anything comparable to Piaget's stages of cognitive development, Chomsky's deep structure, and computer technology as a theoretical model of the mind, is true. Empirical behaviorists have purposely eschewed such concepts in their theories and hypotheses because they are hypothetical variables derived from cultural influences rather than from the data of psychology. Skinner's radical behaviorism and Kantor's natural science philosophy include a postulate which states that the subject matter of psychology is the interaction between a biological individual and circumstances. They also include a postulate that states that all concepts–descriptive, analytical, and theoretical–are traceable to the subject matter. Hence, these kinds of behaviorisms, which should be distinguished from methodological behaviorism and cognitive behaviorism, do not attempt to incorporate unobservable terms, even when they originate in the more prestigious sciences and technologies.

Parent Training

It may be said that behaviorally-oriented parent training came of age in the early 1980s, after two decades of research. The event that marked its maturity was the National Parent Training Convention held in Dallas in 1981 (Dangel & Polster, 1984). Here papers were presented on research and services relating to normal, behavior disordered and developmentally delayed children. Judging by these profferings and a review of the literature, workers in this field were producing more research with better designs and were devoting more attention to evaluating the conditions that promote maintenance and generalization of intervention effects.

To do research with parents whose children have serious conduct problems is understandably difficult. Getting them to adhere to fixed schedules, and to control conditions that maintain behavioral changes present varying obstacles, particularly among parents in marginal socioeconomic situations (Wahler, 1980). Nevertheless, in order for the field to grow, research must be directed to examine the conditions that mitigate against maintenance and generalization.

A word about the current status of parent training for developmentally delayed children is in order. In the United States, the Portage Project home-based model has been used not only in Head Start programs but has also been incorporated in a combination of ways into the program of nursery schools and residential institutions for handicapped children. Abroad, in many countries it has also received wide acceptance. For example, the Asian Conference on Mental Retardation has adopted the model as the standard procedure for parent training and the Japan League for Mental Retardation has sponsored its application on a national basis.

Future Trends

The path of predicting future trends in early childhood education and parent training is beset with obstacles. Future innovations will depend largely on new findings in research, public attitude about educational reforms and the broader social scene, particularly in the political and economic arenas. Nevertheless, we can point out the needs, from a behavioral perspective, and indicate whether conditions will favor or hamper their actualization.

Future Needs

Kindergarten. The kindergarten should undergo a third transformation. You will recall that the first change was from the Froebelian to the developmental-progressive model; the second from the developmental-progressive to the primary grades format. There is now need for a transformation to an authentic developmental model, one with a thoroughgoing individualized orientation. This recommendation is not a call for "turning back the clock" because the kindergarten has never been based on developmental principles. While it is true that the developmental-progressive approach included a few developmental slogans, it was based mostly on Dewey's progressive educational philosophy. At the time of the shift, the field of child study, as it was then called, was just emerging and had practically nothing to offer by way of empirical principles; its contributions were mostly programmatic and attitudinal. But now there is considerable empirical knowledge that is applicable to kindergarten practices.

The primary aim of the individualized developmental program is to help each child enhance basic-stage development. This means providing situations that refine and extend self-help skills, social and language competence, motivation for learning, and value hierarchies. The secondary objective, one closely related to the first, is to ensure that each child progresses smoothly to the next developmental stage, the initial societal stage–the period between the ages of six and ten. This is the period during which a child learns the nature of the larger social environment, the school milieu, and the immediate community. Easy transition between these stages facilitates a child's adjustment in middle childhood and beyond, thus reducing the probability of problem behaviors, school retardation, and failure.

The teaching method in this kind of kindergarten is rooted in learning principles and applied individually so that programs are always appropriate to each child's competence.

This stipulation does not mean that all formal and informal teaching would be done on a one-to-one basis; it simply means that all activities would be designed to enhance each child's development. In other words, every child would always be on his or her own "track."

Adherence to learning principles in instruction and guidance means (1) evaluating developmental status up on enrollment, by criterion referenced texts; (2) matching competencies with tasks, programs, and projects; (3) expediting learning and adjustment on the basis of learning principles; (4) monitoring development; and (5) changing tasks, programs, and projects in accordance with the child's performances. The last component obviously demands a flexible curriculum.

Nursery school. The practices appropriate to the kindergarten apply in essence to the nursery school. They, too, should be based, much more than is presently the case, on the application of developmental principles as described, for example, by Allen and Hart (1984). According to these authors, who have had many years of experience in research and service in two university demonstration schools, the goal of a nursery school is to arrange optimum environments in a variety of settings. The program they advocate emphasizes curriculum implementation rather than specific curricula and concentrates on three kinds of learning experiences: (1) teacher-structured activities which are related, for the most part, to preacademic activities; (2) self-help routines; and (3) discovery-exploratory learning. The foremost requirement of the method is that the teacher arranges, organizes, and adapts both the classroom environment and teaching procedures in such a way that each child experiences these three kinds of activities. The Allen-Hart teaching method is entirely consistent with the instruction and guidance procedures described above in our discussion of the kindergarten.

Although research on early childhood is one of the most active areas in developmental psychology, more investigations are needed which have a bearing on nursery school practices. These include analysis of creative behaviors in specific areas, such as language and social interactions, exploratory behavior, language development, prosocial behavior, self-management, and intellectual processes.

Parent training. Since parent training for parents of children with conduct problems has been evolving mainly from research, its future direction depends on the progress of research. Further improvements in the utilization of sound research designs and more investigations on the outcomes of intervention and consumer satisfaction are only a few of the areas needing additional investigation. If research on these problems is as productive as past research has been and if government support continues, there is no reason why the training of parents whose young children have conduct problems should not become a standard part of clinical psychology along with adult and child diagnosis and treatment.

Inasmuch as we identified and described the Portage Project as the most effective approach to training parents of young developmentally delayed children, we shall restrict our comments here to its future development. Considering the wide acceptance in this country and abroad, and considering the various ways in which it has been combined with other preschool programs, the Portage format should be extended upward through adolescence and should even include prevocational and vocational activities. Many special education teachers and child care workers believe that extending the diagnostic procedure (checklist), the curriculum cards, and the teaching method would produce an invaluable instrument for use in residential institutions, group homes, and upper-age special classes.

Further research on the Portage model is essential to evaluate the long-range consequences of parent training on the children. While it is well documented that young, handicapped children in the program for a year or more make excellent progress, research should be carried on to reveal their adjustment in subsequent academic and social activities. The long-range effects of the program on parents is still another area to explore.

ða

Conditions Influencing Future Trends

Will the country's current readiness for elementary and secondary education reform influence changes in the kindergarten and nursery schools? Many educational administrators are now willing to revamp their elementary and secondary schools for at least two reasons. One is the impact of negative reports from prestigious national panels: *A Nation at Risk: The Imperative for Educational Reform* by the National Commission on Excellence in Education; *Report . . . on Federal Elementary and Secondary Educational Policy* by the Twentieth Century Fund; and *Action for Excellence* by the Task Force on Education for Economic Growth of the Education Commission of the United States. The other reason is the widespread publicity given to the high incidence of severe behavior problems in the junior high and high schools, problems that include violence, vandalism, drug abuse, and teenage pregnancies. The critical question, from the point of view of this paper, is this: Are the policy makers in city, state, and federal governments willing to recognize that in order to upgrade school achievement, enhance motivation for academic learning, and decrease serious problem behaviors, changes must take place not only in elementary and secondary education but also in the kindergarten and nursery school. At the higher levels, recommended revisions would serve to remediate current problems; changes in early childhood education would help to prevent their future occurrence. It seems highly improbable that government officials will consider policy changes with respect to the kindergarten and nursery school as significant preventative measures. It is more likely that their views will be compatible with current thinking that the kindergarten is rightfully a downward extension of the primary grades, and the nursery school is an *ad hoc* agency designed to relieve mothers who must work or who wish to pursue careers.

Will current problems in early childhood education be given proper attention in the 1990s? Current problems refer to the plight of socially disadvantaged and culturally retarded young children, lack of provisions in many states for the education of young, handicapped children, inadequate and insufficient number of nursery schools and day care centers for children of working mothers, lack of recognition of the women's liberation movement, and alarm over excessive TV viewing of young children (estimates of about four and a half hours per day) (Schleicher, 1980). With the current mood of governmental agencies to save money by reducing social programs and to subordinate the significance of human rights to other considerations, primarily economic and political, it would be the height of optimism to expect much, if any, meaningful action in the next decade.

Looking beyond the 1990s, we can only hope that the forces then at play will bring about a national policy for the education of preschool children as in Sweden, Israel, and other highly industrialized countries. The impact of such a policy, if properly conceived and executed, would make itself felt in a number of ways. It would help to upgrade the training of teachers for kindergarten and nursery school placement, help parents to gain control of and seek to improve TV programming for young children, and help school personnel to recruit retired persons to serve as teacher assistants and aides so that individualization of instruction can become a reality, at least in the kindergarten and nursery school.

References

Allen, F.H. (1942). *Psychotherapy with children*. New York: W. W. Norton.

Allen, K.E. & Goetz, E.M. (1982). *Early childhood education*. Rockville, MD: Aspen Publication.

Allen, K.E. & Hart, B. (1984). *The early years: Arrangements for learning*. Englewood Cliffs, NJ: Prentice-Hall.

Berlyne, D.E. (1960). *Conflict, arousal and curiosity*. New York: McGraw-Hill.

Bijou, S.W. (1959). Learning in children. *Monograph of the Society for Research in Child Development, 24*, (No. 5, Whole No. 74).

Bijou, S.W. (1980). Exploratory behavior in infants and animals: A behavior analysis. *Psychological Record, 30*, 483-495.

Bijou, S.W. (1991). Overview of early childhood programs around the world. In J. Herwig & M. Stine (Eds.), *Proceedings from the third international Portage conference*. Portage, WI: Cooperative Educational Service Agency #5.

Bijou, S.W. & Baer, D.M. (1978). *Behavior analysis of child development*. Englewood Cliffs, NJ: Prentice-Hall.

Birnbrauer, J.S. & Lawler, J. (1964). Token reinforcement for learning. Mental Retardation, 2, 275-279.

Dangel, R.F. & Polster, R.A. (Eds.). (1984). *Parent training: Foundations of research and practice*. New York: Guilford Publications.

Dewey, J. (1900). *The school and society*. Chicago: University of Chicago Press.

Doenberg, N., Rosen, B., & Walker, T.T. (1968). *A home training program for young mentally ill children*. Brooklyn, NY: League School for Seriously Disturbed Children.

Etzel, B.C., LeBlanc, J.M., Schillmoeller, K.J., & Stella, E.M. (1981). Stimulus control procedures in the education of young children. In S. W. Bijou and R. Ruiz (Eds.), *Behavior modification: Contributions to education* (pp. 3-37). Hillsdale, NJ: Lawrence Erlbaum Associates.

Evans, E.D. (1975). *Contemporary influences in early childhood education* (rev. ed.). New York: Holt, Rinehart, & Winston.

Forman, G.E. & Fosmot, C.T. (1982). The use of Piaget's Constructivism in early childhood education programs. In B. Spodek (Ed.), *Handbook of research in early childhood education* (pp. 185-211). New York: The Free Press.

Fraigberg, S., Smith, M., & Adelson, E. (1969). An educational program for blind infants. *Journal of Special Education, 3*, 121-139.

Franklin, M.B. & Biber, B. (1977). Psychological perspectives and early childhood education: Some relations between theory and practice. In L. G. Katz (Ed.), *Current topics in early childhood education* (Vol. 1, pp. 1-32). Norwood, NJ: Ablex Publishing Corp.

Freud, A. (1946). *Psychoanalytic treatment of children*. London: Imago Press.

Freud, S. (1925). *Collected papers* (Vol. 3). London: Hogarth Press.

Garcia, E.E. (1982). Language acquisition: Phenomenon, theory, and research. In B. Spodek (Ed.), *Handbook of research in early childhood education* (pp. 46-64). New York: The Free Press.

Gesell, A. & Thompson. H. (1934). *Infant behavior: Its genesis and growth*. New York: McGraw-Hill.

Goetz, E.M. (1982). A review of functional analyses of preschool creative behaviors. *Education and Treatment of Children, 5*, 157-177.

Goetz, E.M. & Allen, K.E. (Eds.). (1983). *Early childhood education: Special environmental, policy, and legal considerations*. Rockville, MD: Aspen Publication.

Goodlad, J.I. (1984). *A place called school: Prospects for the future*. New York: McGraw-Hill.

Hall, G.S. (1883). *The contents of children's minds on entering school*. New York: Kellogg & Co.

Hall, R.V. & Van Houten, R.V. (1983). *Behavior modification: The management of behavior*. Lawrence, KS: H & H Enterprises.

Harris, F.R., Johnston, M.K., Kelley, C.S., & Wolf, M.M. (1964). Effects of positive social reinforcement on regressed crawling of a nursery school child. *Journal of Educational Psychology, 55,* 35-41.

Hawkins, R.P., Peterson, R.R., Schweid, E., & Bijou, S.W. (1966). Behavior therapy in the home: Amelioration of problem parent-child relations with the parent in a therapeautic role. *Journal of Experimental Child Psychology, 4,* 99-107.

Hayden, A.H. & Haring, N.G. (1976). Early intervention for high risk young children: Programs for Down's Syndrome Children. In T.D. Tjossem (Ed.), *Intervention strategies for high risk infants and young children* (pp. 573-608). Baltimore: University Park Press.

Hill-Smith, P. (1916). Kindergartens of yesterday and tomorrow. *National Education Association of the U. S. Journal of Proceedings and Addresses, 1916,* 294-297.

Horton, K.B. (1968). Home demonstration teaching for parents of very young deaf children. *Volta Review, 70,* 97-101, 104.

Hunt, J. McV. (1961). *Intelligence and experience.* New York: The Ronald Press.

Kazdin, A.E. (1982). *Single-case research designs: Methods for clinical and applied settings.* New York: Oxford University Press.

Klein, M. (1949). *The psychoanalysis of children.* London: Hogarth Press.

Lovaas, O.I. & Bucher, B.D. (1974). *Perspectives in behavior modification with deviant children.* Englewood Cliffs, NJ: Prentice-Hall.

Mayer, F. (1960). *A history of educational thought.* Columbus, OH: Merrill.

Morris, E.K., Higgins, S.T., & Bickel, W.K. (1982). Comments on cognitive science in the experimental analysis of behavior. *The Behavior Analyst, 5,* 109-125.

Pearson, G.H.J. (1949). *Emotional disorders of children.* New York: W. W. Norton.

Peniston, E. (1972). *An evaluation of the Portage project.* Unpublished manuscript, The Portage Project, Cooperative Educational Service Agency No. 12, Portage, WI.

Ream, M.A. (1968). *Nursery school education—1966-67.* Washington, DC: Research Division, National Education Association.

Revill, S. & Blunden, R. (1977). *Home training of preschool children with developmental delay: Report of the development and evaluation of the Portage service in South Glamorgan.* Unpublished manuscript, Dept. of Health and Social Security and the Welsh Office, Washington, DC.

Rheingold, H.L. (1977). Sharing at an early age. In B.C. Etzel, J.M. Le Blanc, & D.M. Baer (Eds.), *New developments in behavioral research* (pp. 489-502). Hillsdale, NJ: Lawrence Erlbaum Associates.

Schleicher, K. (1980). Human ecology and television in early childhood education. In L.G. Katz (Ed.), *Current topics in early childhood education* (Vol. 3, pp. 77-90). Norwood, NJ: Ablex Publishing Corp.

Shearer, D.E. & Shearer, M.S. (1972). The Portage Project: A model for early childhood education. *Exceptional Children, 39,* 210-217.

Shearer, D.E. & Shearer, M.S. (1976). The Portage Project: A model for early childhood intervention. In T.D. Tjossem (Ed.), *Intervention strategies for high risk infants and young children* (pp. 335-350). Baltimore, MD: University Press.

Shortinghuis, N.E. & Frohman, A. (1974). A comparison of paraprofessional and professional success with preschool children. *Journal of Learning Disabilities, 1,* 62-69.

Skeels, H.M. & Dye, H.B. (1939). A study of the effects of differential stimulation of mentally retarded children. *Proceedings of the American Association of Mental Deficiency, 44,* 114-36.

Skinner, B.F. (1954). The science of learning and the art of teaching. *Harvard Educational Review, 24,* 86-97.

Skinner, B.F. (1983). Can the experimental analysis of behavior rescue psychology? *The Behavior Analyst, 6,* 9-18.

Spodek, B. (1982a). The kindergarten: A retrospective and contemporary view. In L.G. Katz (Ed.), *Current topics in early childhood education* (Vol. 4). Norwood, NJ: Ablex Publishing Co.

Spodek, B. (Ed.). (1982b). *Handbook of research in early childhood education.* New York: Free Press.

Wahler, R.G. (1980). The insular mother: Her problems in parent-child treatment. *Journal of Applied Behavior Analysis, 13,* 207-219.

Weikert, D. (1967). *Longitudinal results of the Ypsilanti Perry Preschool Project.* Ypsilanti, MI: High/Scope Educational Research Foundation.

Whitehurst, G.J., Kedesdy, J., & White, T.G. (1982). A functional analysis of meaning. In S. Kuczaj (Ed.), *Language development. Vol. 1: Syntax and semantics* (pp. 397-427). Hillsdale, NJ: Lawrence Erlbaum Associates.

Wolf, M.M., Risley, T.R., & Mees, H. (1964). Application of operant conditioning procedures to the behavior problems of an autistic child. *Behavior Research & Therapy, 1,* 305-312.

Influences and Effects of the Behavioral Paradigm in Special Education

Eugene Edgar and Stephen Sulzbacher
University of Washington

*T*he intent of this chapter is not to provide a detailed history of the behavioral movement in special education. Other documents have done a good job on this task (e.g., Nelson & Polsgrove, 1984). Rather, we have attempted to detail the influences of the behavioral paradigm in Public Law 94-142 (the Education of the Handicapped Act), highlight a number of specific research studies by leaders in special education who are greatly influenced by the behavioral paradigm, review some advances in programmed instruction, and speculate on the future of the behavioral paradigm in providing a structure which will generate answers to the many difficult questions facing special education today.

The methods we used to generate this manuscript consisted of several activities on our part. We reflected on our own careers as behaviorists. We were part of the first generation of professionals who grew up believing, vehemently, in the behavioral paradigm. Although we both have at times strayed away from the purist path, we have seen the "behavioral way" progress from a "new upstart theory" to become the prevailing philosophical base in special education. Where once we were wild-eyed radicals, we are now part of the establishment. Where once we pleaded for teachers to try our way, we now listen to teachers tell us why "our way" does (or does not) work. Given this 20-year history, we reflected on our personal experiences over these past years.

As a second activity, we talked to a number of our colleagues who are long-time advocates of behaviorism. We spoke candidly and with a true desire to better understand what was happening—to them as professionals and in terms of behavioral theory. We shared with them our intention to use their comments in our paper—we hope we have adequately reflected their beliefs. We would like to thank Norrie Haring, Tom Lovitt, Wayne Sailor, Fred Weintraub, Cec Harper, and John Kidder for talking with us.

As a third activity, we reflected upon our current personal projects and the role of the behavioral paradigm in our work.

Finally, we read—a little.

These activities were neither systematic, nor comprehensive. However, we attempted to interweave our history and the history of the procession with our current thoughts.

ža

Essential Components of the Behavioral Paradigm

The essence of applied behavior analysis in educational technology can be summarized in seven components: (1) the reliance on precise, observable, measurable behavioral units as the cornerstone of the learning process—*behavioral pinpoints*; (2) the notion of the strength of positive consequences—*reinforcing stimulus*; (3) the temporal relationship between the behavioral pinpoint and the reinforcing stimulus—*contingencies*; (4) the rate of delivery of contingencies—*schedules of reinforcement*; (5) the use of successive small approximations (small steps) in the development of complex behaviors—*shaping*; (6) the provision of ample opportunity to make responses and receive consequences—*practice*; and (7) the use of frequent performance measures to monitor learning—*evaluation*.

These components define the parameters of the behavioral approach. Some of the components can be seen in virtually every special education classroom in our country (behavioral pinpoints, reinforcing stimulus), others are less obvious (schedules of reinforcement), and some (practice) are gaining in popularity as crucial components of instructional technology. Although the precision and expertise of the practitioners vary greatly, there is no doubt that behaviorism rules special education.

ह๛

The Law - P.L. 94-142

The Education of the Handicapped Act, Public Law 94-142, relies heavily on the behavioral paradigm to define appropriate education for handicapped students. The underlying assumption of P.L. 94-142 is that every human is capable of learning given appropriate opportunities (every child, regardless of degree of disability, is guaranteed a free and appropriate public education—FAPE). The definition of appropriate education is the Individualized Educational Program (IEP), which is a statement of student goals and required educational services needed in order to accomplish these goals as agreed upon by the school staff and parents of the student. The IEP is a service contract which guarantees the delivery of specific services in relationship to desired changes in student behavior (goals). While this contract does not guarantee changes in student behavior, it does use measurable student behavior as the singular index of the educational purpose.

In many ways the emergence of P.L. 94-142 can be viewed as an example of the development of public policy through backward mapping. Backward mapping, as defined by Elmore (1979), is a method of implementation of policy through the specification of what's happening at the lowest level of the implementation process. (Forward mapping, on the other hand, is the development of policy at the highest level of authority, then handing this policy to the implementors.) In 1975 and 1976, behavioral technology was the mainstream "theory of choice" among special educators. The policy makers, primarily staff at the Bureau of Education of the Handicapped (BEH) and the Council for Exceptional Children (CEC), were also influenced by behavioral notions as well as the idea of social service contracts (Gallagher, 1972). The law basically reflected what was considered to be state-of-the-art technology as well as what was generally happening in school districts and classrooms (Weintraub, 1984). (The legal right of a free and appropriate education for all children regardless of degree of handicapping condition, due process, and the paperwork and timelines demanded by maintaining the flow of federal dollars to individual children were **not** common practice prior to the passage of P.L. 94-142).

The "bottom-up" approach to setting policy is an effective method of assuring that accepted standards will become customary practice—a legal notion defining what is the acceptable quality of treatment. In this case, the process of education (rather than the content of education) became the standard. So at least two important behavioral components became law: 1) the reliance on precise, observable, measurable behavioral units, and 2) the use of frequent performance measures to monitor learning. Some may argue that the law should have gone much further, than even these components are not stated with sufficient specificity. However, the idea of making a federal law that dictates as much as P.L. 94-142 is almost unprecedented in the social sciences. Even more indicative of the wide-spread acceptance of behavioral programming is that the outcries and protests were centered on procedural issues (timelines, methods of verification, etc.) rather than on substantial ones. The behavioral paradigm has become an accepted part of the special education psyche. Many professionals are not even aware that they are operating within the general behavioral paradigm. As early as 1956, Bergmann could accurately state that every psychologist living today is a behaviorist whether he knows it or not. Without great fanfare, the current generation of special educators who make policy decisions today are basically behaviorists. Resistance to the behavioral paradigm was caused by the older generation, wedded to prior belief systems, who could not accept any challenge to those systems. As noted by Skinner, "I am convinced now that science never progresses by converting. . . . It really takes a new generation [of scientists that can be trained]" (Hall, 1967). This idea was even expressed at an earlier date: "A new scientific truth does not triumph by convincing its opponents and making them see the light, but rather because its opponents eventually die, and a new generation grows up that is familiar with it" (Planck, quoted in Barber, 1961, p. 597). We are a new generation, we are comfortable with the behavioral paradigm, and as such, special education, today, is primarily dominated by behavioral notions.

ॐ

Specifics by Handicapping Category

Although there is considerable debate concerning categorical vs. noncategorical approaches to special education, we would like to briefly review some of the "leading thinkers" by handicapping condition. This is not intended to be a comprehensive review of the literature or current practices. Rather, we hope to point out how leaders in special education are advocating the use of behavioral technology in the development of current instructional procedures.

Learning Disabilities

Whatever "learning disabilities," as a category, is (or is not), the salient feature is a substantial performance deficit in academic skills. The desired behavioral outcomes are increased academic performance in reading, writing, spelling, and arithmetic. Although there are numerous competing theories (information processing, perceptual motor development, and sensory integration), the behavioral approach appears to be the treatment of choice for the majority of practitioners. There are two leading behavioral approaches in this area: the precision teaching model exemplified by Tom Lovitt and the direct instruction approach of Siegfield Engelmann.

Direct Instruction (DI) is very well discussed in Wesley Becker's contribution to this text, Selection II. However, we would like to acknowledge the very believable findings of the DI procedures as related to the Follow Through research (Becker & Carnine, 1980). These data, along with the more recent research findings of DI materials, are powerful indicators of the effectiveness of a number of behavioral principles (e.g., the use of successive approximation in an instructional sequence, the provision of many opportunities to make responses and receive consequences [practice], and frequent performance measures). The DI materials also address the very crucial issue of teacher behavior by providing detailed scripts for the teachers to follow. The DI materials receive many of the criticisms of all behavioral approaches (i.e., too mechanical, no room for creativity, too rigid, does not teach problem solving, etc.). However, when data are collected, DI procedures tend to fare very well.

Precision Teaching has also been thoroughly described (Lindsley, 1964). Tom Lovitt has been identified with Precision Teaching and learning disabilities for a number of years (Lovitt 1976, 1977). Lovitt's work has very systematically enhanced our knowledge of how children with learning problems can best be taught basic academic skills. His methods *always* include: the use of measurable student performance, the sequencing of instructional components, a careful analysis of individual children's reinforcement histories, and frequent evaluation measures of child performance. He is one of the few colleagues we have who almost every day spends considerable time in classrooms, looking, listening, and chatting with teachers and students. His resistance (Lovitt, 1977) has been overcome by his persistence (Lovitt, 1982).

We sought out Dr. Lovitt to ask him several questions about the behavioral paradigm. As with our other respondents, we first asked, "What aspect of behavioral technology do you think is the most powerful, or most important?"

Next we asked, "Given the problems and issues in special education that you find most difficult to resolve today, what role do you see behavior technology (the operant paradigm) playing in resolving those issues?" (This is a multiple choice question:)

1. Systematic experimentation within the behavioral paradigm will undoubtably provide answers.

2. Precise implementation of behavioral methods will provide significant resolution to these problems.

3. Solutions will need to be generated from a new paradigm.

Tom, interrupted while preparing a junior high science worksheet, responded to the two questions after careful thought. Unable to list only one aspect, he enumerated the following: (1) The use of standards (aims) as normed criteria for expected performance provides us with target levels of desired behavior. Nonhandicapped peers provide these standards of performance; (2) Practice; (3) Teachers who use Precision Teaching (Dr. Lovitt prefers to call it Applied Behavior Analysis) tend to have a backlog of interventions. They have multiple interventions that they do not hesitate to use if their "favorite" technique doesn't work; and (4) Pupil management is facilitated with the use of behavioral techniques. This management allows the teacher more time and energy to allot to the instructional process.

When asked to speculate on the future ability of the behavioral paradigm to be useful in resolving current problems, Dr. Lovitt responded, "We need to be more clever in dealing with teachers to get them to use the best practice techniques. We need to become skilled at negotiation and reconciliation and less rigid in our thinking." (Lovitt, 1984).

Behavior Disorders (BD), Emotional Disturbance (ED)

BD and ED children are those children who engage in deviant behaviors, who exhibit too many or too few behaviors, children who are disturbing. Clearly, this group of children comprises two subgroups: those more involved children who do exhibit some deeper central nervous system dysfunction (i.e., autistic, psychotic children), and naughty children—those who are "acting out." The medical model was initially popular in dealing with this group, and the children were viewed as mentally ill. Extending the application of the medical model from the extreme cases of psychosis to "acting out" children resulted in attempts to prescribe for naughtiness—to treat the cause, not the symptoms. School personnel as early as Elizabeth Walsh (1914) noted the need to educationally treat "acting out" children by separating them from others. The adjustment classrooms attempted to contain the naughtiness, in order to decrease the general disruption that affected the other children.

The child study movement of the 1920s focused on the "inner" cause of disturbance and recommended "treatment" of the cause. Teachers were advised not to treat the symptoms but to look for the root cause. The belief prevailed that only psychiatrically- or psychologically-trained professionals could work with these students. Taking a clear cut definition of the population, any naughty child could be so classified. In order to be served as "emotionally disturbed," a child needed to receive a nomination (sort of like the academy awards), usually from the teacher—"I think this kid is weird (emotionally disturbed)". Testing (rotten kid tests) took place, and by some mystical event (psychological reports), eligibility was determined.

Once classified as mentally ill or emotionally disturbed, the child would seldom receive good instruction, but would instead be treated as if sick.

Although we still go through these gyrations, the medical model has been replaced, to a large degree, by the psychological or behavioral model (Ullman & Krasner, 1965). The psychological model states the following assumptions: (1) Behavior, maladaptive and adaptive, is learned and unlearned in the same manner; (2) Basic to learning is the acquisition of a functional connection between an environmental stimulus and some subject response; (3) Discriminative stimuli are those stimuli that mark a time or place of reinforcement; (4) The rates at which reinforcers are delivered are schedules of reinforcement; and (5) Shaping and response chaining are used to build complex behaviors.

Many individuals have applied the behavioral paradigm to the education of emotionally disturbed children (Hewett, 1968; Hobbs, 1966). Haring and Phillips (1962) probably produced the first popular textbook on educating emotionally disturbed children using a behavioral approach. Behavioral targets, use of reinforcement procedures, and frequent performance evaluations became hallmarks of behavioral programming. Behavior modification and M&M therapy were in vogue. The standard criticisms were offered; it's too rigid, behavior modification only treats the symptoms—not the causes, it's too fascist or too liberal, the techniques can be used to make people do things against their will, who wants little robots running around? However, when data was collected, behavioral procedures fared well. And even more impressive was the fact that behavioral technology provided a viable educational intervention for these children.

We found Norrie Haring at a conference on preschool programs for handicapped children and asked him our series of questions. To the first question, what aspect of the behavioral paradigm is most important, Norrie responded, "The systematic approaches which have developed over the years serve as guides—road maps—for teachers. One of the more difficult problems in special education in general, and especially when dealing with 'acting out' children, is [finding] a procedure which provides guidance for teachers. Following the behavioral paradigm, teachers know the instructional sequence: pinpoint, count, apply a contingency, and evaluate. Teachers can be most effective when they have a systematic approach to use and behavioral technology gives them that guide.

"Does the behavioral paradigm offer me guidance in solving the problems I'm working on right now? It sure does. We simply need to apply behavioral strategies in new and novel ways. More precise research and a careful analysis of other research trends [are] the best way[s] to solve today's problems." (Haring, 1984).

Severely Retarded

Instructional procedures for the severely handicapped are almost exclusively drawn from the behavioral paradigm. With the other categories of handicapping conditions there have always been other methods or theories to challenge the behavioral approach. For the severely retarded individual, however, the behavioral paradigm has always been the only alternative to custodial care. This unquestioned predominance can be traced back to the early roots of behaviorism in the work of Itard (1801) with a severely retarded boy. He used Direct Instruction to teach precisely defined functional behaviors. This remains the hallmark of contemporary researchers like Lou Brown and his colleagues in Wisconsin (Brown, Nietupski, & Hamre-Nietupski, 1976), the late Marc Gold (Gold, 1972), and Bud Fredericks at Teaching Research in Oregon (Fredericks, et al., 1976). However, we will highlight Wayne Sailor and Doug Guess as contemporary exemplars.

Wayne Sailor and Doug Guess have a long history of working with severely retarded individuals. Their work with Don Baer and the "Kansas Group" is well documented. The current state of the art (Sailor & Guess, 1983) is a detailed prescriptive approach to the education of severely and profoundly retarded people. Task analysis, the systematic presentation of antecedents, use of behavioral pinpoints, a functional curriculum, shaping procedures, and precise evaluation techniques are all integral parts of this approach. With this population, improvements can only be viewed over time and through the use of precise measurement systems. Almost all the behaviors in the individual repertoires are those which are directly taught—there is very little incidental learning. Generalization must be specifically taught. Acquisition curves are gradual–practice is required for each increment. This population is new to public school special education and many of the procedures are still being developed. Additionally, there has been some debate over the educability of these students—both in terms of real outcomes and in terms of ethics (Kaufman & Krouse, 1981).

We caught Dr. Sailor Sailor as he was preparing to teach one of his courses. Without hesitation, Dr. Sailor nominated measurement systems for tracking student performance as the most crucial aspect of the behavioral paradigm for those working with the severely handicapped. As to the power of behavioral theory in providing answers to current questions, Dr. Sailor was less optimistic. He felt that too much time and too many resources are spent on demonstrations that "the system works" rather than on new discovery. Replications are important but without expansion into new areas we will not advance beyond our current status. We all need to be more creative and probably need to greatly expand the behavioral paradigm if we are to discover more effective ways to achieve increased skills with this population (Sailor, 1984).

We interviewed two other individuals who were active in behavioral research with severely retarded children in the early 1960s: Cecelia Tague Harper and John D. Kidder. Both were teachers in Bijou's programmed learning classroom (Birnbrauer, Wolf, Kidder, & Tague, 1965). Harper is now a school district administrator, and Kidder continues to teach in a special education classroom, where he also continues to do curriculum research. Both Kidder and Harper also agree that the measurement system is the most enduring and important feature of the behavioral paradigm. Kidder remains confident that this paradigm will continue to provide the answers to educational questions we need (Kidder, 1984), whereas Harper believes we will need to find some new directions, growing largely out of the behavioral viewpoint, however. (Harper, 1984).

ॐ

Programmed Instruction in Special Education: A Case History

Dr. Vargas (1985) has presented a detailed early history of programmed instruction through 1976. Let us now selectively review some of the research of the early '70s, and then pick up in early 1976 to follow one case example through today and into tomorrow in regard to programmed instruction and teaching machines.

These old photos were taken in the programmed learning classroom at Rainier School, a residential institution near Seattle, in the early 1960s (see Figures 6.1 and 6.2). The series of pictures illustrates the progression of programming and technological sophistication of Dr. Bijou and his associates in applying the principles of behavior modification to special education. Initially, there were relatively simple pencil and paper tasks, with the teachers trying to be specific about learning objectives. In Figure 6.2 you'll notice that a clock was placed on the table to facilitate keeping rate data.

The next advancement was to replace prepared texts and have the children fill in blanks on worksheets with a slider. This was the beginning of incorporating more and more programmed instruction and programming techniques in the Rainier School classroom. At the same time, Skinner and others were working on improving teaching machines (Skinner, 1961) and writing programmed texts (Holland & Skinner, 1961). The University of Washington researchers were also heavily influenced by the work of Terrace (1963) and of Stoddard and Sidman (1967) on errorless learning. In subsequent research (Sulzbacher & Kidder, 1979), analysis of error patterns has allowed for "error windows" of about 10%. This enables careful teachers to isolate the few words which seem to cause most of the errors for individual learners. Often, it is possible to skip such words (or substitute synonyms) and the learner can continue through the program at an acceptable level of few errors.

In Figure 6.3, John Kidder, a coworker of Bijou's still teaching in a Seattle-area classroom, is using a Min-Max machine, which for years was the standard classroom teaching machine. They stopped making those machines about six to eight years ago, and many of us scurried about collecting them against the time they'd be unavailable, because those machines often broke and had to be taken apart, fixed with a part from another one, and put back together. Nevertheless, those old blue plastic machines were very important in the development of programmed instruction as we know it today. In the late 1960s, the University of Washington researchers began an analysis of the components of reading. The most obvious component is word call: saying the word when presented with the written stimulus. The next component is more complex: reading comprehension. This involves the use of the language meaning of the written word. Two types of lesson were devised to teach these language concepts: direction books and picture phrase matching. In the latter, the pupil picks the one of several phrases (composed of previously learned words) which correctly

FIGURE 6.1

Kids in PLC at Rainier School

FIGURE 6.2

Kids in PLC at Rainier School

FIGURE 6.3

Kidder Using an Early Teaching Machine

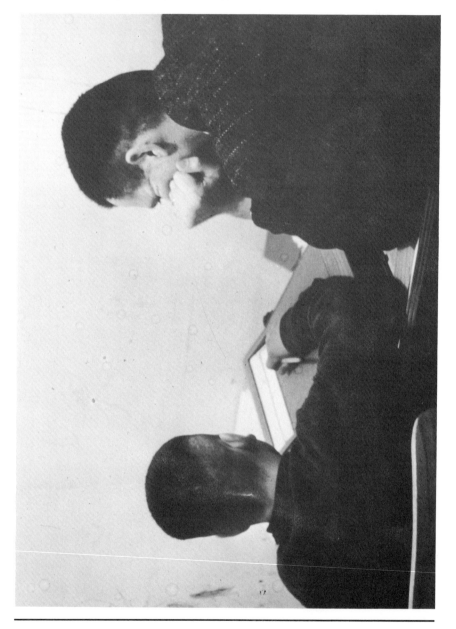

matches a picture. In the direction books, there is only one phrase or paragraph and the student uses that information to arrange pictures on a board according to the given "directions." By correctly completing these lessons, the student demonstrates reading comprehension and understanding of the language.

Of course, all of this reading research was conducted within the context of a classroom reinforcement system (Birnbrauer & Lawler, 1964; Birnbrauer, et al., 1965). When the children finished all their work correctly, they got marks in their "mark books" to turn in at the "store": a token economy. Figure 6.4 shows how daily data on student progress was kept in that classroom. A distinguishing feature of the Rainier classroom program was that the reinforcement system, the classroom and social environment, and the curriculum were all carefully integrated. Because much of the curriculum required one-to-one instruction, each student became the tutor for subsequent learners, as he or she mastered a given lesson. Thus, the students learned to see both the curriculum and the reinforcement system from a teacher's perspective as well as their own. This feature may well have had a significant effect on the subsequent success of these students (Sulzbacher and Kidder, 1975).

By 1972, the materials had been rewritten and assembled in a kit form which is currently commercially available[1]. The Program illustrates important features of teaching reading and teaching language. To use the Program, a student must be able to point on command, but no language skills are required. The student either has to be able to sign or have the physical capability of saying a word. Table 6.1 shows a beginning word recognition lesson. The order of presentation of words and distractors is determined by a program redundancy matrix which is consistent throughout the Program. *Horse* is the first word taught in the Program.

The direction books were made transportable by using little cards instead of objects. The child has to place the cards in the proper place in the proper order. Figure 6.5 shows picture phrase cards, where the child now has to recognize a picture, and search with his newly learned skills to put the textual label on the picture. These two types of lessons teach the "language" use of written words as they are learned. Short stories in a book

1 The Edmark Reading Program®, printed and software, and the Touch Window® computer touch screen are products of the Edmark Corporation, Box 3218, Redmond, WA 98073. Illustrations in this chapter are reproduced by permission.

FIGURE 6.4

Rainier School PLC Student Daily Data Records

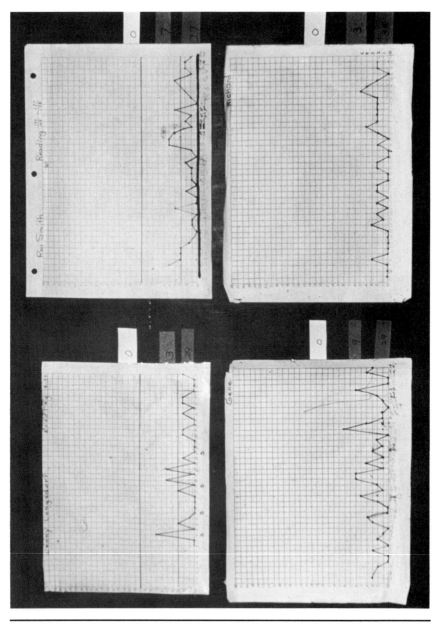

TABLE 6.1

Example of Increasing Complexity of Distractors

The instructions for frames 1, 5, 8, and 11 are "point to the word 'horse' . . . read the word." In the other frames, the child just points to the word "horse" (Edmark, 1972)[1].

wr 1-1	horse	—	—
wr 1-2	ft	horse	un
wr 1-3	ros	fuvx	horse
wr 1-4	sho	horse	rwao
wr 1-5		horse	
wr 1-6	horse	erh	lemz
wr 1-7	osr	cmxe	horse
wr 1-8		horse	
wr 1-9	horse	see	yellow
wr 1-10	a	horse	car
wr 1-11		horse	

---

allow the child to experience "reading a book" after learning to recognize only a few words. The prereading section of the Program teaches stimulus discrimination, first with pictures and then with letters and letter combinations. Figure 6.6 illustrates that basic format, which has also been used diagnostically and as a measure of perceptual skills in research projects.

After over a year and a half of development work, the Edmark Reading Program was programmed for the Apple computer. This effort illustrated a number of applications of the principles of behavior modification. In reviewing this example of computer software for special education, some examples of the use of programming, systematic data management, and effective reinforcement are evident. These are things to look for in evaluating any curriculum or computer software.

FIGURE 6.5

Picture Phrase Lesson from the Edmark Reading Program (Level 1)

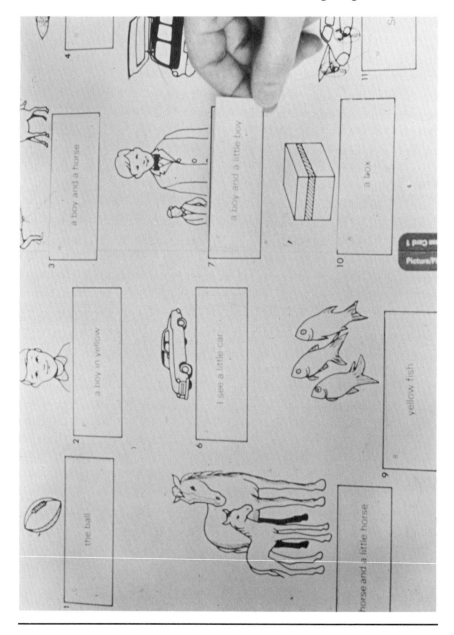

FIGURE 6.6

Prereading Lessons from the Edmark Reading Program (Level 1)

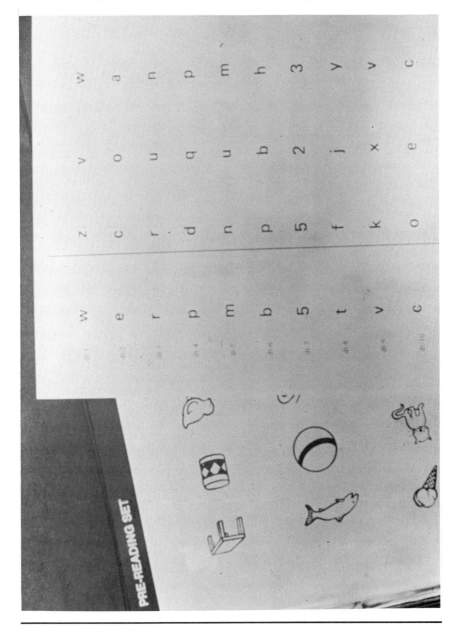

The Edmark software requires the student to use a joystick or Touch Window[1] to "point." Since teaching reading, not "computer literacy," is the goal of the Program, the student need not ever touch (or even see) the computer keyboard. Furthermore, with more reliable and less expensive "touch screen" technology now available, it is possible to eliminate the joystick and have the student respond directly to the text and stimulus material presented on the video monitor (see Figure 6.7).

The student must learn to respond to only two vocal commands from the speech synthesizer in the computer (Street Electronics, 1982), "point" and "find one like it," although the Program can be run without the synthesizer.

Reinforcement is provided after each correct response, but these reinforcers are intentionally simple and avoid use of fancy computer graphics or "bells and whistles." The reinforcers are "very good" if a child's first response is correct, "good" if the second response is correct, and "okay" if the third try is correct. The technological expertise of the computer programmers should be evident in the attractiveness (and intrinsic reinforcement) of the stimulus material to be learned, not in any "bells and whistles" presented after correct or incorrect responses as putative reinforcers.

ﺯﻪ

Why Use a Computer at All?

A feature which distinguishes special education from "regular" education is the higher ratio of teachers to students. The reasons typically given for this are the need for: (1) greater individualization of curriculum, (2) more precise record keeping, and (3) dealing with student inattention and disruptive behavior. A computer can help with these three needs because: (1) stimulus material is presented precisely and systematically with automatic error checking; (2) each student progresses at his or her own pace; (3) the computer can easily and automatically manage student performance records to allow data-based curriculum changes and to generate progress reports, IEPs, etc.; and (4) the colorful graphic images on the video monitor are clearly more intrinsically attractive than printed material in maintaining student attention, and should thus reduce classroom behavior problems.

The Edmark Reading Program has built-in criteria for allowing a student to continue. If the student begins to make errors or takes too long

FIGURE 6.7

Computer Presentation of a Prereading Lesson from the Edmark Reading Program

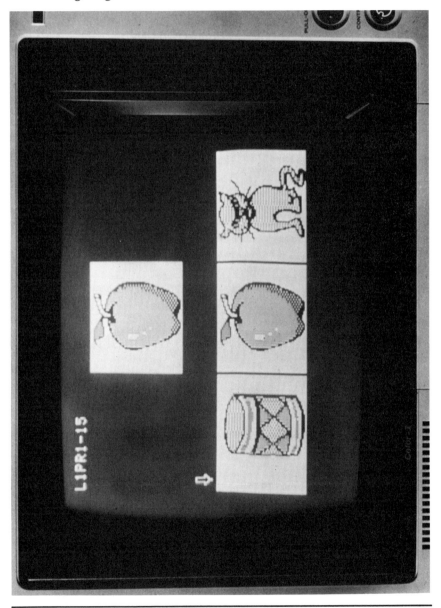

to respond, the computer prompts "call your teacher," and stops until someone checks the data. The computer displays the reason for the break and the place in the Program where the student was working (see Figure 6.8). The teacher can then reset the Program or return to an earlier lesson for review. It is necessary for the teacher to review all the student data at least daily and to update all the permanent student records at the end of each day. If records are not updated, this must be done before the Program can be run again the next day. From the behavior analysis viewpoint, the data recording/management functions a computer can perform are probably its greatest assets. Figures 6.9 and 6.10 are sample printouts of the daily and permanent data records generated by this program.

Figures 6.11 and 6.12 present examples of the computer graphics employed to teach the student to use newly taught sight words to describe a picture and to match pictures of objects to the words which describe them. These components of the Program specifically bridge the traditional gap between reading instruction and language training.

Returning to the rhetorical question of why we need computers in special education classrooms, we can conclude that they are a convenient teaching tool, but clearly secondary to employing sound behavioral principles in curriculum and classroom management. Various programmed instruction approaches have been proven effective (Greene, 1966; Vandever, Maggart, & Nasser, 1976; Becker, 1985), but the bulk of behavioral research has still been concerned with the parameters of reinforcement. Perhaps the main contribution of the classroom microcomputer to special education will be that, after the past decade or two when consequences and reinforcement were the object of most of the behavioral research interest, this device has again focused attention on the programming of antecedent events (curriculum).

The most obvious immediate research question is whether the classroom microcomputer can really improve student skill acquisition. Do students learn faster or is this just another gimmick? (We all remember when TV sets in each classroom were going to revolutionize education!) If the computer is effective, will skills acquired in this medium generalize to other media, like the printed page? These questions all lead us back to behaviorism's strong suit: the methodology for making data-based decisions. Here we do see an obvious new use for microcomputers: gathering precise data

FIGURE 6.8

Example of an Error Message in the Edmark Reading Program

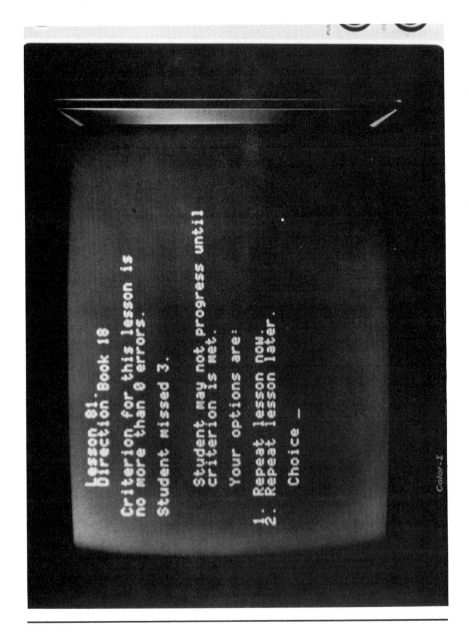

FIGURE 6.9

Data Summary of Student Performance on a Lesson in the Edmark Reading Program

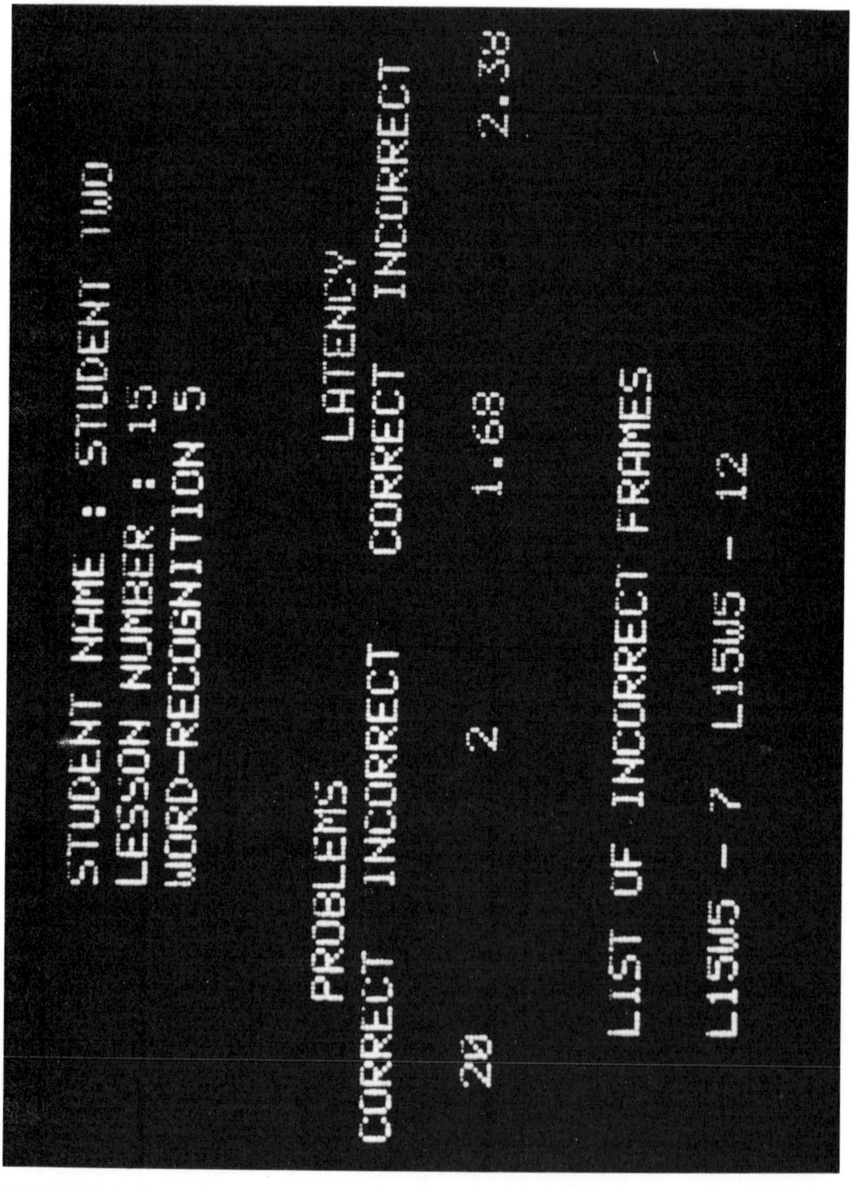

FIGURE 6.10

Summary Report for a Class Using the Edmark Reading Program

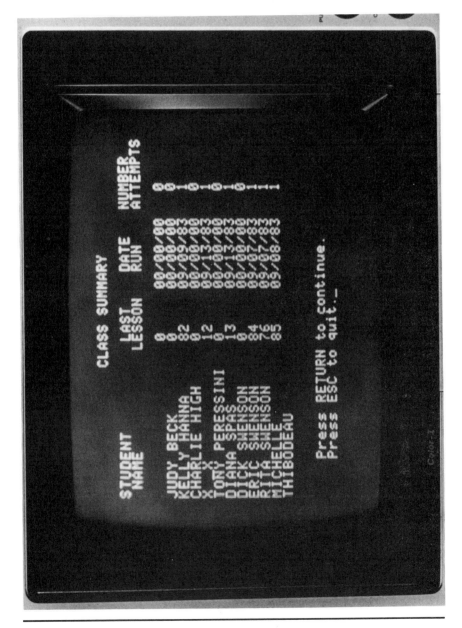

FIGURE 6.11

Computer Display of a Picture-phrase Lesson from the Edmark Reading Program

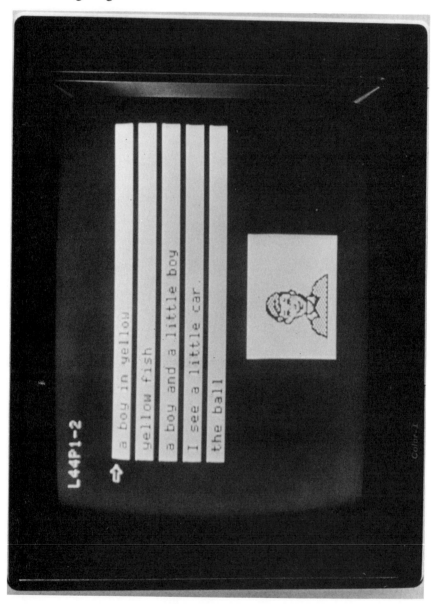

FIGURE 6.12

Direction Book Lesson from the Edmark Reading Program Software

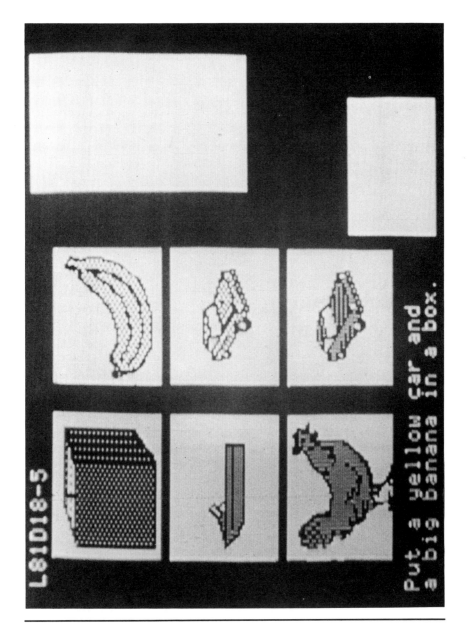

automatically in the classroom setting, without a huge investment of time and effort by the teacher (cf, Figures 6.8, 6.9).

ঝ

Future Issues for Special Education and Behaviorism

Special education appears to be at a crossroads of sorts, as does behaviorism. We think the future contributions of behaviorism to the field of special education, in general, should be in the area of research on antecedent events. Past research has focused on reinforcement, and this work has revolutionized the field. If we continue to focus on that success with consequence management, we will stagnate. Refinement of curriculum (the stimulus side of the equation) and further research on prosthetic devices, like microcomputers, and prosthetic environments (also part of the antecedent event side of the equation) seem to be the areas where the next great advances in understanding and modifying behavior will be made.

The case example we discussed in this paper, the Edmark Reading Program, was chosen because it illustrates these future trends. The program uses a consistent reinforcement system, is designed to maximize correct responses, and incorporates data decision rules. These features reflect the research of the past several decades and are examples of good "standard practice" of behavioral principles. However, we believe the design of the curriculum itself reflects careful scientific analysis of the language elements and a precise matrix of presentation of words, based on behavior analysis research design. This curriculum was well researched before being programmed for computer presentation. Research-quality data collection procedures are built into the curriculum to enable users to conduct further behavioral analyses of the "software" and to analyze the relative effectiveness of computer presentation with various special education populations.

Other examples could have been chosen; Alan Hofmeister and his research group at Utah State University are conducting highly significant research on videodisks as a mode of stimulus presentation in special education (Hofmeister & Friedman, 1985; Thorkildsen, Allard, & Reid, 1983). The impact of videodisks and videocassettes could be as great for these populations as the printing press was for all a few centuries ago. For most of us, the book is a convenient reference file for routines we do infrequently or which are complex. When tuning a car, many of us have a step-by-step manual (usually with many illustrations) at hand to follow. Most computer users are very dependent upon the printed documentation to enable them to use even fairly simple computer programs. Imagine the nonreader being able to select a videodisk with a picture of someone "Getting Dressed" on the cover, and then being led, step-by-step, through the routine of selecting color coordinated clothing, suitable for the season. Similar disks (or cassettes) could be on the shelf in a developmentally delayed person's room, with titles like "Toothbrushing," "Breakfast," "Using the Telephone," etc. In other words, we could create videodisks as prosthetic devices for an individual who currently needs supervision for many self-help tasks. Such behavioral analysis could also involve concurrent use of several devices, for example, a disk entitled "Keeping Track of Your Money" could provide reminders on identifying and sorting coins and bills, and take an individual through a program to use a pocket calculator to help them assume some responsibility for managing their money and even paying bills. Properly designed "do it yourself" disks like this could allow greater independence to individuals who do not have the independent arithmetic skills for unaided computation. Obviously, these ideas would cause us to revise much of the special education curriculum as it exists today.

ða

Has the Behavioral Paradigm Aged?

Thomas Kuhn, in *The Structure of Scientific Revolutions* (1970), notes that few theoretical paradigms exist forever. Rather, paradigms pass through predictable stages of development. First is a stage of rejection by the mainstream scientific community; this is followed by acceptance of the theory (usually by a new generation of scientists); this stage is conducive to theory expansion and the development of solutions to real problems; during the mature phase, scientists generally speak only to themselves through minute and highly technical reports; finally a new paradigm is championed by a fringe group while threatening the acceptance of the now old theory (stage one of the new paradigm). The passing of an old thought pattern to a new is not an indication that the old ideas were wrong. Rather, any new idea is due, in part, to the very existence of the old ideas. However, when a paradigm is no longer useful in answering today's questions, a new paradigm will probably develop which, in time, will replace the prevailing theory. The question we pose is, "Has the behavioral paradigm run its course?"

There is considerable evidence that (at least in special education) behavioral theory does not provide a viable framework for generating answers to today's problems. For instance, in the area of learning disabilities, a major issue today is how to get school systems to use best-practice techniques (the Lovitt question). Clearly, in most cases, students labeled as LD do not receive the best instructional technology available. How do we get systems to be responsive? In the areas of behavior disabilities and emotional disturbance, the real issues are ecological and system related (Bronfenbrenner, 1977) rather than clinical. Poverty, lack of family support systems, job opportunities, health maintenance, and access to the "goods of our society" are major barriers to assisting families and schools in handling acting out behavior. For the more severely involved, those with documented central nervous system deficits, including autistic and psychotic children, pharmacology is more likely to provide an answer than is learning theory. A good case for lack of strength (effectiveness) of mainstream interventions is the amount of divergent (quack) treatment which is used by the general population. Injecting fetal lamb brain cells into retarded people to stimulate brain growth does occur, whereas there is no market for such a treatment for polio prevention. Spinning, hopping, and twirling is recommended for children with reading problems at a fairly common level in North America. The treatment for scurvy has few competing "popular" methods. Divergent, nontraditional treatment only grows when standard treatments are ineffective. Special education is a hotbed for weird treatments. Why? A major reason must be that our standard treatments don't work! Remember, the behavioral paradigm rules special education.

If science evolved in a linear fashion, we would expect the accumulation of research data to lead us to new treatments for handicapped children. However, Kuhn and others clearly disagree that science advances in a linear fashion—we have revolutions in thought. (See James Watson, *The Double Helix*, 1968, for a personal view of the development of new knowledge.) Some of these revolutions are brought on by technology (e.g., glass grinding, telescopes, and microscopes) (Boorstin, 1983), others by new ideas (such as the alphabet), some by careful theory development (relativity), some by careful analysis of existing data coupled with theory building (DNA), and some by straight out revolution (Copernicus).

Selection VI

We are at a crucial time in terms of our dependence on the behavioral paradigm. We are believers. The model has served us well in the past. We have solved difficult problems by being faithful. We gather together to support one another in our quests. We strongly reject unproven theories. We point at quackeries. We demand data. Are we the generation that must die before the new generation comes along and advances the cause? Or is the behavioral paradigm different than all the others?

References

Barber, B. (1961). Resistance by scientists to scientific discovery. *Science,* *134,* 596-602.

Becker, W.C. (1992). Direct instruction: A twenty year review. In R.P. West & L.A. Hamerlynck (Eds.), *Designs for excellence in education: The legacy of B.F. Skinner* (Selection II). Longmont, CO: Sopris West.

Becker, W.C. & Carnine, D.W. (1980). Direct instruction: An effective approach to educational intervention with the disadvantaged and low performers. In B.B. Lahey and B. K. Kuzdin (Eds.), *Advances in clinical and child psychology* (Vol. 3). New York: Plenum.

Bergmann, G. (1956). The contribution of John B. Watson. *Psychological Review, 63,* 270.

Birnbrauer, J.S. & Lawler, J. (1964). Token reinforcement for learning. *Journal of Mental Retardation, 2,* 275-279.

Birnbrauer, J.S., Wolf, M.M., Kidder, J.D., & Tague, C. (1965). Classroom behavior of retarded pupils with token reinforcement. *Journal of Experimental Child Psychology, 2,* 219-235.

Boorstin, D.J. (1983). *The discoverers.* New York: Random House.

Bronfenbrenner, U. (1977). Toward an experimental ecology of human development. *American Psychologist,* 513-530.

Brown, L.J., Nietupski, J., & Hamre-Nietupski, S. (1976). Criterion of ultimate functioning. In M.A. Thomas (Ed.), *Hey! Don't forget about me: Education's investment in the severely, profoundly and multiply handicapped.* Reston, VA: Council for Exceptional Children.

Elmore, R.E. (1979). Backward mapping: Implementation research and policy decisions. *Political Science Quarterly, 94,* 601-616.

Fredericks, H.N., Riggs, C., Furey, T., Grave, D., Moore, W., McDonnell, J., Jordon, E., Hanson, W., Baldwin, U., & Wadlow, M. (1977). *The teaching research curriculum for moderately and severely handicapped.* Springfield, IL: Charles C. Thomas.

Gallagher, J.J. (1972). The special education contract for mildly handicapped children. *Exceptional Children, 78*, 527-536.

Gold, M.W. (1972). Stimulus factors in skill training of retarded adolescents on a complex assembly task: Acquisition, transfer, and retention. *American Journal of Mental Deficiency, 76*(5), 517-526.

Greene, F.M. (1966). Programmed instruction techniques for the mentally retarded. In N.R. Ellis (Ed.), *International Review of Research in Mental Retardation, 2*, 228.

Hall, M.H. (1967). An interview with "Mr. Behaviorist" B.F. Skinner, *Psychology Today, 1*(5), 20-23, 68-71.

Haring, N.G. (1984). Personal communication.

Haring, N.G. & Phillips, E.L. (1962). *Educating emotionally disturbed children.* New York: McGraw-Hill.

Harper, C. (1984). Personal communication.

Hewett, F.M. (1968). *The emotionally disturbed child in the classroom.* Boston: Allyn & Brown.

Hobbs, N. (1966). Helping the disturbed child: Psychological and ecological strategies. *American Psychologist, 21*, 1105-1115.

Hofmeister, A.M. & Friedman, S. (1985). The application of technology to the education of the severely handicapped. In R. Horner, L.M. Voeltz, & B. Fredericks (Eds.), *Education of learners with severe handicaps: Exemplary service strategies.* (in press). Seattle: Association for the Severely Handicapped.

Holland, J.G. & Skinner, B.F. (1961). *The analysis of behavior.* New York: McGraw-Hill.

Itard, J.M.G. (1801). *De l'education d'un homme savage.* Goujon, Paris.

Kaufman, J.M. & Krouse, T. (1981). The cult of educability: Searing for the substance of things hoped for, the evidence of things not seen. *Analysis and Intervention in Developmental Disabilities, 1*, 53-60.

Kidder, J. (1984). Personal communication.

Kuhn, T.S. (1970). *The structure of scientific revolutions* (2nd ed.). Chicago: The University of Chicago Press.

Lindsley, O.R. (1964). Direct measurement and prosthesis of retarded behavior. *Journal of Education, 147,* 62-81.

Lovitt, T.C. (1976). Applied behavior analysis technique and curriculum research: Implications for instruction. In N.G. Haring & R.L. (Eds.), *Teaching special children.* New York: McGraw-Hill.

Lovitt, T.C. (1977). *In spite of my resistance I've learned from children.* Columbus, OH: Charles E. Merrill.

Lovitt, T.C. (1982). *Because of my persistence I've learned from children.* Columbus, OH: Charles E. Merrill.

Lovitt, T.C. (1984). Personal communication.

Nelson, C.M. & Polsgrove, L. (1984). Behavior analysis in special education: White rabbit or white elephant? *Remedial and Special Education, 5,* 6-17.

Sailor, W. (1984). Personal communication.

Sailor, W. & Guess, D. (1983). *Education of the severely handicapped.* Columbus, OH: Charles E. Merrill.

Skinner, B.F. (1961). Why we need teaching machines. *Harvard Educational Review, 32,* 377-398.

Stoddard, L.T. & Sidman, M. (1967). The effects of errors on children's performance of a circle-ellipse discrimination. *Journal of the Experimental Analysis of Behavior, 10,* 261-270.

Street Electronics Corp. (1982). *The Echo II speech synthesizer.* Carpinteria, CA: Author.

Sulzbacher, S. & Kidder, J.D. (1975). Following up on the behavior analysis model: Results after ten years of early intervention with institutionalized mentally retarded children. In E. Ramp & G. Semb (Eds.), *Behavior analysis: Areas of research and application* (pp. 62-70). Englewood Cliffs, N.J.: Prentice-Hall.

Sulzbacher, S. & Kidder, J.D. (1979). Teaching sight words to severely retarded children and adolescents. In J.E. Button, T.C. Lovitt, & T.D. Rowland (Eds.), *Communications research in learning disabilities and mental retardation* (pp. 113-124). Baltimore: University Park Press.

Terrace, H.S. (1963). Discrimination learning with and without "errors." *Journal of the Experimental Analysis of Behavior, 6,* 1-27.

Thorkildsen, R., Allard, K.E., & Reid, R.C. (1983). Interactive videodisc for special education technology: Presenting CAI to handicapped students. *The Computing Teacher, 10.*

Ullman, L.P. & Krasner, L. (1965). *Case studies in behavior modification.* New York: Holt, Rinehart and Winston.

Vandever, T.R., Maggart, W.T., & Nasser, S. (1976). Three approaches to beginning reading instruction for EMR children. *Mental Retardation, 14,* 29-32.

Vargas, E.A. & Vargas, J.S. (1992). Programmed instruction and machines that teach. In R.P. West & L.A. Hamerlynck (Eds.), *Designs for excellence in education: The legacy of B.F. Skinner* (Selection I). Longmont, CO: Sopris West.

Walsh, E.A. (1914). Ungraded classes work in New York City–Methods and results. *Journal of Psycho-Asthenics, 19,* 59-66.

Watson, J.D. (1968). *The double helix.* New York: Signet.

Weintraub, F. (1984). Personal communication.

Applied Behavior Analysis in Sport and Physical Education: Past, Present, and Future

Garry L. Martin, University of Manitoba

*D*uring the past 20 years, applied behavior analysis has made considerable inroads in sport and physical education. Perhaps it should not come as a surprise that applied behavior analysis would be accepted in these areas. In sports in particular, there has long been an emphasis on measurable behaviors, and the awarding of consequences for successful performances. Can applied behavior analysts improve upon the natural measurement and contingency management systems frequently used by many coaches and physical educators? Research to date suggests a definite "yes." In this paper, we will trace the history, examine current applications, and suggest future trends of applied behavior analysis in sport and physical education.

❧
The Past

It is a relatively easy task to discuss the historical development of applied behavior analysis in sport and physical education from the seminal research to the initial applications. That's because the history is brief and it mainly involves two people - Brent Rushall and Daryl Siedentop. The initial applications were described in their book, *The Development and Control of Behavior in Sport and Physical Education* (Rushall & Siedentop, 1972). Written within an operant conditioning framework, their book contains numerous practical strategies for shaping new sport skills, maintaining existing skills at high levels, and generalizing practiced skills to competitive settings.

Published research in this area prior to 1972 appears to consist of one paper. Rushall and Pettinger (1969) compared the effects of several different reinforcement contingencies on the amount of swimming performed by members of an age-group swimming team. In general, candy and money contingencies resulted in more laps swum than coach's attention and control contingencies. While both Rushall and Siedentop have published applied behavior analyses of both sport and physical education since 1972, Rushall has concentrated mainly on sport, and Siedentop's efforts have been directed mainly at physical education.

From 1971 to 1975, Rushall taught at the School of Physical Education at Dalhousie University in Nova Scotia. From 1975 through 1986, he directed the applied behavior analysis research program at the School of Physical Education and Outdoor Recreation at Lakehead University in Ontario. Since that time he has been professor of physical education at San Diego State University. As indicated by the review later in this paper, he has examined behavioral analysis techniques for coaching both youth and elite athletes, and has served as the team psychologist to Canadian Olympic teams in several sports (Rushall, 1977a).

While Rushall was developing the first operant conditioning research program in sport at Dalhousie in the early 1970s, Daryl Siedentop was pioneering the first behavior analysis research program in physical education at Ohio State University. Studies there were directed primarily at improvement of student teaching as well as on replication of classroom research using behavior analysis techniques. The first physical education applications in schools were theses (Young, 1973; Hughley, 1973) super-vised by Siedentop. Siedentop published books (1976, 1983a) to help physical education teachers to develop applied behavior analysis skills. Throughout his books, he maintained a strong emphasis on the importance of continuous data collection, and the use of feedback and reinforcement techniques for accomplishing behavioral goals with students.

Rushall and Siedentop were classmates in the doctoral program in physical education at Indiana University in the late 1960s. Together, they launched research and applications in applied behavior analysis in sport and physical education with their pioneering book published in 1972. They have continued to provide exemplary leadership in these areas, with Rushall directing most of his energy to sport and Siedentop concentrating on physical education.

ءهـ
Update to the Present: Physical Education

This section provides a review of research and applications of applied behavior analysis in physical education. Unpublished papers and unpub-lished graduate theses were not included. (Unpublished papers and theses prior to 1980 were reviewed by Donahue, Gillis, & King, 1980.) Also, only papers that fit within the applied behavior analysis tradition, at least in a loose sense, were reviewed. To be included, a paper had to have at least one of the following characteristics: draw mainly from operant conditioning principles and procedures; use single-subject research designs; or include several of the dimensions of applied behavior analysis identified by Baer, Wolf, & Risley (1968, 1987).

Descriptive Reports and Books

Many of the published papers on applied behavior analysis and physical education do not describe research. Nonresearch papers have emphasized the value of training in applied behavior analysis for physical educators (Evans, 1974; Rushall, 1972; Siedentop, 1972), defined and described principles and procedures of operant conditioning for physical educators (Martin & Hrycaiko, 1983b; Siedentop & Rushall, 1972), and described how the proper application of reinforcement contingencies can rectify many unsatisfactory situations found in physical education (McKenzie & Rushall,

1973). Other papers illustrated, with examples, how various behavioral techniques could be applied in physical education settings. Articles have discussed behavioral contracts (Coulon, 1989; Fast, 1971), token systems (McDonald, 1971), backward chaining (Chelladura & Stothart, 1978), contingency management (Darst, 1979), personalized systems of instruction (Siedentop, 1973; Tousignant, 1983), and a technique referred to as backward shaping (Rushall & Ford, 1982). The backward shaping procedure appears to involve backward chaining with behavioral shaping of topography at each of the steps that are added to the sequence in a backward fashion.

Some of the nonresearch papers and chapters have offered detailed task analyses of behaviors to be taught in various physical education settings. The task analyses, along with mastery criteria for instructional purposes, are of obvious benefit to curriculum development for physical educators. Examples include behavioral objectives and mastery criteria for teaching badminton (Siedentop & Rife, 1974), a component checklist for freestyle swimming (Martin, LePage, & Koop, 1983), and a behavioral sequence and mastery criteria for teaching golf (O'Brien & Simek, 1983).

Finally, several of the nondata papers have emphasized the need for physical educators to be accountable and to assess their effectiveness in terms of data collected on the progress of the behavior of their students (Allard & Rife, 1980; Dodds, 1976, 1977, 1978; Siedentop, 1983b), and to use single-subject designs (Rife & Dodds, 1978; Siedentop, 1982).

Three books since 1972 describe behavioral analysis procedures for physical educators. Siedentop (1976, 1983a) designed his books to help prospective teachers, during their field experience, to develop skills in various areas of teaching including classroom management, interpersonal relations, planning for instruction, execution of instruction, school policies, and professional role development. Presbie and Brown (1977) described the technicalities of behavioral procedures for use by physical educators in field settings. Their book presented techniques for increasing behaviors, decreasing problem behaviors, skill development, and self-modification procedures for personal physical fitness.

Although the papers described in this section were primarily descriptive reports, there has been considerable research on applied behavior analysis and physical education. Research papers will be reviewed under three topics: observations of physical education classes, development of teaching skills of physical educators, and decreasing problem behaviors of students.

Research: What's Happening in the Gym?

Considerable effort has been directed to developing reliable observation systems for monitoring the behavior of physical education teachers and students in order to provide information on "What's happening in the gym?" (Anderson, 1980; Cheffers, 1977; Darst, 1976; Darst, Zakrajsek, & Mancini, 1989; Fishman & Anderson, 1971; Grant & Martens, 1982; Metzler, 1981; Quarterman, 1980; Rushall, 1981; Siedentop, 1973, 1989; Siedentop & Hughley, 1975; Siedentop & Tousignant, 1982; Wilson, Buzzell & Jensen, 1975). Not all of these studies were conducted within a strict applied behavior analysis framework. Moreover, there is still disagreement as to what constitutes the effective teaching of physical education. Nevertheless, some tentative generalizations on "what's happening in the gym" can be made. Several studies have found that physical educators present very low rates of consequential responses (rewards, feedback, correcting, prohibiting) in general, and of the consequences that are provided, more negative than positive consequences are the rule. Also, physical activity of students in physical education classes tends to be low. For example, Rushall (1981) observed that, when observation intervals were expressed in units of 10%, the model class interval for physical activity of students was 10 to 20%. This was the lowest of all of the sport practices he observed which included swimming, volleyball, basketball, and ice hockey along with physical education classes. While such generalizations might be somewhat discouraging from the point of view of a behavioral analysis of what should happen in the gym (e.g., see Dickinson, 1977; Dodds, 1976; Siedentop, 1983a), these observational studies of the behavior of physical education instructors provide a growing database that can be used to develop an effective technology of teaching in this area.

Research: Behavioral Teaching Skills for Physical Educators

A major advance in applied behavior analysis and physical education is the increased acceptance of "behavioral teaching skills" as important components for preparation programs for physical educators. Siedentop and Taggert (1984) indicated that it is now routinely accepted that physical education trainees must become proficient at praising students for appropriate behavior, providing positive feedback for skill development attempts, shaping skills to increasing complexity, and so forth. The research foundation for this advance includes a number of studies. While reviewing research on modeling, McKenzie (1982) and Rife (1979) illustrated its implications for physical education teachers. Westcott (1977, 1979, 1980) clearly demonstrated the benefits of modeling by physical education teachers for influencing children's peer encouragement behavior. When physical education instructors provide frequent praise contingent upon learner efforts, for example, the students show increased rates of peer encouragement.

Several studies have examined strategies for increasing the frequency with which physical education teachers praise on-task pupil behavior and provide instructional feedback, and decrease the frequency with which they react negatively to off-task pupil behavior. In some cases, the intervention package to modify teacher behavior was a multiple-component, competency-based package (Anderson, Cooper, DeVault, Dickson, Johnson, & Weber, 1973; Darst, 1976; Darst & Steeves, 1980; Elam, 1972; Houston & Howsam, 1972). Other studies successfully increased praise and feedback rates of physical education teachers by using an audio cueing device (Van Der Mars, 1987, 1988, 1989), and a post hoc analysis of tape recorded teacher/student interactions (Devoe, 1990).

Hughley (1979) demonstrated the effectiveness of behavioral contracting for helping a physical education instructor objectively evaluate and improve the performance of physical education students completing requirements in a swimming credit course. Dodds (1977, 1979) applied a behavioral training package to improve rates and percentages of verbal teaching behaviors of physical education majors completing teacher certification practicum requirements. In this study, fellow student teachers systematically gathered the data and provided feedback to peers about verbal teaching behaviors, while functioning as change agents for each other in the program.

In a series of studies, McKenzie and his colleagues (Clark, McKenzie, & McKenzie, 1982; McKenzie, 1983; McKenzie, Clark, & McKenzie, 1984; Williams & McKenzie, 1978) compared machine pacing to instructor pacing for prompting student behavior during drills and fencing classes. They also monitored the frequency with which the instructor provided feedback and gave instructions during the two conditions. Student performance was slightly better under machine pacing. Interestingly, rates of teacher feedback were much higher under machine pacing while rates of giving instructions and modeling were reduced. The results suggest the potential benefits of producing labor saving devices to augment teaching techniques.

Wilkinson (1992) described a training program to teach qualitative skill analysis—observation of a student performing a skill, and on the basis of the observation, identifying discrepancies between actual and desired response characteristics. Subjects observed an instructional videotape to learn how to analyze three different volleyball skills. Introduced in a multiple-baseline across volleyball skill behaviors, the intervention effectively increased the subjects' ability to make accurate judgements about the correctness of the performance of volleyball skills. The study has implications for helping physical education teachers make accurate judgements about sport skill analysis.

These and other studies (e.g., McKenzie, 1981; Rushall & McEachern, 1977; Ocansey, 1988; Siedentop, 1980a, 1983b; Taggart, 1988) have demonstrated effective strategies for developing behavioral teaching skills of physical educators. Many of the earlier studies demonstrated desirable improvements in the behavioral teaching strategies of the physical educators while they were interns in a ten-week intern experience (Siedentop, 1981).

Research: Decreasing Problem Behaviors in the Gym

Behavioral strategies are now routinely applied to decrease a variety of behavioral excesses in many settings (e.g., Martin & Pear, 1992). There is also increased acceptance of behavior management strategies for decreasing problem behaviors in physical education classes (Dunn & Fredericks, 1985; Lavay, 1986; Siedentop & Taggart, 1984).

In a recent survey of 76 elementary and secondary school physical education teachers for mild and moderate behavior disturbances, the most frequently used tactic was simple praise of appropriate behavior (Vogler & Bishop, 1990). For severe disturbances, the most frequently used strategy was timeout, and the next most used strategy was loss of privileges. Overall, the survey suggested that physical educators frequently use behavior management strategies in sensible ways. Some of their strategies are illustrated by the following examples.

Pearce and Risley (1974) examined strategies for reducing disruptive behavior of youths at an urban recreation center. The disruptive behaviors included leaving trash in the game room, leaving pool cues lying around, and leaving trash in the halls. Such behaviors were clearly identified as rule violations. When rule violations were consistently consequated by shortening of recreation time, they were dramatically reduced. McKenzie (1980) described several studies in which student teachers in physical education, during field experiences, were able to apply behavioral strategies to decrease such behaviors as loud verbalizations, a variety of aggressive behaviors, and several types of off-task behaviors. The student teachers were able to quickly learn and implement behavioral techniques to effectively change student behaviors in desired directions. Vogler and French (1983) examined the effects of a group reinforcement contingency (the good behavior game first described by Barish, Saunders, & Wolf, 1969) for improving on-task behavior of a class of behavior disordered students in physical education. The group reinforcement contingency effectively increased on-task behavior with a younger group (mean age of 7.8 years) and an older group (mean age of 11.2 years), and there were no individuals within either group who did not respond favorably to treatment. In a study described by Hall (1979), the target population consisted of sophomore physical education majors at Ohio State University, rather than children in a grade school physical education class. The students taught by Hall participated in a self-instructional course in behavioral self-modification. All students were required to focus upon personal behavior problems as a part of the course. The students provided evidence in AB designs of decreasing a wide variety of personal behavior problems.

In summary, inroads have been made in several areas of applied behavior analysis in physical education, including: the development of reliable observation systems for monitoring the behavior of physical education teachers and students in order to provide usable information on "what's happening in the gym"; the increased acceptance of "behavioral teaching skills" as important components for teacher preparation programs, and demonstrations that these skills can be acquired in ten-week practice teaching situations; and increased acceptance of behavioral strategies to help physical educators manage a variety of behavioral difficulties of students.

ঞ

Update to the Present: Sports

Since the early 1970s, there has been a growing desire on the part of practicing coaches for more applied sport science experimentation, particularly in the area of sport psychology (Gowan, Botterill, & Blimkie, 1979). The 1970s saw the development of both national and international organizations devoted to sport psychology, including the International Society for Sport Psychology, the North American Society for the Psychology of Sport and Physical Activity, and the European Sport Psychology Association. Then in 1985, the Association for the Advancement of Applied Sport Psychology was founded. Applied behavior analysts have contributed to this rapidly growing field in several ways. After summarizing descriptive studies and books in the next section, research on applied behavior analysis and sports will be reviewed under the topics of skill development, increasing the frequency of practice behaviors, decreasing problem behaviors, changing the behavior of coaches, and "sport psyching" for competition.

Descriptive Reports and Books

As was the case with physical education, many of the published reports on applied behavior analysis and sports are not formal research reports. Papers have described application guidelines for coaches (Botterill, 1978, 1983; McClements & Botterill, 1980; Rushall, 1977b; Siedentop, 1980b; Smoll, Smith, & Curtis, 1978), summarized behavioral principles and procedures (Martin & Hrycaiko, 1983b; Siedentop & Rushall, 1972) and illustrated them with case histories with before and after data (Lynch & Stillman, 1979; Martin et al., 1983; Rushall, 1970, 1988), or with reference to research published elsewhere (Liskevych, 1979; Rushall, 1976), discussed the benefits of applied behavior analysis for sports (Rushall, 1975), called for more single-subject research designs for evaluating sport psychology interventions (Bryan, 1987; Wollman, 1986), and described characteristics of effective behavioral coaching (Martin & Hrycaiko, 1983c).

Several books have also described applied behavior analysis procedures for coaches and athletes. Dickinson (1977) offered an insightful Skinnerian analysis of the contingencies that both promote and deter participation in sports. He also examined the effects of contingencies of reinforcement and punishment on the acquisition of skills and the social behaviors with which sports are associated. Martin and Hrycaiko (1983a) published an edited volume of behavior modification procedures for coaches, and Martin and Lumsden (1987) described how-to strategies for use by coaches in youth sports. Another book that was directed primarily at coaches of kids or beginners is that of Orlick and Botterill (1975). They were concerned with the overemphasis on winning in youth sports and the possible deleterious effects that such an emphasis can have. Their book stressed the need for coaching behaviors that might increase the probability of young athletes participating in and enjoying sports. Rushall (1979b), on the other hand, described detailed steps that a coach might follow to help elite athletes learn to emit specific precompetition behaviors (those that occur on the day of competition up to the time of the event itself) and competition behaviors (those that occur just before and during competition) to improve competitive performance.

Four of the books with a behavioral approach fall within the self-modification arena. Orlick (1980, 1986a, 1986b) relying mainly on the behavioral self-control literature, outlined competitive strategies to help advanced athletes improve athletic performance. Some of the recommended strategies include coping self-statements to cope with stress and improve concentration just before competition, progressive relaxation to control excessive nervousness, realistic goal setting strategies, and imagery rehearsal of "best" performances to maximize performance at competitions. While Orlick's books are directed primarily at elite athletes, Simek and O'Brien (1981) described detailed training steps with mastery criteria for beginning golfers.

Research: Skill Development

A number of studies have clearly demonstrated that various operant conditioning strategies can be advantageously applied to develop athletic skills and/or decrease errors in open-ended team sports and in closed-ended individual sports. The strategies can be applied with individuals as young as seven and with adults in their forties and fifties, and in practices as well as in competition conditions. Successful interventions have ranged from complex multiple-component packages to improve swimming technique (Koop & Martin, 1983) to a simple auditory click contingent upon an error in putting (Simek & O'Brien, 1978). Sports studied have included classical ballet (Fitterling & Ayllon, 1983), baseball (Osborne, Rudrud, & Zezoney, 1990), bowling (Kirschenbaum, Ordman, Tomarken, & Holtzbauer, 1982), football (Allison & Ayllon, 1980; Komaki & Barnett, 1977), golf (Johnston-O'Connor & Kirschenbaum, 1986; O'Brien & Simek, 1983, Simek & O'Brien, 1978), gymnastics (Allison & Ayllon, 1980; Wolko, Hrycaiko, & Martin, in press), racquetball (Darst & Model, 1983), tennis (Allison & Ayllon, 1980; Buzas & Ayllon, 1981; Ziegler, 1987), track (Shapiro & Shapiro, 1985), soccer (Rusch & Ayllon, 1984), and swimming (Fueyo, Saudergas, & Bushall, Jr., 1975; Hazen, Johnstone, Martin, & Srikameswaran, 1990; Koop & Martin, 1983). Collectively, these studies illustrate some of the benefits of applied behavior analysis for skill development in sports provided that: (1) the behaviors that are critical to success are precisely defined; (2) there is accurate and frequent recording of those behaviors before, during, and after behavioral intervention to demonstrate progress; and (3) there is consistent and individualized application of specific behavioral strategies.

However, several limitations should be noted. First, considering the theoretical potential for applied behavior analysis for skill development, there have been applications to only a few sports. Practitioners should be encouraged to adapt and demonstrate behavioral procedures with many additional sports. Second, when complex interventions are used, procedural reliability should be included to ensure replicability of the intervention strategy (Koop & Martin, 1983; Peterson, Homer, & Wonderlich, 1982). However, procedural reliabilities on interventions are a rarity in this area. Third, most of the studies had the benefit of the involvement of a doctoral-level, trained applied behavior analyst. It's one thing for a graduate student or coach in collaboration with such a person to demonstrate the effectiveness of applied behavior analyses in studies such as those cited above. It's another thing for full-time or part-time coaches, paid or volunteer, to consistently apply behavioral procedures on their own, and to obtain results comparable to those in the above studies. Thus, an important need is the development of effective self-instructional manuals, such as that by Simek and O'Brien (1981) for golf. These must be followed by experimental demonstrations so that coaches can follow the manuals and more effectively improve skills than when following "traditional" coaching procedures.

Research: Increasing the Frequency of Practice Behaviors

How can a coach effectively improve attendance at practices, motivate athletes to get the most out of practice time, organize practices so that there is very little down time in which athletes are inactive, and still make practices fun? Studies in this area have focused on two general strategies—consequence management by coaches or self-management packages for the athletes.

To some extent, studies on consequence management by coaches demonstrate the obvious: (1) making various reinforcers contingent upon improved practice performance leads to improved practice performance; and (2) the effectiveness of specific events as reinforcers varies across groups and individuals. With youth competitive swimmers, for example, allowing swimmers to earn candy and money for swimming more laps was more effective than coach praise as a consequence for increased workout volume (Rushall & Pettinger, 1969). With members of a university women's varsity volleyball team, however, the opportunity for private instruction with the coach was a more effective reinforcer for improving practice performance than was money (McKenzie & Liskevych, 1983). Cracklen and Martin (1983) demonstrated that a natural reinforcer (the opportunity to choose sides for a relay race at the end of a swim practice) led to improved practice performance when it was behavior-based (contingent upon all of the swimmers performing above a minimum level) rather than when it was time-based (scheduled at the end of every practice). Interestingly, the great majority of participants preferred to "earn" the reinforcer rather than having it made available on a noncontingent basis.

Studies with youth swimmers (Critchfield, 1989; Critchfield & Vargas, 1991; McKenzie & Rushall, 1974), a university swim team (Bell & Patterson, 1978), and young figure skaters (Hume, Martin, Gonzalez, Cracklen, & Genthon, 1985) all demonstrated positive effects with self-management packages that included goal setting, self-monitoring, and feedback for progress towards goals as a potent strategy for improving practice performance.

Collectively, the studies in this area suggest that improving practice performance depends upon effective goal setting (Locke, 1991; Locke & Latham, 1985), monitoring a variety of athletic behaviors during practices, and making better use of existing reinforcers to increase the behaviors that are monitored. A limitation of this research is that demonstrations of strategies for increasing practice behaviors have examined short-term applications. Future studies should be directed at designing sport environments for maintaining an increased frequency of desirable practice behaviors over the long term.

Research: Decreasing Problem Behaviors in Sport Environments

Only five studies were encountered on decreasing problem behaviors in sport environments. The small number of published studies may mean that coaches are not familiar with behavioral strategies for decreasing disruptive behaviors. Alternatively, it may mean that disruptive behaviors are infrequent in sport environments.

McKenzie and Rushall (1974) effectively applied public self-recording and charting of attendance and arrival on time to decrease late arrivals and missed practices by youth competitive swimmers. McKenzie and Rushall (1980) compared coach management of undesirable behaviors during swimming practices (e.g., changing stroke, stopping, not pushing off, etc.) to a behavioral game managed by the players. In the coach management condition, the coach praised desirable behaviors, reprimanded undesirable behaviors, and recorded both types of behaviors on a display board. In the behavioral game, players could disqualify other players for inappropriate behaviors, and list them on a display board. While both strategies led to a decrease in inappropriate behavior, the game conditions showed the greatest suppression.

Three studies examined strategies for decreasing problem behaviors in public sport environments. In a study designed to decrease the number of weights on the floor in a college weight room, Darden and Madsen (1972) found that subjects responded best to clearly stated rules and regulations with specific warnings and punishments for failure to comply, as compared to signs alone or signs plus a point system with backup rewards. Walley, Graham, and Forehand (1982) examined instructions distributed via leaflets for influencing spectators at baseball games to increase their praise of desirable plays, teams, coaches, and umpires. While questionnaire follow-up data indicated that observers believed that the leaflets increased their positive verbalizations, objective data indicated no change in positive verbalizations. Yu and Martin (1987) compared educational sign prompting versus a weekly lottery to influence golfers at a public golf course to repair their ballmarks on putting greens. Because both interventions were approximately equally effective in decreasing unrepaired ballmarks on greens, both were favorably received by golfers, and because the educational sign prompting was almost cost-free, the educational sign prompt was adopted by the golf course at the completion of the study. This study suggests that effective, low-cost behavioral techniques that have been applied in community behavioral psychology (Geller, Winett, & Everett, 1982; Martin & Osborne, 1980) deserve serious consideration for preserving public sport environments.

Research: Assessing and Developing Behavior Management Skills of Coaches

Coaches have a very difficult job. From an applied behavior analysis perspective, a coach must effectively instruct, set goals, praise, reprimand, and perform a wide variety of other activities that, collectively, greatly determine his or her effectiveness as a behavior manager. Studies that have examined interactions between coaches and athletes suggest several generalizations. First, coaches in many sports generally show low rates of positive reinforcement (McKenzie & King, 1982; Rushall, 1977c, 1981). Second, behavioral intervention strategies can be used effectively to influence coaches to provide higher frequencies of positive reinforcement and feedback (Rushall & Smith, 1979; Smith, Smoll, & Curtis, 1979; Ziegler, 1980). Third, teaching coaches to be better behavior managers leads to higher ratings of the coach by the athletes (Smith et al., 1979). Fourth, players of more successful coaches received significantly more of several types of interactions than players of less successful coaches (Claxdon, 1988; Markland & Martinek, 1988).

An important series of studies in this area was conducted by Ron Smith and Frank Smoll and their colleagues at the University of Washington concerning the assessment and modification of behaviors of Little League baseball coaches. Using an assessment device called the Coaching Behavioral Assessment System (CBAS), Curtis, Smith, and Smoll (1979) demonstrated a number of significant relationships between coaches' behavior and players' perceptions of both the coaches and themselves. Interestingly, perceptions of their own behavior by coaches didn't relate to data provided by observers and players. Studies by this group have indicated that observers can be trained to use the CBAS with a high degree of reliability and accuracy in coding behaviors of baseball coaches (Smith, Smoll, & Hunt, 1977), that a variety of factors exert influence on players' attitudes toward both the coach and the game (Smith, Smoll, & Curtis, 1978), and that an effective training program for coaches can exert a significant and positive influence on both player-perceived and overt coaching behaviors (Smith et al., 1979). The research of this group has led to the development of a coach effectiveness training program for youth coaches (Smith & Smoll, 1991; Smoll &

Smith, 1987). In general, this model emphasizes formal goal setting and technical instruction, use of encouragement and positive reinforcement to increase desirable behaviors, and an overall socially supportive environment. The model has been extended and adapted for the Houston Astros minor league player development program (Smith & Johnson, 1990).

Assessing and developing behavior management skills of coaches may be one of the most important areas of applied behavior analysis and sports. No amount of research on skill development, increasing frequency of practice behaviors, or decreasing disruptive behaviors is likely to lead to significant and permanent changes in the behavior of coaches until behavior management techniques are applied to and by the coaches themselves. Coaches must be encouraged to self-monitor or invite others to frequently evaluate their performance using checklists of behaviors that define effective behavioral coaching (Martin & Lumsden, 1987). Such coaching behaviors as encouraging athletes to set individual goals, praising athletes at every practice for progress shown, frequently assessing the many components of various skills of individual athletes, and dispensing a higher frequency of rewards and praise than reprimands are ones that all coaches do at some time or another. It is a rare coach, however, who consistently performs such behaviors in all practices and employs detailed data systems to consistently improve his/her effectiveness. Coaches, like the athletes they train, learn, make progress, and change as the season unfolds. They are most likely to master behavior management techniques if they themselves are assessed, receive frequent prompts on how well they do, and receive positive consequences for improving (Martin & Lumsden, 1987).

Research: Sport Psyching

In general, mental preparation or "sport psyching" refers to psychologically-based strategies that athletes might follow to maximize sport performance at competitions. The techniques typically used involve some combination of relaxation and arousal management, imagery or mental rehearsal, self-instruction and self-monitoring, goal setting, and training under simulations of competitive conditions. Reports describe applications of these techniques with Olympic level (*The Sport Psychologist*, Special Theme Issue, December, 1989), professional (*The Sport Psychologist*, Special Theme Issue, December, 1990), collegiate (e.g., Elko & Ostrow, 1991; Ravizza & Osborne, 1991), recreational (Kirchenbaum, Ordman, Tomarken, & Holtzbauer, 1982), and youth (Martin, 1989) athletes. Detailed how-to strategies in this area have been described for coaches and athletes (Orlick, 1986a, 1986b).

Most of the research in this area has been conceptualized within a cognitive behavioral framework, and has examined sport psyching interventions using control group designs. Reviews of this research can be found in Greenspan & Feltz (1989), Kirschenbaum (1984), Weinberg (1982), and Whelan, Mahoney, & Meyers (1991). A few reports in this area, however, have been conceptualized within an applied behavior analysis framework. Martin (1989) offered a behavioral interpretation of sport psyching and described a program for young figure skaters. The program focused on the identification of stimuli that are present in the competitive environment, and emphasized practice strategies to bring figure skating skills under the control of similar stimuli at practices. Although only self-report data has been gathered to date, preliminary results are very positive.

Several studies have examined self-talk packages for improving competitive performance. Athletes are taught to bring skilled athletic performance under the control of specific cue words or self-talk in practice environments, and then to use the self-talk to cue desirable athletic performance in competitive situations. This approach capitalizes on rule-governed control of behavior and uses a generalization programming strategy referred to as "program common stimuli" (Martin & Pear, 1992). In practice environments, studies have demonstrated positive effects of self-talk for improving performances in rowing (Rushall, 1984), cross-country skiing (Rushall, Hall, Roux, Sasseville, & Rushall, 1988), tennis (Ziegler, 1987), and figure skating (Martin, 1989). Only one study to date has utilized a single-subject design to examine a sport psyching intervention on actual competitive performance. Kendall, Hrycaiko, Martin, & Kendall (1990) investigated the effects of a self-talk package (that included imagery, rehearsal, and relaxation) on the performance of the execution of a defensive skill during games with four female intercollegiate basketball players. The intervention was clearly effective in enhancing basketball skill in a multiple-baseline across subject design, and social validity measures were very positive.

Two studies examined the game performance of baseball players from a behavioral analysis perspective. In a delightful report of a season traveling with a barnstorming (semipro) baseball team, Heward (1978) described the effects of small amounts of money (the players were poorly paid) contingent upon a player's efficiency average. The efficiency average is a numerical description of a player's overall contribution to his team's run production, and was considered to be a better measure of overall contribution than traditional baseball statistics. In an ABAB design, six of nine players compiled higher efficiency averages during intervention than during baseline conditions. Howard, Figlerski, & O'Brien (1982) took advantage of the change in the method of payment of major league baseball players to do a naturalistic, AB field study. Prior to 1977, most players negotiated contracts at the end of each season on the basis of the previous year's performance. Beginning in 1977, multiyear, guaranteed contracts became increasingly common. Both within subject and control groups, comparisons indicated that pitchers signed under high pay, long-term guaranteed contracts showed steady improvement until the guaranteed contract was signed, and steady decline in performance after the contract took effect.

è.

Future Directions

Applied behavior analysis in physical education and sports has a solid foundation. But what directions should we take in the future?

Physical Education

While it is clear that considerable progress has been made in applied behavior analysis in physical education, several areas have been identified as requiring further study. First, Luke (1989) has argued that definitions of behaviors in the management of problem behaviors in physical education classes need to be improved. Second, in spite of several pleas that physical educators take specific, detailed, and frequent measures of student performance, and that they use those measures as the primary means for evaluating the effectiveness of specific teaching tactics (Dodds, 1976, 1977; McKenzie, 1979; Siedentop, 1972, 1976, 1983a), there appears to be little accountability placed on teachers in terms of student performance gains (Siedentop & Taggart, 1984). Direct and frequent measurement of individual student behavior is much more likely to be a feature of applied behavior analysis in education than in physical education. Siedentop and Taggert (1984) suggested three possible reasons for this. First, in physical education, larger spaces, frequent movement of students, and the pace of change all create problems of measurement that are accentuated in comparison to a classroom setting. Second, relevant responses in physical education classes (e.g., exercise movements) do not leave permanent products, such as the test results in education classes. Third, there is less agreement on what constitutes important outcome measures in physical education than in education classes. In a variety of interactive team games and dual activities, for example, considerable work needs to be done to identify important outcome measures that go far beyond simple win/loss records.

An important step to influencing future physical educators is to incorporate more applied behavior analysis in physical education curricula at colleges and universities. The kind of training provided for graduate students in physical education by Siedentop and his colleagues at Ohio State University is exemplary. Such training is clearly effective in influencing physical educators to learn applied behavior analysis procedures and to demonstrate behavioral competencies in teaching situations. What is needed is for similar training to be made available for undergraduate physical education majors. Graduates from undergraduate programs in physical education in North America fulfill a wide variety of recreational, instructional, and coaching needs in elementary and secondary schools, community centers, and service organizations. We can anticipate a greater impact of applied behavior analysis on physical education as relevant undergraduate courses become increasingly common in physical education departments at colleges and universities.

Sports

What about coaching kids and beginners? Components of effective behavioral coaching have been described (Martin & Hrycaiko, 1983c; Martin & Lumsden, 1987). And there are mechanisms available to provide coaches of youth sports with a variety of coaching competencies. In Canada, for example, the Canadian National Coaching Certification Program offers courses and certification in some 50 sports and operates in all provinces of Canada. In the United States, a private program that has similar characteristics is the American Coaching Effectiveness Program, distributed by Human Kinetics Publishers. But, with the exception of isolated demonstration projects (e.g., Smith et al., 1979), there is no evidence that such courses or certification programs do anything other than change the coach's verbal behavior. There is evidence from other areas that the most effective way of influencing people to apply behavior modification is to reinforce them for doing so in real life settings (Reid & Whitman, 1983). Future investigators need to examine ways to develop and disseminate practicum components for enhancing coaching competencies in applied behavior analysis in field experiments. Additional prescriptions for increasing the practice of effective behavioral coaching would include more social validity from the point of view of the athletes, and more adequately field tested "how-to" instructional packages similar to the Simek and O'Brien (1981) book on golf. Another need in the area of youth sports is to encourage sport psychology trainees at universities to emphasize the life skill features of "sport psyching" strategies when working with young athletes. Teaching young athletes how to relax, set goals, compete against self-improvement standards (rather than always focusing on winning), and monitoring progress toward goals are skills that have applicability far beyond any particular sport. They are skills that characterize successful adjustment in everyday living (Martin & Osborne, 1989).

Concerning coaching at the national and international levels, Rushall (1979a, 1982) has identified a number of needs including greater individualized strategies, refined self-control techniques for athletes to manage precompetition and competition behaviors, greater use of a variety of behavioral measures as opposed to more simple-minded outcome measures, greater integration of applied behavior analysis preparation with physical and technical preparation for competition, and increased frequency with which coaches provide individual as opposed to group feedback. Prescriptions for influencing the sporting world to respond to these needs would include educating elite athletes to ask for what behavioral psychology has to offer, and the establishment of demonstration projects within and across different sports.

In summary, applied behavior analysis in sport and physical education has a short past, a solid foundation, and a promising future. As in other areas of applied behavior analysis, emphasis is placed on specific and detailed measurement of athletic performance, the use of these measures to evaluate the effectiveness of specific teaching and coaching techniques, and a strong reliance on the principles of operant and Pavlovian conditioning for conceptualizing intervention strategies. Applied behavior analysis has much to offer physical educators, coaches, and athletes of all levels and ages.

References

Allard, R. & Rife, F. (1980). A teacher directed model of peer supervision in physical education. *The Physical Educator, 37*(2), 89-94.

Allison, M.G. & Ayllon, T. (1980). Behavioral coaching in the development of skills in football, gymnastics, and tennis. *Journal of Applied Behavior Analysis, 13,* 297-314.

Anderson, D.W., Cooper, J.M., DeVault, M.V., Dickson, G.E., Johnson, C.E., & Weber, W.A. (1973). *Competency based teacher education* (p. 304). Berkeley: McCutchan Publishing.

Anderson, W. (1980). *Analysis of teaching physical education.* St. Louis, MO: Mosby.

Baer, D.M., Wolf, M.M., & Risley, T.R. (1968). Some current dimensions of applied behavior analysis. *Journal of Applied Behavior Analysis, 1,* 91-97.

Baer, D.M., Wolf, M.M., & Risley, T.R. (1987). Some still-current dimensions of applied behavior analysis. *Journal of Applied Behavior Analysis, 20,* 313-328.

Barrish, H.H., Saunders, M., & Wolf, M.M. (1969). Good behavior game: Effects of individual contingencies for group consequences on disruptive behavior in a classroom. *Journal of Applied Behavior Analysis, 2,* 119-124.

Bell, K.F. & Patterson, M.R. (1978). A self-monitoring technique for enhancement of swimming performance. *Swimming Technique, 14,* 103-106.

Botterill, C. (1978). Psychology of coaching. *Coaching Review, 1*(4), 46-55.

Botterill, C. (1983). Goal-setting for athletes with examples from hockey. In G.L. Martin & D. Hrycaiko (Eds.), *Behavior modification and coaching: Principles, procedures, and research.* Springfield, IL: Charles C. Thomas.

Bryan, A.J. (1987). Single-subject designs for evaluation of sport psychology interventions. *The Sport Psychologist, 1,* 283-292.

Buzas, H.P. & Ayllon, T. (1981). Differential reinforcement in coaching skills. *Behavior Modification, 5,* 372-385.

Cheffers, J.T.F. (1977). Observing teaching systematically. *Quest, 28,* 17-28.

Chelladura, P. & Stothart, C. (1978). Backward chaining: A method of teaching motor skills. *Canadian Association for Health, Physical Education and Recreation Journal, 45*(1), 26-29, 36-37.

Clark, E.K., McKenzie, T.L., & McKenzie, R.E. (1982). Instructional strategies: Influence on teacher behavior and student motor engagement rates in university fencing classes. *Research papers: 1982 AHPERD Convention.* Reston, VA: AHPERD.

Claxdon, D.B. (1988). A systematic observation of more and less successful high school tennis coaches. *Journal of Teaching in Physical Education, 7,* 302-310.

Coulon, S.C. (1989). Behavioral contracts: Uniting the student teaching triad. *The Physical Educator, 46,* 94-98.

Cracklen, C. & Martin, G.L. (1983). Earning fun with correct techniques. *Swimming Technique, 20,* 29-32.

Critchfield, T.S. (1989). Self-recording mutually exclusive multiple responses. *Behavior Modification, 13,* 361-375.

Critchfield, T.S. & Vargas, E.A. (1991). Self-recording, instructions, and public self-graphing: Effects on swimming in the absence of coach verbal interaction. *Behavior Modification, 15,* 95-112.

Curtis, B., Smith, R.E., & Smoll, F.L. (1979). Scrutinizing the skipper: A study of leadership behaviors in the dug-out. *Journal of Applied Psychology, 64,* 391-400.

Darden, E. & Madsen, C.H. (1972). Behavior modification for weightlifting room problems. *College Student Journal, 6,* 95-99.

Darst, P.W. (1976). Effects of competency-based intervention on student-teacher and pupil reaction. *Research Quarterley, 47,* 336-345.

Darst, P.W. (1979). Contingency management learning system. *AAHPER Research Consortium Symposium Papers* (Vol. 2, Book 1, pp. 81-85). Washington, DC: AAHPER.

Darst, P.W. & Model, R.L. (1983). Racquetball contracting: A way to structure your learning environment. *Journal of Physical Education, Recreation and Dance, 54*(7), 65-67.

Darst, P.W. & Steeves, D. (1980). A competency-based approach to secondary student teaching in physical education. *Research Quarterley, 51*(2), 274-285.

Darst, P.W., Zakrajsek, D.B., & Mancini, V.H. (1989). *Analyzing physical education and sport instruction.* Champaign, IL: Human Kinetics Publishers.

Devoe, D.E. (1990). The effects of self-assessment on selecting teaching behaviors of an elementary school student. *The Physical Educator, 47,* 37-41.

Dickinson, J. (1977). *A behavior analysis of sport.* Princeton, NJ: Princeton Book Company.

Dodds, P. (1976). Love and joy in the gymnasium. *Quest, 26,* 109-116.

Dodds, P.S. (1977). Behavior analysis model for student teacher supervision. *The Association of Health, Physical Education & Recreation Journal, May,* pp. 12, 13, 36.

Dodds, P.S. (1978). Behavior analysis of students: What students can tell teachers without ever saying a word. *Motor Skills: Theory into Practice, 3*(1), 3-10.

Dodds, P.S. (1979). A peer assessment model for student teacher supervision. *Research Quarterley, 50*(1), 18-29.

Donahue, J.A., Gillis, J.H., & King, K. (1980). Behavior modification in sport and physical education: A review. *Journal of Sports Psychology, 2,* 311-328.

Dunn, J.M. & Fredericks, B. (1985). The utilization of behavior management in mainstreaming in physical education. *Adapted Physical Activity Quarterly, 2,* 338-346.

Elam, S. (1972). Performance-based teacher education: What is the state of the art? *Quest, 18,* 14-19.

Elko, P.K. & Ostrow, A.C. (1991). Effects of a rational-emotive education program on heightened anxiety levels of female collegiate gymnasts. *The Sport Psychologist, 5,* 235-255.

Evans, J. (1974). Implications of behavior modification techniques for the physical education teacher. *The Physical Educator, 31,* 28-32.

Fast, B.L. (1971). Contingency contracting. *Journal of Health, Physical Education, and Recreation, 42,* 31-32.

Fishman, S.E. & Anderson, W.G. (1971). Developing a system for describing teachers. *Quest, 17,* 9-16.

Fitterling, J.M. & Ayllon, T. (1983). Behavioral coaching in classical ballet: Enhancing skill development. *Behavior Modification, 7,* 345-368.

Fueyo, U., Saudergas, R.A., & Bushall, D., Jr. (1975). Two types of feedback in teaching swimming skills to handicapped children. *Perceptual and Motor Skills, 40,* 963-966.

Geller, E.S., Winett, R.A., & Everett, P.B. (1982). *Preserving the environment: New strategies for behavior change.* New York: Pergamon.

Gowan, G.R., Botterill, C., & Blimkie, C.J. (1979). Bridging the gap between sport science and sport practice. In P. Klavora and J. Daniel (Eds.), *Coach, athlete, and sport psychologist.* Toronto: School of Physical and Health Education, University of Toronto.

Grant, B. & Martens, F. (1982). Teacher effectiveness in elementary physical education. *Canadian Association for Health, Physical Education and Recreation Journal, 48*(4), 7-10.

Greenspan, M.J. & Feltz, D.L. (1989). Psychological interventions with athletes in competitive situations: A review. *The Sport Psychologist, 3,* 219-236.

Hall, W.D. (1979). Behavioral self-modification in teacher education. *AAHPER Research Symposium Papers* (Vol. 2, Book 1, pp. 70-77). Washington, DC: AAHPER.

Hazen, A., Johnstone, C., Martin, G.L., & Srikameswaran, S. (1990). A videotaping feedback package for improving skills of youth competitive swimmers. *The Sport Psychologist, 4,* 213-227.

Heward, W.L. (1978). Operant conditioning of a .300 hitter? The effects of reinforcement on the offensive efficiency of a barnstorming baseball team. *Behavior Modification, 2*(1), 25-40.

Houston, W.R. & Howsam, R.B. (Eds.). (1972). *Competency-based teacher education.* Chicago, IL: Science Research, Inc.

Howard, F.R., Figlerski, F.W., & O'Brien, R.M. (1982). The performance of major league baseball pitchers on long-term guaranteed contracts. In R.M. O'Brien, A.M. Dickinson, & M.P. Rozow (Eds.), *Industrial behavior modification: A management handbook.* New York: Pergamon.

Hughley, C. (1973). Modification of teacher behaviors in physical education. Unpublished doctoral dissertation, Ohio State University, Columbus, OH.

Hughley, C. (1979). Evaluting the behavior contract. *AAHPER Research Consortium Symposium Papers* (Vol. 2, Book 1, pp. 60-64). Washington, DC: AAHPER.

Hume, K.M., Martin, G.L., Gonzalez, P., Cracklen, C., & Genthon, S. (1985). A self-monitoring feedback package for improving freestyle figure skating practice. *Journal of Sport Psychology, 7,* 333-345.

Johnston-O'Connor, E.J. & Kirschenbaum, D.S. (1986). Something succeeds like success: Positive self-monitoring in golf. *Cognitive Therapy and Research, 10,* 123-136.

Kendall, G., Hrycaiko, D., Martin, G.L., & Kendall, T. (1990). The effects of an imagery rehearsal, relaxation, and self-talk package on basketball game performance. *Journal of Sport and Exercise Psychology, 12,* 157-166.

Kirschenbaum, D.S. (1984). Self-regulation and sport psychology: Nurturing an emerging symbiosis. *Journal of Sport Psychology, 6,* 159-183.

Kirschenbaum, D.S., Ordman, A.M., Tomarken, A.J., & Holtzbauer, R. (1982). Effects of differential self-monitoring and level of mastery of sports performance: Brain power bowling. *Cognitive Therapy and Research, 6,* 335-342.

Komaki, J. & Barnett, F.T. (1977). A behavioral approach to coaching football: Improving the play execution of the offensive backfield on a youth football team. *Journal of Applied Behavior Analysis, 7,* 199-206.

Koop, S. & Martin, G.L. (1983). A coaching strategy to reduce swimming stroke errors with beginning age-group swimmers. *Journal of Applied Behavior Analysis, 16,* 447-460.

Lavay, B. (1986). Behavior management in physical education, recreation, and sport. *The Physical Educator, 43,* 103-112.

Level III Coaching Theory Manual (1981). Canadian National Coaching Certification Program, Ottawa, Canada.

Liskevych, T.N. (1979). Applications of behavior modification in athletic environments. *AAHPER Research Consortium Symposium Papers* (Vol. 2, Book 1, pp. 55-59). Washington, DC: AAHPER.

Locke, E.A. (1991). Problems with goal setting research in sports—and their solution. *Journal of Sport and Exercise Psychology, 8,* 311-316.

Locke, E.A. & Latham, G.P. (1985). The application of goal setting to sports. *Journal of Sport Psychology, 7,* 205-222.

Luke, M.D. (1989). Research on class management and organization: Review of implications for current practice. *Quest, 41,* 55-67.

Lynch, A.R. & Stillman, S.M. (1979). Behavior modification in coaching. *Journal of Physical Education and Recreation, May,* pp. 38, 61.

Markland, R. & Martinek, T.J. (1988). Descriptive analysis of coach augmented feedback given to high school varsity female volleyball players. *Journal of Teaching in Physical Education, 7,* 289-301.

Martin, G.L. (1989). *Sport psyching: A behavioral interpretation; and a program for young figure skaters.* Presentation to the XXI Banff Conference on Behavioral Science, Banff, Alberta, Canada.

Martin, G.L. & Hrycaiko, D. (1983a). *Behavior modification and coaching: Principles, procedures and research*. Springfield, IL: Charles C. Thomas.

Martin, G.L. & Hrycaiko, D. (1983b). Principles and procedures of applied behavior analysis with illustrations from sport and physical education. In G.L. Martin & D. Hrycaiko (Eds.), *Behavior modification and coaching: Principles, procedures and research*. Springfield, IL: Charles C. Thomas.

Martin, G.L. & Hrycaiko, D. (1983c). Effective behavioral coaching: What's it all about? *Journal of Sport Psychology, 5*, 8-20.

Martin, G.L., LePage, R., & Koop, S. (1983). Applications of behavior modification for coaching age-group competitive swimmers. In G.L. Martin & D. Hrycaiko (Eds.), *Behavior modification and coaching: Principles, procedures and research*. Springfield, IL: Charles C. Thomas.

Martin, G.L. & Lumsden, J. (1987). *Coaching: An effective behavioral approach*. St. Louis, MO: Times Mirror/Mosby.

Martin, G.L. & Osborne, J.G. (1980). *Helping in the community: Behavioral applications*. New York: Plenum.

Martin, G.L. & Osborne, J.G. (1989). *Psychology, adjustment, and everyday living*. Englewood Cliffs, NJ: Prentice-Hall.

Martin, G.L. & Pear, J.J. (1992). *Behavior modification: What it is and how to do it* (4th ed). Englewood Cliffs, NJ: Prentice-Hall.

McClements, J.D. & Botterill, C. (1980). Goal-setting and performance. In R. M. Suinn (Ed.), *Psychology in sports: Methods and applications*. Minneapolis, MN: Burgess.

McDonald, L.J. (1971). An elective curriculum. *Journal of Health, Physical Education and Recreation, September,* 29.

McKenzie, T.L. (1979). Accountability in the gymnasium: A behavior analysis approach. *AAHPER Research Consortium Symposium Paper* (Vol. 2, Book 1, pp. 65-69). Washington, DC: AAHPER.

Selection VII

McKenzie, T.L. (1980). Behavioral engineering in elementary school physical education. In P. Klavora & K. Whipper (Eds.), *Psychological and sociological factors in sport* (pp. 194-203). Toronto: University of Toronto.

McKenzie, T.L. (1981). Modification, transfer, and maintenance of the verbal behavior of an experienced physical education teacher: A single-subject analysis. *Journal of Teaching in Physical Education, 1*(1), 48-56.

McKenzie, T.L. (1982). Research on modeling: Implications for teacher educators. *Journal of Teaching in Physical Education, 1*(3), 23-30.

McKenzie, T.L. (1983). Machine-paced instruction: Innovations for improving teaching in physical education. In T. Templin & J. Olson (Eds.), *Teaching in physical education, Big Ten Body of Knowledge* (Vol. 14, pp. 224-231). Champaign, IL: Human Kinetics Publishers.

McKenzie, T.L., Clark, E.K., & McKenzie, R.E. (1984). Instructional strategies: Influence on teacher and student behavior. *Journal of Teaching in Physical Education, 3*(2), 20-28.

McKenzie, T.L. & King, H.A. (1982). Analysis of feedback provided by youth baseball coaches. *Education and Treatment of Children, 5*, 179-188.

McKenzie, T.L. & Liskevych, T.N. (1983). Using the multi-element baseline design to examine motivation in volleyball training. In G.L. Martin & D. Hrycaiko (Eds.), *Behavior modification and coaching: Principles, procedures and research.* Springfield, IL: Charles C. Thomas.

McKenzie, T.L. & Rushall, B.S. (1973). The neglect of reinforcement theory in physical education. *Canadian Association for Health, Physical Education and Recreation Journal, 39*, 13-17.

McKenzie, T.L. & Rushall, B.S. (1974). Effects of self-recording on attendance and performance in a competitive swimming training environment. *Journal of Applied Behavior Analysis, 7*, 199-206.

McKenzie, T.L & Rushall, B.S. (1980). Controlling inappropriate behaviors in a competitive swimming environment. *Education and Treatment of Children, 3,* 205-216.

Metzler, M. (1981). A multi-observational system for supervising student teachers in physical education. *The Physical Educator, 38*(3), 152-159.

O'Brien, R.M. & Simek, T.C. (1983). A comparison of behavioral and traditional methods for teaching golf. In G.L. Martin & D. Hrycaiko (Eds.), *Behavior modification and coaching: Principles, procedures and research.* Springfield, IL: Charles C. Thomas.

Ocansey, R.P.A. (1988). The effects of a behavioral model of supervision on the supervisory behaviors of cooperating teachers. *Journal of Teaching in Physical Education, 8,* 46-62.

Orlick, T. (1980). *In pursuit of excellence.* Ottawa: Coaching Association of Canada.

Orlick, T. (1986a). *Coaches training manual to psyching for sport.* Champaign, IL: Leisure Press.

Orlick, T. (1986b). *Psyching for sport.* Champaign, IL: Leisure Press.

Orlick, T. & Botterill, C. (1975). *Every kid can win.* Chicago, IL: Nelson-Hall.

Osborne, K., Rudrud, E., & Zezoney, F. (1990). Improved curveball hitting through the enhancement of visual cues. *Journal of Applied Behavior Analysis, 23,* 371-377.

Pearce, C.H. & Risley, T.R. (1974). Improving job performance of neighbourhood youth core aids in an urban recreational center. *Journal of Applied Behavior Analysis, 7,* 207-215.

Peterson, L., Homer, A.L., & Wonderlich, S.A. (1982). The integrity of independent variables in behavior analysis. *Journal of Applied Behavior Analysis, 15,* 477-492.

Presbie, R.J. & Brown, P.L. (1977). *Physical education: The behavior modification approach.* Washington, DC: National Education Association.

Quarterman, J. (1980). An observational system for observing the verbal and nonverbal behaviors emitted by physical educators and coaches. *The Physical Educator, 37*(1), 15-20.

Ravizza, K. & Osborne, T. (1991). Nebraska's 3 R's: One-play-at-a-time preperformance routine for collegiate football. *The Sport Psychologist, 5,* 256-265.

Reid, D. & Whitman, T. (1983). Behavioral staff management in institutions: A critical review of effectiveness and acceptability. *Analysis and Intervention in Developmental Disabilities, 3,* 131-149.

Rife, F.N. (1979). Emphasizing teacher behavior as an educational tool. *AAHPER Research Consortium Symposium Papers* (Vol. 2, Book 1, pp. 75-80). Washington, DC: AAHPER.

Rife, F.N. & Dodds, P.S. (1978). Developing evidential bases for educational practice through the single-subject research paradigm. *Motor Skills: Theory into Practice, 3*(1), 40-48.

Rusch, D.B. & Ayllon, T. (1984). Peer behavioral coaching: Soccer. *Journal of Sport Psychology, 6,* 325-334.

Rushall, B.S. (1970). Some applications of psychology to swimming. *Swimming Technique, 7,* 71-82.

Rushall, B.S. (1972). Operant conditioning as a realistic method for physical education. *Canadian Association for Health, Physical Education, and Recreation Journal, March,* 31-33.

Rushall, B.S. (1975). Applied behavior analysis for sports and physical education. *International Journal of Sports Psychology, 6,* 75-88.

Rushall, B.S. (1976). A direction for contemporary sport psychology. *Canadian Journal of Applied Sport Sciences, 1,* 13-21.

Rushall, B.S. (1977a). The scope of psychological support services for Canadian Olympic athletes. *Canadian Journal of Applied Sport Sciences, 2,* 43-47.

Rushall, B.S. (1977b). Using applied behavior analysis for altering motivation. In V. Wilson (Ed.), *Proceedings of the Art and Science of Coaching Seminar.* Toronto: York University.

Rushall, B.S. (1977c). Two observation schedules for sporting and physical education environments. *Canadian Journal of Applied Sport Sciences, 2,* 15-21.

Rushall, B.S. (1979a). Observations of psychological support services for elite sport teams. In P. Klavora & J. Daniel (Eds.), *Coach, athlete and the sport psychologist.* Champaign, IL: Human Kinetics Publishers.

Rushall, B.S. (1979b). *Psyching in sports.* London, England: Pelham.

Rushall, B.S. (1981). Coaching styles: A preliminary investigation. *Behavior Analysis of Motor Activity, 1,* 3-19. Also reprinted in G. L. Martin & D. Hrycaiko (Eds.), *Behavior modification and coaching: Principles, procedures and research.* Springfield, IL: Charles C. Thomas.

Rushall, B.S. (1982, Sept. 23-26). Future directions for coaching elite athletes: Seven principles. A keynote address presented at the Psycholgoical Skills and Attributes in Sport Symposium, Winnipeg.

Rushall, B.S. (1984). The content of competition thinking. In W.F. Straub & J.M. Williams (Eds.), *Cognitive sport psychology* (pp. 51-62). Lansing, NY: Sport Science Associates.

Rushall, B.S. (1988). Covert modeling as a procedure for altering an elite athlete's psychological state. *The Sport Psychologist, 2,* 131-140.

Rushall, B.S. & Ford, D. (1982). Teaching backwards—an alternative skill instruction progression. *Canadian Association for Health, Physical Education and Recreation Journal, 48*(5), 16-20.

Rushall, B.S., Hall, M., Roux, L., Sasseville, J., & Rushall, A.C. (1988). Effects of three types of thought content instructions on skiing performance. *The Sport Psychologist, 2,* 283-297.

Rushall, B.S. & MacEachern, J.A. (1977). The effect of systematic behavioral feedback on teaching behaviors of student physical education teachers. *Canadian Journal of Applied Sport Sciences, 2,* 161-169.

Rushall, B.S. & Pettinger, J. (1969). An evaluation of the effects of various reinforcers used as motivators in swimming. *The Research Quarterly, 40*, 540-545.

Rushall, B.S. & Siedentop, D. (1972). *The development and control of behavior in sport and physical education.* Philadelphia: Lea & Febinger.

Rushall, B.S. & Smith, K.C. (1979). Coaching effectiveness of the quality and quantity of behavior categories in a swimming coach. *Journal of Sport Psychology, 1*, 138-150.

Shapiro, E.S. & Shapiro, S. (1985). Behavioral coaching and the development of skills in track. *Behavior Modification, 9*(2), 211-224.

Siedentop, D. (1972). Behavior analysis and teacher training. *Quest, 16*, 26-32.

Siedentop, D. (1973). How to use personalized systems of instruction in college teaching. *NCPEAM Proceedings, 77th Annual Meeting* (pp. 116-125). Kansas City, KS: NCPEAM.

Siedentop, D. (1976). *Developing teaching skills in physical education.* Boston: Houghton Mifflin Co.

Siedentop, D. (1980a). The Ohio State University behavior analysis research program in physical education and sport, 1973-1978. In P. Klavora & K. Whipper (Eds.), *Psychological and sociological factors in sport* (pp. 188-193). University of Toronto: Publications Division, School of Physical and Health Education.

Siedentop, D. (1980b). The management of practice behavior. In W.F. Straub (Ed.), *Sports psychology: An analysis of athletic behavior.* Ithica, NY: Mouvement Publications.

Siedentop, D. (1981). The Ohio State University's supervision research program: Summary report. *Journal of Teaching in Physical Education, 2*, 30-38.

Siedentop, D. (1982). Teaching research: The interventionist view. *Journal of Teaching in Physical Education, 2*, 46-50.

Siedentop, D. (1983a). *Developing teaching skills in physical education.* Palo Alto, CA: Mayfield Publishing Co.

Siedentop, D. (1983b). Recent advances in pedagogical research in physical education. *The Academy Papers* (pp. 82-94). Washington, DC: American Association of Health, Physical Education, and Dance.

Siedentop, D. (1989). The effective elementary specialist study [Monograph]. *Journal of Teaching in Physical Education, 8,* 187-270.

Siedentop, D. & Hughley, C. (1975). OSU teacher behavior rating scale. *Journal of Health, Physical Education and Recreation, 46,* 45.

Siedentop, D. & Rife, F.N. (1974). Developing a learning environment for badminton. *The Ohio High School Athlete, 33,* 17-19.

Siedentop, D. & Rushall, B.S. (1972). An operant model for skill acquisition. *Quest, 17,* 82-90.

Siedentop, D. & Taggart, A. (1984). Behavior analysis in physical education and sport. In W.L. Heward, T.E. Heron, D.S. Hill, & J. Trapp-Porter (Eds.), *Focus on behavior analysis in education.* Columbus, OH: Charles E. Merrill.

Siedentop, D. & Tousignant, M. (1982). *ALT-PE coding manual.* Columbus, OH: Ohio State University.

Simek, T.C., & O'Brien, R.M. (1978). Immediate auditory feedback to improve putting quickly. *Perceptual and Motor Skills, 47,* 1133-1134.

Simek, T.C. & O'Brien, R.M. (1981). *Total golf: A behavioral approach to lowering your score and getting more out of your game.* New York: Doubleday. (Now available from B-Mod Associates, Suite 109, 4230 West Hempstead Turnpike, Bethpage, NY 11714.)

Smith, R.E. & Johnson, J. (1990). An organizational empowerment approach to consultation in professional baseball. *The Sport Psychologist, 4,* 347-357.

Smith, R.E. & Smoll, F.L. (1991). Behavioral research and intervention in youth sports. *Behavior Therapy, 22,* 329-344.

Smith, R.W., Smoll, F.L., & Curtis, B. (1978). Coaching behaviors in Little League baseball. In F.L. Smoll & R.W. Smith (Eds.), *Psychological perspectives in youth sports.* Washington, DC: Hemisphere.

Smith, R.E., Smoll, F.L., & Curtis, B. (1979). Coaching effectiveness training: A cognitive behavioral approach to enhancing relationship skills in youth sport coaches. *Journal of Sport Psychology, 1,* 39-73.

Smith, R.E., Smoll, F.L., & Hunt, E. (1977). A system for the behavioral assessment of athletic coaches. *Research Quarterly, 48,* 401-407.

Smoll, F.L. & Smith, R.E. (1987). *Sport psychology for youth coaches: Personal growth to athletic excellence.* Washington, DC: National Federation for Catholic Youth Ministry.

Smoll, F.L., Smith, R.E., & Curtis, B. (1978). Behavioral guidelines for youth sport coaches. *Journal of Physical Education and Recreation, 49,* 46-47.

The Sport Psychologist. Special Theme Issue, December, 1989. Champaign, IL: Human Kinetics Publishers.

The Sport Psychologist. Special Theme Issue, December, 1990. Champaign, IL: Human Kinetics Publishers.

Taggart, A.C. (1988). The systematic development of teaching skills: A sequence of planned pedagogical experiences. *Journal of Teaching in Physical Education, 8,* 73-86.

Tousignant, M. (1983). PSI in PE - it works! *Journal of Physical Education, Recreation and Dance, 54*(7), 33-34.

Van Der Mars, H. (1987). Effects of audio cueing on teacher verbal praise of students' managerial and transitional task performances. *Journal of Teaching in Physical Education, 6,* 157-165.

Van Der Mars, H. (1988). The effects of audio cueing on selected teaching behaviors of an experienced elementary physical education specialist. *Journal of Teaching in Physical Education, 8,* 64-72.

Van Der Mars, H. (1989). Effects of specific verbal praise on off-task behavior of second-grade students in physical education. *Journal of Teaching in Physical Education, 8,* 162-169.

Vogler, E.W. & Bishop, P. (1990). Management of disruptive behavior in physical education. *The Physical Educator, 47,* 16-26.

Vogler, E.W. & French, R.W. (1983). The effects of a group contingency strategy on behaviorally disordered students in physical education. *Research Quarterly, 54*(3), 273-277.

Walley, P.B., Graham, G.M., & Forehand, R. (1982). Assessment and treatment of adult observer verbalizations at youth league baseball games. *Journal of Sport Psychology, 4,* 254-266.

Weinberg, R.S. (1982). The relationship between mental preparation strategies and motor performance: A review and critique. *Quest, 33*(2), 105-213.

Westcott, W. (1977). Teaching by example and increasing one's modeling influence. *Journal of Physical Education, 75,* 15.

Westcott, W. (1979). Physical educators and coaches as models of behavior. *Journal of Physical Education and Recreation, 50,* 31-32.

Westcott, W. (1980). Effects of teacher modeling on children's peer encouragement behavior. *Research Quarterly, 51*(3), 585-587.

Whelan, J.P., Mahoney, M.J., & Meyers, A.W. (1991). Performance enhancement in sport: A cognitive behavioral domain. *Behavior Therapy, 22,* 307-327.

Wilkinson, S. (1992). A training program for improving undergraduates' analytical skill in volleyball. *Journal of Teaching in Physical Education, 11,* 177-194.

Williams, D. & McKenzie, T.L. (1978). Student responses to machine-paced skills in physical education. *The Association of Health, Physical Education and Recreation Journal, Fall,* 10, 11, 60, 61.

Wilson, S., Buzzell, N., & Jensen, M. (1975). Observational research: A practical tool. *The Physical Educator, 32,* 90-93.

Wolko, K.L., Hrycaiko, D.W., & Martin, G.L. (in press). A comparison of two self-management packages to standard coaching for improving practice performance of gymnasts. *Behavior Modification.*

Wollman, N. (1986). Research on imagery and motor performance: Three methodological suggestions. *Journal of Sport Psychology, 8,* 135-138.

Young, R.M. (1973). The effects of various reinforcement contingencies on a second-grade physical education class. Unpublished doctoral dissertation, Ohio State University, Columbus, OH.

Yu, D. & Martin, G.L. (1987). Low-cost procedures to preserve a public sport environment. *Behavior Modification, 11*(2), 241-250.

Ziegler, S. (1980). Applied behavior analysis: From assessment to behavioral programming. In P. Klavora & K. Whipper (Eds.), *Psychological and sociological factors in sport* (pp. 204-214). University of Toronto: Publications Division, School of Physical and Health Recreation.

Ziegler, S.G. (1987). Effects of stimulus cueing on the acquisition of ground strokes by beginning tennis players. *Journal of Applied Behavior Analysis, 20,* 405-411.

PART THREE

Designs for Excellence:
Systematic Approaches

The Teacher as Strategic Scientist: A Solution to Our Educational Crisis?

R. Douglas Greer
Columbia University Teachers' College

*T*he solution to the educational dilemma is tied necessarily to the ability of teachers to ensure that their students achieve learning objectives that are germane to the survival of the culture and the species. The growing body of scientifically-based practices necessary to eliminate the existing educational crisis is briefly outlined. It is argued that these practices can be implemented by

Portions of this paper were presented at the XVIth Banff Conference on Behavior Modification in March of 1984. The conference and the paper were dedicated to B.F. Skinner. The current paper is also dedicated to B.F. Skinner, one of the few who recognized the critical role of education to the survival of the species and the one who has contributed most to a potential solution to our educational crisis. This paper is reprinted and adapted with permission. A version of this paper appeared in *Behavior and Social Issues*, Volume 1, Number 2 (1991), published by the Cambridge Center for Behavioral Studies, 11 Waterhouse Street, Cambridge, MA 02138. Permission to reproduce this paper must be obtained from the Cambridge Center for Behavioral Studies as well as Sopris West, Inc.

teachers who function as strategic scientists. The science used by such teachers includes research findings and teaching models incorporating that research (Precision Teaching, Direct Instruction, Programmed Instruction, Personalized System of Instruction). In order to train, support, and motivate the pervasive and sustained application of effective pedagogy by teachers who function as strategic scientists, behavior analysis must be applied to all components of schooling—students, parents, teachers, and supervisors. One model for doing so has developed over the last decade. Research studies and applications in six schools for disabled children in this country and abroad suggest that this comprehensive application of behavior analysis to schooling (CABAS) is effective, efficient, and viable.

ะ๑

The Educational Crisis

The greatest experiment in education in the history of the world, that of free and available public schooling, has failed to realize its potential (C. Greer, 1972).[1] Does this mean that the country that launched the experiment is in peril? The figures on crime in schools, the exodus of the middle class from public schools, and the ineptness of graduates to meet the requirements of employers are alarming signs of a national crisis. Moreover, our inability to compensate for abuses to minorities by providing them with adequate skills with which they can command the respect of the marketplace suggests that schools may even exacerbate the dilemma. Students in the U.S. have performed dismally when compared with students from similar industrial nations for the last six years (Hitchens, 1990). Today's children of even well-to-do parents will have to compete with the better educated child in Osaka, not the child from schools in the ghetto. Even more importantly, will the children of today be able to cooperate in intelligent ways as adults so that the species will survive (Skinner, 1984)?

The key to adequate schooling (a prerequisite to excellence) is the teacher. Teachers have more responsibility for the futures of children than any other professionals. School-age children spend the major portion of

---

1 Collin Greer (1972) documents the ineffectiveness of the New York City schools of the past in acculturating the waves of emigrants to the U.S. In fact, he presents convincing evidence that the schools actually functioned to thwart upward mobility. Rather than educating, the schools functioned to select out students.

their day with teachers. Only parents have a greater role and, increasingly, teachers spend more waking hours with children than do many parents. Despite the responsibility and opportunity, teaching as a profession has never had the *power* (defined as tools and science) to realize its charge to educate.[2] American education is a process of selection, not of education (Keller, 1978).

Everyone, from presidential commissions to leaders of teachers unions (Shanker, 1984), has noted with increasing urgency that there is a crisis. There have been attempts to meet the crisis by well-intentioned governmental agencies, universities, and foundations. Proposals for solutions have included increased teachers' pay, stronger liberal arts backgrounds for those entering the profession, voucher systems, and more stringent graduation requirements. Unfortunately, all of these potentially useful approaches simply increase the responsibility of the teacher without increasing the ability and power of teachers to teach. Some educators have defended the current teaching practices by asserting that schools are but a reflection of society and until society is fixed, schools will remain unchanged (Cremin, 1982). One wonders how society is to be salvaged if a unit as small as a school is beyond reach.

The necessary component for any solution is the practice of an effective pedagogy by teachers. None of the reform efforts deal with pedagogy; it is as if . . . "pedagogy is a dirty word" (Skinner, 1984). It is commonly assumed that the medical crisis created by AIDS will be laid to rest only when a scientific solution is found. It is no less true for education. The key to the educational dilemma is to apply the existing science of teaching or pedagogy and expand that science throughout America's school systems.

---

2 The term *power* is used here in the sense of shared, recognized tools for teaching based on a science. In the engineering of computers, the development and *widespread* use of the chip is an analogous example of the professional power of engineers to produce computers capable of certain functions. The invention and use of the wheel is another example. The presence of the wheel provided the species with the power to transport goods at previously impossible levels. The problems of education have been in place for centuries. The fact that there are now tools is understandably perplexing to those who do not know about them.

❧

Pedagogy: What Science Exists?

The problem is indeed one of a science and technology of teaching (R.D. Greer, 1983). The pedagogical practices that are widely used are inadequate for the responsibility given teachers for improving the prognosis for our culture.

Some presume that inadequate teaching can be rectified with the introduction of more sophisticated hardware. However, equipment such as the overhead projector, the VCR, or the computer can help only if there is a better science and technology of pedagogy. Sophisticated electronic devices will compound the problem by magnifying the application of inadequate teaching practices.

Even educational researchers bemoan what they presume is the lack of a science of pedagogy (Brophy, 1983). Schools of education have been blamed for this inadequacy, but in reality, schools of education have obtained their research tools from other parts of the university, particularly from psychology and the other social sciences. Only one small branch of psychology has provided a science and technology, and that branch, behaviorology, is a small minority with little political clout (R.D. Greer, 1983). Thus the science is known by only a few educators.

The scientific practices adopted by most educational researchers were ones based on actuarial statistical assumptions and a hypothetico-deductive epistemology anchored to a mind/body dualism (Zuriff, 1986). Psychology has offered theories of development based on age and performance correlations (still another way to select earlier on), theories of personality, theories of learning, theories of memory (but is memory the problem?), psychodynamics, and other byproducts of environment/behavior interactions that tell us little about how to teach more and faster. Remunerative tests for traits or hypothetical constructs have proliferated, and while they may tell us about the distribution of such traits and hypothetical constructs, they are useless to pedagogy. In fact, they impede. For example, one supposedly new notion asserts that children have multiple intelligences (Gardner, 1990). Such a notion is strongly reminiscent of trait psychology of the early twentieth century and serves as another example of an explanatory fiction that makes the objectives of instruction even more inaccessible,[3] thereby providing a new rationalization for inadequate instruction.

Using tools from psychology, educational researchers set out to determine what *existing* educational practices were most useful. They assessed team teaching, audiovisual aids, counseling and other support services, the salary of teachers, child-centered (explore and discover) versus teacher-oriented (authoritarian) strategies, conceptual questioning versus drill, problem-solving approaches, money spent per pupil, and warmth of the teacher. The answers were overwhelmingly equivocal (Stephens, 1967) because the tools used were the wrong ones to use and because the questions asked were the wrong ones to ask.

Inadequate Methodology

The statistically-based assumptions underlying group comparison research will continually produce norm-shaped curves with the same distribution of problems. If one pretests, exposes groups to comparative procedures for a fixed period of time, and posttests, at best, the mean for one group may be higher but the distribution will remain the same.[4] The variability will remain, even for the best procedure. A methodology is needed that will apply scientific procedures to the individual. Such scientific procedures predate Mendelian and Gaussian statistical approaches. They are found in the natural sciences (Johnston & Pennypacker, 1980; Mach, 1960; Sidman, 1960). In such approaches, procedures that are effective in individual cases are replicated across individuals until principles of behavior are inductively obtained. The variability between individuals becomes the source for future research rather than a residual artifact to be averaged out. The phylogenetic and ontogenetic differences should contribute to different instructional procedures, not selection. The principal differences in the methodologies is tied, however, to the questions asked. Rather than asking what are the comparative effects of traditional approaches to teach-

3 Whether there are multiple or single intelligences clouds the real issue. Of what benefit is an IQ test with regard to education? The real problems reside in epistemological assumptions about behavior that predate a science of behavior.

4 Certainly the field of statistics has been an important tool in the advancement of some scientific practices. We can predict elections, the spread of epidemics, and the probability of consumer satisfaction. Indeed, there are numerous uses for statistics in education; however, research in pedagogy is currently a field in which the wholesale application of statistics is unwarranted (R.D. Greer, 1983).

ing in traditional settings, a science of pedagogy must ask: What does the teacher need to do to produce mastery and fluency for *each student?*

⁊⦁

The Right Question and Adequate Methodology

Teachers require pedagogical tools commensurate with their responsibility—ones that are powerful enough to teach all children until they have fluent mastery of repertoires needed for their well-being and that of society. The variability in the effectiveness of the procedures must not be allowed to spread across the population in a bell-shaped curve, allowing some to exceed the mean, most to perform at mediocre levels, and some to fail. Rather, the variability should lie in the spread required by students to achieve mastery (e.g., number of instructional trials/opportunities). The quests of effective teaching and an effective instructional science are the same. Increase the number of instructional opportunities and decrease or eliminate errors for each individual. Bit by bit the inductive procedure will lead to accrual of more powerful principles and tactics.

However, asking the old questions and using the group methodology, educational researchers had by the end of the eighties found one useful fact. Students in classrooms who were taught by teachers who induced their children to be more task-engaged were more successful. Also, those teachers had their students respond often. They measured the accuracy of student responses frequently and directly (Stallings, 1980). Yet this research effort had not produced a literature on what pedagogy teachers had used to produce more engaged students (Brophy, 1983). It is ironical that at the same time a set of sophisticated scientific principles, tactics, and methodologies were developed (in another literature) that prescribed effective pedagogical practices. Moreover, the literature of this scientific approach specified better measures—measures of absolute units such as correct responses of behaviors taught at the time taught. These measures were in contrast to projective tests of achievement done after the fact (posttest with standardized test) or task engagement.

The best and hardest measures of instruction are mastery and fluency of the responses needed for the specific setting and problem encountered by the student. "Retention" must be measured similarly. And if the instruction is adequate and the environment and setting event are the same, the student will respond similarly. Pedagogical questions about maintenance and generalization involve searches for differences and similarities in controlling stimuli, not individuals. The literature of behavior analysis and its related epistemology has supplied a basic technology of pedagogy and, more importantly, a means to an even more powerful science and technology of pedagogy (R.D. Greer, 1983).

ᶻᵃ

Spread of a Science of Pedagogy

There is evidence that many substansive findings from the science of behavior are entering gradually into the educational literature, if not into wide-spread schooling practices. These findings include emphasis on (1) presentation of frequent opportunities to respond and tactics such as tutoring to ensure more opportunities (Greenwood, Delquadri, & Hall, 1984), (2) increased student responding, and (3) direct measurement of student responding. Still, much of the literature asks the wrong questions (e.g., student cognitive styles based on theories of cognition) and relies on hypothetico-deductive scientific procedures.

A science of behavior continues to develop even though practiced by a minority. The pioneers (Keller, 1968; Skinner, 1968) continue to call out for its acceptance (Keller, 1978; Skinner, 1984) along with their fellow scientist-practitioners (Barrett, 1987). The existence and parameters of that effort have been defended and described elsewhere (R.D. Greer, 1983; R.D. Greer, 1989). The lessons that behavior analysis offers provide the basis for effective schooling. Schools can be developed in which children learn. The model of pedagogy that is needed is one that casts the teacher in the role of a strategic scientist of instruction. This will require revolution in the way teachers work and the way in which they are supported.

ᶻᵃ

Teacher as Strategic Scientist

The teacher who applies the existing science of teaching behaves more as an applied scientist than as a traditional teacher. The principles of behavior derived from the basic science and its evolving status with issues such as stimulus equivalence, the matching law, response deprivation, and establishing operations are the cutting edge of effective practice. Tactics drawn from 25 years of applied behavior analysis are integral components of the practice of the effective teacher. Tactics and strategies from Precision Teaching (Lindsley, 1990), Direct Instruction (Engelmann & Carmine, 1982), Personalized System of Instruction (Keller, 1968), and potentially programmed instruction (Skinner, 1968) are also substantive components of the science of teaching.

The teachers who can solve the educational crisis are strategic scientists of the behavior of their students. The requisite skills of the teacher/scientist may be categorized into three repertoires, each with multiple levels of skill attainment. These three repertoires are: (1) contingency-shaped behaviors of teaching, (2) verbal behavior about the science, and (3) verbally-mediated behaviors of teaching.

ï&

Contingency-shaped Teaching

Many if not all teaching repertoires are shaped directly by the contingencies of the classroom. Teachers have learned to "manage" group instruction based on acquiring classroom survival skills. These contingency-shaped repertoires have been acquired, unfortunately, in the existing school wherein the model is badly designed and does not lead to mastery and fluency by each individual student. Fortunately, special education has changed the old model by drawing on behavior analysis in responding to a law which requires individualized education plans for all students enrolled in special education. Moreover, the requirement that these individualized plans be accountable paved the way for data-based instruction. These requirements changed the contingencies of the classroom for the special education teacher. Each individual student's behavior became a controlling variable for the behavior of the teacher. The demand set the stage for effective instructional procedures.

The contingency-shaped behaviors of the teacher operating in an appropriately designed special education classroom that is devoted to the individual student include: (1) designing instructional objectives based on direct assessments of deficits in all learning domains, (2) designing instructional methodology with scripted teacher procedures, (3) measuring directly the responses of students to instructional presentations, (4) consequating student responses to all instruction in a manner that increases correct responses while decreasing incorrect responses, and (5) increasing productivity (more three-term-contingency trials) and increasing quality (more correct responses and fewer incorrect responses in less time).

A teacher trained and functioning in a well-designed classroom manages to collect reliable data, consequate incorrect responses appropriately, reinforce correct responses, use multiple negative exemplars when necessary, use stimulus and response delays as needed, use peer models effectively, devise establishing operations, and manage individualized instruction continuously based on graphs of student behaviors (Sulzer-Azaroff & Mayer, 1986). Appropriate contingency-shaped behaviors for teachers, however, can develop only in well-designed and properly supervised classrooms. Otherwise, punitive and ineffective procedures will prevail as they have in the past (Skinner, 1968), and teachers will measure sporadically using inadequate and inappropriate measures. Thus, good contingency-shaped teaching skills can be acquired most efficiently only in a classroom designed to reflect the science of behavior.

ะ๑

Verbal Behavior About the Science

Verbal behavior about the science is initially a separate repertoire for the teacher. Like most behavior, verbal behavior is independent of contingency-shaped behavior until the verbal behavior comes to function as accurate tacts of classroom events.[5] Even independently, it is an important repertoire. Teachers who are practicing scientists are called on to defend what they do. They must write and present vocally the basic tenets of the science with reference to their own practices. All verbal behavior about the science used on the job takes the form of speaker-writer behavior, not listener behavior (i.e., multiple choice questions) (Skinner, 1957). Hence, all examinations used to train teachers about the science should be essay exams or brief sophisticated recitations.

5 The term *tact* is from Skinner's *Verbal Behavior* (1957). It denotes verbal behavior that contacts the nonverbal environment. It is under the control of nonverbal antecedents, certain establishing operations, and generalized reinforcers. In science the use of tacts (e.g., mammals, chemical compounds, behavioral principles) occurs when the phenomenon is verbally identified without verbal antecedents.

As the teacher acquires verbal behaviors about the science simultaneously with the acquisition of contingency-shaped teaching behavior in the classroom, the verbal behaviors make contact with classroom practices and come to tact (Skinner, 1957) instructional repertoires. These two repertoires converge into verbally-mediated teaching repertoires.[6]

ৰ৶

Verbally-mediated Teaching Repertoires

This third repertoire (initially termed rule-governed behavior by Skinner, 1957, and renamed by Vargas, 1988) is crucial, and is based on the accumulated responses derived from the contingency-shaped and verbally-mediated responses. Note that the term "creative teaching" is missing from the discussion. Yet all of the benefits for children of such teachers occur with teachers trained in verbally-mediated repertoires. Moreover, the procedures are operational. One can replicate them and teach them to novice teachers.

Teachers with verbally-mediated repertoires of the science learn to deal with plateaus of student responding by drawing on visual inspections of their students' data, the literature of the basic science, the literature of applied practices, and their own contingency-shaped behavior. Such teachers can deduct from strategies and tactics to individual cases, and induct from individual cases to general strategies and tactics. Tactics consist of findings from the applied science while strategies consist of the principles of behavior and their related epistemology. Inadequate stimulus presentations, response prompts, teacher consequences, and inappropriate controlling variables are replaced with adequate antecedents, responses, and consequences (Selinske, Greer, & Lodhi 1991).

---

6 Verbally-mediated repertoires encompass acts of viewing data (antecedent) and locating sources that serve to verbally direct the application of scientifically-based procedures to the teaching of a student, which in turn results in the desired behavior change for the student. In addition, tacts of processes in operations result in application of verbal summaries of the science (principles and tactics) to still other scientific applications.

꒰꒱

Levels of Pedagogical Expertise

Each of these repertoires involve several levels of expertise. One level of expertise consists simply of keeping all students engaged at individual tasks and occasionally at group tasks. At this level, the teacher learns instructional control over his or her students through contingency-shaped, verbal, and verbally-mediated behaviors that use, describe, and design practices from the science. A more advanced level involves increasing response opportunities, lowering incorrect responses while increasing correct responses, and increasing the effectiveness of teaching assistants. Still more advanced levels include applying new findings of the science to intractable student behaviors or deficits and developing new tactics based on strategies. At the most advanced levels, student environment/behavior relations are analyzed quickly and effective procedures introduced for other teachers who are at less advanced levels of expertise. The subcomponents of this repertoire are described in the following sections.

꒰꒱

Subcomponents of Teaching Repertoires

Each of the three generic repertoires of effective teaching are tied to basic practices from the science of behavior. The prominent subcomponents are: (1) measurement, (2) evaluation of stimulus control (research design), (3) analyzing and acting on the data, (4) use of the existing substantive findings and packaged models, (5) reliance on a thoroughgoing behavioral epistemology (Zuriff, 1986), and (6) application of logical and behavior analytic principles to the identification of curricular goals and their subobjectives.

Measurement

Measurement must be direct, quantified in absolute units, product-rather than process-oriented, and continuous. These characteristics of the science prescribe the criteria for the measurement of pedagogical efforts. They were characteristics of the evolution of the bench science (Skinner, 1938) and the first applications forged by Lindsley (1990). Schooling must be designed such that measurement that meets these criteria is the central thread that runs through all aspects of instruction. Even the existing body of practices found to be effective requires individually-tailored applications that are possible only through pervasive individualized measurement.

Design

Similarly, the application of existing procedures and the development of new ones require the application of Method of Disagreement (Mill, 1950) or experimentation at the individual level. Practices developed in the natural sciences and behavior analysis are feasibly incorporated into classrooms with an adequate database.

Applications

The research literature provides tactics and include applications for reading (Lindsley, 1990; Sidman & Wilson-Morris, 1974; Trovato & Bucher, 1980), mathematics (Ferritor, Buckholdt, Hamblin, & Smith, 1972; Lovitt & Curtiss, 1968), spelling (Ollendick, Matson, Esveldt-Dawson, & Shapiro, 1980), physical fitness and sports (Koop & Martin, 1983), speech training (R.J. Ingham, 1984), language acquisition (Hart & Risely, 1974, 1980), writing (Guess, Sailor, Rutherford, & Baer, 1968), language structure (Steinam, 1977; Whitehurst & Vasta, 1975), the development of verbal behavior (Lodhi & Greer, 1989; Simic & Bucher, 1980), and even the development of musical skills and aesthetics (R.D. Greer, 1980). In each of these experiments and numerous others (Sulzer-Azaroff & Mayer, 1986), there are models of effective measurement tactics wedded to effective pedagogical practices.

Data Analysis

The strategies and tactics governing how teachers make instructional decisions derived from the data and scientific manipulation of pedagogical practices are critical. Is the student's progress adequate or optimal? Does the instruction need to be changed and what are the tested instructional tactics appropriate for the student? What tactics of evaluation need to be used to tease out the controlling variables (Johnston & Pennypacker, 1980)? Should the data be collapsed, blocked, or broken down into minute intrasession analyses? Is there cyclical variability? What are the stimulus controls and are they being transferred appropriately? These and other critical decisions require a sophisticated application of the science by the teacher.

Epistemology

When the need arises for procedures not found in the existing substantive findings, the philosophy of the science of behavior offers directions (Skinner, 1974). These guidelines are succinctly prescribed in Precision Teaching (Lindsley, 1990) and compared with procedures that are unsuccessful by Zuriff (1986) and R.D. Greer (1983). These prescriptions provide the direction for the teacher functioning as strategic scientist.

Curriculum

Engelmann and Carnine (1982) provide logical tools for analyzing curricular goals and their components. Similarly, programmed instruction provides guidelines for shaping stimulus control (Skinner, 1968). However, there is still a need for task analyses of repertoires that are critical to the performance of students in the work force and the culture. What are the real repertoires of scientists, musicians, social workers, mechanics, chefs, and parents? While philosophy may suggest logical goals, a behavior analysis of the true repertoires may provide more precise objectives.

Many behavior analysts who have been concerned with education have erred on one important issue (R.D. Greer & Dorow, 1976). That is, the assumption was often made that all that behavior analysts needed to do was provide a science and the tactics for training target behaviors (pedagogy). Society and specifically educators were believed to possess a ready set of clearly defined goals to be achieved. This was just not so. The ultimate goals need to be analyzed and determined by tools of behavior analysis as well as logic. The advantage of the logically analyzed, scripted curriculum from Direct Instruction is clear. Similarly, without the functional perspective of verbal behavior (Skinner, 1957), the goals of language instruction will be left to the structural perspective of linguists only. Behavior analytic strategies for determining curriculum and what students and society should do must be developed much more extensively than they have been in the past. Strategies and tactics for determining goals of instruction are embryonic yet are needed to revolutionize instructional presentations. A critical step concerns the identification of curricular goals. Goals need not be derived necessarily only through authoritative consensus; the science of behavior provides tools to identify essential goals. Such goals need to produce not only individuals with employable skills, but citizens who can protect and draw from a democracy in a manner that functions for the well-being of the culture and the individual. Individuals must also have repertoires for consumption of the heritage of the culture as well as its protection (Hitchens, 1990).

^{ta.}

Teacher Packages

The science has provided some basic models and packages of instruction that increase the probability that contingency analysis will control teacher intervention. These include Direct Instruction (Becker, 1977; Becker & Carnine, 1981), Personalized System of Instruction (Sherman, Raskin, & Semb, 1982), the consulting behavior analyst model from Kansas (Greenwood et al., 1984), and the Precision Teaching Model (Lindsley, 1990). The Follow Through Project report provides not only evidence for the success of some of the behavioral models, despite the long controversy, but descriptions of the inadequacy of opposing views (Engelmann & Carnine, 1982).

^{ta.}

Comprehensive Application of Behavior Analysis to Schooling (CABAS)

What has been missing is a systemic comprehensive application of behavior analysis to schooling, one that incorporates the teaching packages and individual studies, and one that applies behavior analysis to all components of schooling—students, teachers, supervisors, and their interactions. Such an approach simultaneously provides an appropriate setting for training and studying teachers and supervisors as strategic scientists while providing a continuous modification of the schooling system based on the flow of data.

Teachers learn their real teaching repertoires, whether poor or competent, in the environment in which the repertoires are used. As long as the schooling system is inadequate, only inadequate repertoires will prevail. However, a model for adequate schooling has developed with little fanfare, and no grant money, and has been replicated on a small scale. The proposal advocated in this paper is no longer an inference from the research but a functional schooling model.

ఌ

CABAS Model and Research

Over the last decade, a model of schooling has provided small system-wide settings for the comprehensive application of behavior analysis to the schooling effort. The model, CABAS (R.D. Greer, 1989), is comprehensive in several ways. First, CABAS is comprehensive in that behavior analytic strategies and tactics are applied to all parties involved in the school process—students, teachers, supervisors, and parents. Second, it is comprehensive in that the substantive findings from individual studies in the literature and packages using the principles of the science (Precision Teaching, PSI, Programmed Instruction, Direct Instruction) (Engelmann & Carnine, 1982; Keller, 1968; Lindsley, 1990; Skinner, 1968; Sulzer-Azaroff, Drabman, Greer, Hall, Iwata, & O'Leary, 1988) are incorporated. Third, the measurement of student, teacher, and supervisor responses occurs on a continuous basis. The model measures the behaviors of the teachers and supervisors as well as of the students. A cybernetic system based on a thoroughgoing operant paradigm evolved within the constraints and opportunities engendered in the daily operation of the schools.

The effectiveness of the total package and the role of several components have been investigated. Greer, McCorkle, and Williams (1989) found correlations between certain student, teacher, and supervisor behaviors in a CABAS school. This analysis represented the most extensive test known to the author of relationships between students, teachers, and supervisors that showed concomitant variance between specific supervisor, teacher, and student behaviors in a functioning school across an entire year. Although the relationships found were only correlational, the control of procedures, the extent of reliable measurement of absolute units, and the completeness of the analysis were unique. Furthermore, Babbitt (1986) found a functional relationship between specific supervisor and teacher behavior and, in turn, student responses. That is, increased numbers of supervisor observations resulted in greater teacher effectiveness, reflected in greater numbers of correct responses by students and increased opportunities to respond.

Ingham and Greer (in press) found that the use of the specific observation procedures of teachers used in the CABAS model by supervisors resulted in educationally significant increases in accurate teacher presentations, student responding, and correct student responses. No other CABAS procedures were used with these teachers, suggesting that the observation procedures alone can be beneficial. The changes occurred without the use of workshops, and through training in the classroom simply with the use of the Teacher Performance Rate/Accuracy Observation procedure (which is discussed in greater detail below). Thus, this component was cost effective.

Selinske, Greer, and Lodhi (1991) studied the effect of the application of the entire CABAS package. The study involved all of the parties in a small school for children with multiple disabilities across a three-year period. The results showed functional relationships between the package and students' correct responses, teacher presentations, and objectives achieved. The data from the year following the experiment showed maintenance of the effects. These results were replicated recently in an Italian school for disabled children (Lamm & Greer, 1991). Lamm and Greer also compared the first year of data in the Italian program with the first year of data in four American CABAS schools. The data were comparable.

The CABAS model emphasizes high rates of presentation of three-term contingency trials. The term "trial" is not used in the traditional meaning associated with maze trials or medical/clinical trials. Rather they (three-term contingency trials or learn units) involve all instruction in which a student contacts an antecedent stimulus that is under teacher control, actively responds, and receives a corrective or reinforcing consequence from a teacher, tutor, or an automated device. In the CABAS model these are referred to as learn units. The learn units may occur in massed, discrete, programmed, or incidental forms. They include free operant as well as controlled presentations. These learn units are measured continuously in all five CABAS schools at the level of student, teacher (all students), supervisor (groups of teachers), and the total school. Learn units are graphed as total opportunities and correct responses in allotted time, with the visual difference representing incorrect responses, or they are displayed as rate per minute correct or incorrect. These data show the determination of average (mean) latency per pupil between instructional opportunities and mean latency between correct responses. When used in conjunction with the systematic assessment of target and standardized learning objectives, the latency measure provides a prediction of instructional effectiveness. While standardized tests of pupil achievement may show correlations with instructional effectiveness, they provide at best only indirect measures. They can be useful as calibration indices for daily instruction at the school and teacher level, but only if the questions on the standardized test have validity for the goals of the classroom or the needs of society.

Teacher behavior is measured in terms of student responses to learn units in a teacher's class and teacher performance on frequent observations of student/teacher interaction using the Teacher Performance Rate/Accuracy Observation procedure (Ingham & Greer, in press). Supervisor task accomplishment is measured by having supervisors log their accomplishments that are related potentially to student care or behavior change. The accomplishment of some of these tasks was found to be related to student behavior change and teacher behavior change in five research studies (Babbitt, 1986; Greer, McCorkle, & Williams, 1989; Ingham & Greer, in press; Lamm & Greer, 1991; Selinske, et al., 1991). Although it is not known whether all supervisor tasks are related to student performance, the teacher observation procedure has been directly or indirectly related to all of the studies.

In addition to an individualized and scripted curriculum for the students, each teacher receives an ongoing individualized instructional program devoted to acquiring or improving skills in applications of behavior analysis. Each module of instruction includes readings and exercises which increases the teacher's sophistication with (1) contingency-shaped teaching behavior, (2) verbal behavior about the science, and (3) verbally-mediated behavior. These repertoires were defined and described earlier. The repertoires are taught to mastery and fluency through PSI procedures. Completion of clusters of modules lead to promotions and increases in salary.

While the relationships of these teacher training procedures have not been tested experimentally in all cases, the importance of continuous visual displays of each teacher's performance has been found to increase teacher productivity (more learn units) and teacher quality (more student correct responses and fewer student incorrect responses per minute). Dorow, McCorkle, and Greer (1989) found that setting teacher criteria for CABAS units individually and at successively higher levels of productivity resulted in increases in productivity and correspondingly higher correct responses without increasing incorrect responses.

The CABAS package has been successfully implemented in one school for ten years, demonstrating that the behavior analytic school can be operated day in and day out (R.D. Greer, et al., 1989). This particular school is a residential school for severely disabled children with severe behavior problems. None of the children or adolescents in the program receive psychotropic drugs. The most common behavior reduction procedures are nonsecluded time out from reinforcement, response cost, DRI, DRO, and in a few cases, overcorrection. More importantly, instruction is frequent and always directly measured. In another school for behaviorally disordered preschoolers, the primary behavior reduction procedure is time out in a chair (5 to 20 seconds) in the child's classroom. Most of these children are reading before they attend kindergarten. Teacher disapproval occurs infrequently and positive reinforcement occurs continuously even in those classrooms for children with very problematic behaviors. Consequently the children enjoy school and learn. Many of the procedures in the CABAS model need additional study, particularly with other school populations. However, the strategy of applying behavior analysis to teachers and supervisors as well as students is key to more effective schooling.

ঽৄ

Conclusion

While the development of teachers as strategic scientists will not be sufficient alone to eliminate all of the problems plaguing our schools, the development of schools with such teachers is a necessary step. The development of teachers as strategic scientists in schools for nondisabled children will require more research, wider applications, and continuous modification.[7] Even with the problems facing the spread of effective teaching, the fact that such a sophisticated model has been developed, improved, and

---

7 The notion of the teacher as researcher was promulgated by Vance Hall in the first issue of the *Journal of Applied Behavior Analysis* in a research paper by the same name. The notion of the school as a center of inquiry came from Robert Shaeffer in a book by that name. Both of these influences affected the conception of the teacher as strategic scientist. However, Skinner's *Behavior of Organisms* (1938), Sidman's *Tactics of Science* (1960), Johnston and Pennypacker's *Strategies and Tactics of Human Behavioral Research* (1980), and the influence of presentations by Ogden Lindsley were also critical. In addition, the data generated in the CABAS schools—consisting of millions of recorded responses of teachers, supervisors, students, and parents—shaped the profile of the teacher as strategic scientist.

maintained against seemingly overwhelming odds holds promise. It can be argued that the problems in schools for the disabled are significantly more difficult (or at least no more difficult) than those encountered in even the worst of schools for nondisabled children. There are no alternatives on the horizon that have not been shown wanting. There are signs that many critical social issues can be solved only by the development of effective schooling for all children. Model schools have been developed that demonstrate that a science of the behavior of schooling is feasible, effective, and sustainable. The evidence and the dilemma warrant more comprehensive applications of behavior analysis to schooling. The development of teachers who are strategic scientists of pedagogy is a necessary step to the solution of the educational crisis. Such teachers will need to be trained and supported in schools committed to pervasive applications of behavior analysis to all components of education.

References

Babbit R.L. (1986). Computerized data management and the time distribution and rate of tasks performed by supervisors in a data-based educational organization. *Dissertation Abstracts International, 47,* 3737a.

Barrett, B. (1987). Excerpt from the August 1987 Report to Council of the Right to Effective Education Task Force. *The Behavioral Educator, 4,* 9-10.

Becker, W.C. (1977). Teaching reading and language to the disadvantaged. *Harvard Educational Review, 47,* 518-543.

Becker, W.C. & Carnine, D.W. (1981). Direct instruction: A behavior therapy model for comprehensive educational intervention with the disadvantaged. In S.W. Bijou & R. Ruiz, *Behavior modification: Contributions to Education* (pp. 146-207). Hillsdale, NJ: Lawrence Erlbaum.

Brophy, J.E. (1983). If only it were true: A response to Greer. *Educational Researcher, 12,* 10-13.

Cremin, L.S. (1982). *Teachers' College in the 1980s and 1990s.* New York: Teachers' College, Columbia University.

Dorow, L.G., McCorkle, N., & Greer, R.D. (1989). *Setting teacher performance criteria to increase teacher productivity.* Paper presented at the annual meeting of the Association for Behavior Analysis, Philadelphia, PA.

Engelmann, S. & Carnine, D.W. (1982). *Theory of instruction: Principles and applications.* New York: Irvington.

Ferritor, D.E., Buckholdt, D., Hamblin, R.L., & Smith, L. (1972). The noneffects of contingent reinforcement for attending behavior on work accomplished. *Journal of Applied Behavior Analysis, 5,* 299-310.

Gardner, H. (1990, April 29). New views on human intelligence. *New York Times Magazine,* 16-27, 30.

Greenwood, C.R., Delquadri, J., & Hall, R.V. (1984). Opportunity to respond and student academic performance. In W. Heward, T. Heron, D. Hill, & J. Trap-Porter (Eds.), *Behavior analysis in education* (pp. 58-88). Columbus, OH: Charles E. Merrill.

Greer, C. (1972). *The great school legend: A revisionist interpretation of American public education.* New York: Basic Books.

Greer, R.D. (1980). *Design for music learning.* New York: Teachers' College Press.

Greer, R.D. (1983). Contingencies of the science and technology of teaching and pre-behavioristic research practices in education. *Educational Researcher, 12,* 3-14.

Greer, R.D. (1989). A pedagogy for survival. In A. Brownstein (Ed.), *Progress in behavioral sciences* (pp. 7-44). Hillsdale, NJ: Lawrence Erlbaum.

Greer, R.D. & Dorow, L.G. (1976). *Specializing education.* Dubuque, IA: Kendall Hunt.

Greer, R.D., McCorkle, N., & Williams, G. (1989). A sustained analysis of the behaviors of schooling. *Behavioral Residential Treatment, 4,* 113-141.

Guess, D., Sailor, W., Rutherford, G., & Baer, D.M. (1968). An experimental analysis of linguistic development: The productive use of the plural morpheme. *Journal of Applied Behavior Analysis, 1,* 297-306.

Hart, B. & Risely, T.R (1974). Using preschool materials to modify the language of disadvantaged children. *Journal of Applied Behavior Analysis, 7,* 243-256.

Hart, B. & Risely, T.R. (1980). In vivo language intervention: Unanticipated general effects. *Journal of Applied Behavior Analysis, 13,* 407-432.

Hitchens, C. (1990, May 13). Why we don't know what we don't know. *New York Times Magazine, 32,* 59-62.

Ingham, M. & Greer R.D. (in press). Function relationships between supervisors' observation of teachers and generalization to unobserved settings. *Journal of Applied Behavior Analysis.*

Ingham, R.J. (1984). *Stuttering and behavior therapy.* San Diego, CA: College Hill Press.

Johnston, J.M. & Pennypacker, H.S. (1980). *Strategies and tactics of human behavioral research.* Hillsdale, NJ: Lawrence Erlbaum.

Keller, F.S. (1968). "Goodby, teacher...". *Journal of Applied Behavior Analysis, 1,* 79-89.

Keller, F.S. (1978). Instructional technology and educational reform: 1977. *The Behavior Analyst, 1,* 48-53.

Koop, S. & Martin, G.L. (1983). Evaluation of a coaching strategy to reduce swimming stroke errors with beginning age-group swimmers. *Journal of Applied Behavior Analysis, 16,* 447-460.

Lamm, N. & Greer, R.D. (1991). CABAS at OASI: An international replication and comparative analysis. *Journal of Behavioral Education, 1,* 427-444.

Lindsley, O.R. (1990). Precision teaching: By teachers for children. *Teaching Exceptional Children, 22,* 10-15.

Lodhi, S. & Greer, R.D. (1989). The speaker as listener. *Journal of the Experimental Analysis of Behavior, 51,* 353-359.

Lovitt, T.C. & Curtiss, K.A. (1968). Effects of manipulating an antecedent event on mathematics response rate. *Journal of Applied Behavior Analysis, 1,* 329-334.

Mach, E. (1960). *The science of mechanics* (T.J. McCormack, Trans.). Lasalle, IL: Open Court.

Mill, J.S. (1950). A system of logic. In E. Wagel (Ed.), *John Stuart Mill's philosophy of scientific method* (pp. 20-105). New York: Harper.

Ollendick, T.H., Matson, J.L., Esveldt-Dawson, K., & Shapiro, E.S. (1980). Increasing spelling achievement: An analysis of treatment procedures utilizing an alternating treatments design. *Journal of Applied Behavior Analysis, 13,* 645-654.

Selinske, J., Greer, R.D., & Lodhi, S. (1991). A functional analysis of the comprehensive application of behavior analysis to schooling. *Journal of Applied Behavior Analysis, 24,* 220-249.

Shanker, A.T. (1984, March 4). *New York Times*, p. C5.

Sherman, J.G., Raskin, R.S., & Semb, G.B. (1982). *The personalized system of instruction: 48 seminal papers.* Lawrence, KS: TRI.

Sidman, M. (1960). *Tactics of scientific research.* New York: Basic Books.

Sidman, M. & Willson-Morris, M. (1974). Testing for reading comprehension: A brief report on stimulus control. *Journal of Applied Behavior Analysis, 7,* 327-332.

Simic, J. & Bucher, B. (1980). Development of spontaneous manding in language deficient children. *Journal of Applied Behavior Analysis, 13,* 523-528.

Skinner, B.F. (1938). *The behavior of organisms.* New York: Appleton-Century-Crofts.

Skinner, B.F. (1957). *Verbal behavior.* New York: Appleton-Century-Crofts.

Skinner, B.F. (1968). *The technology of teaching.* New York: Appleton-Century-Crofts.

Skinner, B.F. (1974). *About behaviorisms.* New York: Alfred A. Knopf.

Skinner, B.F. (1984). The shame of American Education. *The American Psychologist, 39,* 947-954.

Stallings, J. (1980). Allocated academic learning time revisited, or beyond time on task. *Educational Researcher, 9,* 11-16.

Steinam, W.M. (1977). Generalized imitation and the setting event concept. In B.C. Etzel, J.M. LeBlanc, & D.M. Baer (Eds.), *New Developments in Behavioral Research* (pp. 103-110). Hillsdale, NJ: Lawrence Erlbaum.

Stephens, J.M. (1967). *The process of schooling.* New York: Holt, Rinehart, & Winston.

Sulzer-Azaroff, B., Drabman, R.M., Greer, R.D., Hall, R.V., Iwata, B.A., & O'Leary, S. (Eds.). (1988). *Behavior analysis in education 1968-1987 from the Journal of Applied Behavior Analysts.* Lawrence, KS: Journal of Applied Behavior Analysis.

Sulzer-Azaroff, B. & Mayer, G.R. (1986). *Achieving educational excellence using behaior strategies.* New York: Holt, Rinehart, & Winston.

Trovato, J. & Bucher, B. (1980). Peer tutoring with or without home-based reinforcement for reading instruction. *Journal of Applied Behavior Analysis, 13,* 129-141.

Vargas, E.A. (1988). Event governed and verbally governed behavior. *The Analysis of Verbal Behavior, 6,* 11-22.

Whitehurst, G.J. & Vasta, R. (1975). Is language acquired through imitation? *Journal of Psycholingusitic Research, 4,* 37-59.

Zuriff, G. (1986). *A conceptual reconstruction of behaviorism.* New York: Columbia University Press.